Acknowledgements

I want to thank those who have helped me assemble this tribute to my husband, Dewey Sullivan. Thanks to the *Salem Statesman Journal* for permission to reprint the Timothy Gonzalez photo for the cover as well as other articles and photos, and to the *McMinnville News-Register* for permission to reprint the Tom Ballard photo and other articles and photos from the archives. Thanks to Jim Connelly and Mike Dixon for the research done in their booklets, *X's and O's with Dewey and Emory and Roger 1928 – 1994*, and *The Tradition of Dayton Football – 1995 – 2005* – and to the hundreds of players and many teams that Dewey coached as well as the students that he loved and enjoyed.

I also wish to thank David Bischoff who helped immensely in this writing (for his editorial advice and for his skill) – to Shiela Henry for her advice – to those who have asked questions and offered suggestions -- to those who have been patient with me in this endeavor – and to Lyn Schroeder and Madeline Jepson (and the Upward Bound Program at Linfield) – to Wendy Stetina of Outskirts Press for her assistance and encouragement. I apologize to those who have struggled with me through this venture and are not mentioned.

Thanks to Sandi Colvin of Hidden Treasures for her help in assembling the photo tribute to Dewey -- and thanks to Lora Kearns for her assistance. Thanks to the Dayton community for the love and the respect shown him during his time on the football field and off.

And finally -- thanks to those who have helped with the Dewey Sullivan Classic -- for their efforts and endeavors in making it such a success.

Without the help of many this work would never have reached completion. Thank you! Thank you! Thank you!

A Barefoot Boy from Oklahoma

A Barefoot Boy from Oklahoma

The Dewey Sullivan Story

Vera Sullivan

Outskirts Press, Inc.
Denver, Colorado

I would like to dedicate this labor of love to God, to my husband, Dewey Sullivan, and to my children, Candy, Barry, Brent and Brenda. They have encouraged me in this writing, and I appreciate the love that everyone has shown me during the time I have spent in putting together this volume. This has been a labor of love and I have enjoyed it so much that I hate to let it go. But, as all children must leave home, I am releasing it to fly on its own. Thanks to all.

The opinions expressed in this manuscript are solely the opinions of the author and do not represent the opinions or thoughts of the publisher. The author has represented and warranted full ownership and/or legal right to publish all the materials in this book.

A Barefoot Boy from Oklahoma
The Dewey Sullivan Story
All Rights Reserved.
Copyright © 2009 Vera Sullivan
v4.0

Cover photo and newspaper article Reprinted with permission of the Statesman Journal.

This book may not be reproduced, transmitted, or stored in whole or in part by any means, including graphic, electronic, or mechanical without the express written consent of the publisher except in the case of brief quotations embodied in critical articles and reviews.

Outskirts Press, Inc.
http://www.outskirtspress.com

ISBN: 978-1-4327-3890-7

Library of Congress Control Number: 2009926556

Outskirts Press and the "OP" logo are trademarks belonging to Outskirts Press, Inc.

PRINTED IN THE UNITED STATES OF AMERICA

Preface

"They will soar on wings like eagles; they will run and not grow weary. They will walk and not faint."
-- Isaiah 40:36

"Most of us live our lives mired in mediocrity, but a few of us soar with the eagles. Dewey soared with the eagles, and I consider myself the wind beneath his wings."
-- Vera Sullivan (2008)

Every fall his footsteps could be heard echoing down the halls of Dayton High School, and each autumn evening I waited expectantly for the sound of tires on gravel as he came from football practice.

It's fall again, and the leaves are beautiful in their autumn splendor. Each evening I wait expectantly for the sound of his car coming home. Then I realize afresh that he really is not coming home; that he is already home; that he has gone to heaven to be with God.

I know I will see him again one day, not here on earth, but in heaven to come. He is not really gone. He lives on in my memory, and his spirit will never die. I miss him every day, but I miss him most of all when the autumn leaves start to fall. I celebrate his life daily.

His name was Dewey Sullivan, and I was married to him for more than fifty-three years. The last time his tires crunched up our driveway was in September 2006. In November of 2006, he died after two months of suffering, as he tried to recover from surgery to remove a brain tumor.

My name is Vera Sullivan, and he was my best friend, my hero, and my husband. We met in the sixth grade and began dating as juniors in high school. It was not love at first sight, but when it took over it really was true love. Our love endured for fifty-five years through struggles and sacrifices. This is our story.

CHAPTER 1

It's Not Just a Game

I can see him now, standing on the sidelines of the field in Dayton. His broad shoulders fill out his jacket, and his arms are crossed. Above the roar of the crowd is heard, "Stay low . . . stay low!" His blue eyes look out resolutely at the flurry of flashing uniforms and pigskin. He hears the thud of impact as body meets body. Cleats flash in the light and sod heaves as the team moves as one to accomplish a common goal. This is all beneath the intent watch of those resolute eyes.

I know those eyes, and they twinkle with humor as they relish the sight of young men in high school wearing helmets and learning skills as they encounter the thrill of the game, the thrill of life. The lines around his eyes crinkle in delight as a play goes as designed. His lips lift in a smile. Touchdown!

BUT THIS IS NOT VINCE LOMBARDI OF THE GREEN BAY PACKERS.

THIS IS DEWEY SULLIVAN OF THE DAYTON PIRATES!!

(In the eyes of Dayton, Oregon, he was our Vince Lombardi. He was this and much more. He was a father to those who did not have one. He encouraged those who were discouraged. He made those laugh that felt like crying.)

I lived with this big man for a long time. I learned to love football, and I was there rooting for him every game he coached, not just because I loved him, but because I loved what he was doing, what he was accomplishing.

Dewey coached football at Dayton, Oregon for forty-two years. In that time, he won more games than any other football coach west of the Mississippi River, and he was inducted into the National Hall of Fame for his achievements. His life touched many and his influence lives on. Now, I feel compelled to tell his story.

Dewey was more than a sports icon in Oregon history, and those wins weren't what prompted nearly three thousand people to attend a celebration of his life in the McMinnville Community Center, (the largest venue we could find for the occasion). And his story is not important because of the football games he won, but rather for how he helped others.

It was standing-room-only at the service, and many could not get in, but had to stand outside. People came from New York, California, Colorado, Utah, Washington, Nebraska and other far reaches, and one former player even came from overseas.

Attendees started arriving two hours before the ceremonies began. If they weren't there early, they stood in the balcony, lined the lower level, or stood outside to hear. All the seats were filled and people crowded three or four deep around the balcony and the auditorium. Grief hung over the room like a thick fog. Tears obscured my view of the surroundings.

A small stage provided seating for twelve individuals. Pastor Steven Funk, the minister of the Dayton Baptist Church delivered the eulogy. Also seated were five senior football players from the 2006 Dayton football team. Jordan May was the representative from that group, and gave a tribute to Dewey.

Garnet Wright and Jean Rowland represented Dewey's graduating class at Boone High School, and Max Wall spoke. Former players, Randy Freeborn from the class of 1971, Caleb Kearns from the 2002 championship team, and Roger Lorenzen, the principal at Dayton High School at the time of Dewey's death had amusing stories.

IT'S NOT JUST A GAME

Displayed was a cardinal Dayton football jersey with "#42" on it, as well as "352-84-2" (Dewey's coaching record while at Dayton) and "'85,' '86,' '95,' '96,' and '02'" (the years Dayton teams won state championships while he coached the Pirates). Also displayed were a large arrangement of roses, a football, a floral arrangement in the shape of a football, many other floral arrangements and plants, a native African shield brought from Africa on Dewey's first trip, and a hat he purchased in Mazatlan on his April 2006 trip.

A large banner proclaimed: *"WE LOVE YOU DEWEY SULLIVAN! YOU LIVE IN OUR HEARTS FOREVER!!"*

As people filed in, two players from the Oregon Symphony provided music. Dave Bowlin, a former Dayton High School football player, played the guitar and sang a song written by Roger Lorenzen dedicated to Dewey: *The Forty Year Reign.*

A rolling video of *The Life and Times of Dewey Sullivan* was aired. The haunting sounds of Nana Mouskouri singing, *I Believe in Angels*, one of Dewey's favorite songs hung in the air. (That song was played almost continuously while Dewey was hospitalized. He loved it!) The eulogy was delivered, and tributes were paid. Several people spoke, but we could not have an open mike, as the service would have lasted for hours.

Dewey brought all that he touched together, and in some small way, made them feel as though they were part of the Sullivan family. One person in attendance described the celebration as, "a big family reunion." Family isn't only blood — it's the people you love across the generations and Dewey loved many.

(Most people who knew Dewey, those who were students of his, those who played football for him, or those who just met him have a story or two to tell.) Tributes were paid to him on *carepages.com* and on *YouTube*. Type in "Dewey Sullivan" on *Google*, and get ready to be overwhelmed with webpages mentioning him. The *McMinnville News-Register* reported, *Dewey Plays to a Packed House.*

But Dewey Sullivan did not realize the impact he had on so

many. He knew he was loved, but he did not know how many lives he touched during his lifetime. He was referred to as, "A man with many victories but few words." But his life was about more than victories on the football field. It was about human relationships -- about caring and compassion.

CHAPTER 2

More Than Just a Football Coach

When we moved to Dayton, Oregon more than forty years ago, we did not know Dewey would coach football there for forty-two years. Dewey had applied at several California schools, and we thought we were on our way to California, the land of "milk and honey." But when Dewey learned of the opening at Dayton, he was intrigued, and applied there also. When he was offered the contract at Dayton, we thought we would stay for a couple of years.

Two days after signing the contract at Dayton he had an offer from a school in California. Three days separated Dayton and California. Three days impacted his decision to go to Dayton rather than California. I had no idea it was the town where he would die forty-two years later.

What attracted Dewey to this backwater? Well, quite simply, its football team seemed to be a winner. The Dayton Pirates won first place in the Yawama League in 1964. With that title Dewey thought he could start his coaching days in Oregon with momentum.

Highway I-5 cuts a path from Vancouver, British Columbia down to San Diego, California, running through the western part of both Washington and Oregon. It goes from the border of Canada and the United States, skirting Seattle, and then running through Portland, just below the Columbia River. When Dewey accepted the position at Dayton, we were living in the town of Chehalis located between Seattle and Portland.

Dayton, which is just a bit to the southwest of Portland, near the larger town of McMinnville, is a rural community. If the name, *Dayton*, reminds you of a far bigger town there's a good reason. When Andrew Smith co-founded it in 1850 he named it after his hometown of Dayton, Ohio.

The other founder, Joel Palmer, was the Superintendent of Oregon Indian Affairs and built a flour mill there. Palmer ran for governor of Oregon in 1870, and was defeated by less than seven hundred votes.

When it was first settled, Oregon was considered only fit for the raising of cattle. But when the fertility of the land became evident, it was learned that it was agriculturally viable.

People have the idea that Oregon is a dark and gloomy place, so crowded with trees you can hardly move and that you are bedeviled with rain . . . rain . . . rain.

There's a good chance that, when the first wave of settlers started becoming prosperous and noticed the problems of high-density populations in the southern and eastern states, they collectively decided to encourage this myth.

Western Oregon has its dark days in the winter, and it does rain a good deal then. But it's quite mild weather-wise. In the summer it hardly rains at all. In the spring there are beautiful peonies, irises, azaleas, rhododendrons and a wealth of other flowers. Cherry, apple and other fruit trees bloom in breath-taking beauty, and they take their time going from green to multi-colored.

In a town like Dayton, with its block house and its houses from a hundred years ago there is a unique vibrant western touch minus the dreadful cold and snow of winter.

One of the top restaurants of the Pacific Northwest, the *Joel Palmer House*, is downtown. And Dayton is at the epicenter of the burgeoning *Oregon Winery Community*.

But in 1965, there weren't any wineries to speak of. There was Dayton High School which needed both a biology teacher and a football coach. Dewey got both positions.

CHAPTER **3**

Letters from Dewey

When Dewey Sullivan met the Dayton Pirate team for the first time in August of 1965, he was greeted by nineteen football players; nineteen from a list of thirty-nine potential players. *NINETEEN?* Nineteen!! You can't field an eleven-man football team with nineteen players. The Dayton Pirates won the league title in 1964 and participated in the state playoffs. That was something that had not happened for sixteen years. In fact, the Dayton Pirates had only five winning seasons in the sixteen years between 1948 and 1964 but Dewey was unaware of that. The league championship in 1964 was one of the lures that brought him to Dayton, and he looked with anticipation to the '65 season. He was not aware of the dearth of championships, so he was devastated by such a small turnout.

But he made the best of what he had. With only nineteen players, he definitely questioned his decision — why had he chosen Dayton over California?) He was disappointed, but undaunted. He and Barry went to Dayton to spend the first two weeks — the two weeks before we could move into the home we had rented. I received several letters from him at that time.

◄ A BAREFOOT BOY FROM OKLAHOMA

August 1965

Dear Vera,

I had two practices today and I'm worried. Only 19 players showed up to check out gear. I have a list of 39 players so I asked where the others are. The kids said there was an assembly the day they signed up for football and they could miss it if they signed up. Most players work for the local farmers during the day, so if I want to have daily doubles I'll be the only one there. The farmers keep them until after 5:00 or so. I guess I'll have evening practices. Barry and I have been sleeping on the stage at the high school and that works okay, but I'll be glad to get things moved and have you and the kids with me.

Also, I have other bad news for you. Your grandmother's china cabinet blew off the pickup on my way to Dayton and it's now in small pieces. I gathered it up and it's a mess. I wouldn't blame you if you never want to see me again. I feel so bad about it. I'll see you this weekend and I hope you can forgive me.

Love, Dewey

August 1965
Dear Vera,

I don't know what I'm doing here. This is not what I expected. I went around town yesterday and tried to get more players. One young man said he would come out so I'll wait and see. I talked with several, but they said they don't want to try football. Last year was the first good team in about twenty years. I guess winning league is not enough to build a football team on. As I left practice last night I overheard one of the players say "That crazy coach. I just came with 'so-and-so' for him to suit up and that coach had me in a uniform before I could turn around. Does he think I'm crazy? I've seen what he has on his team." (And, you know, the funny thing is, he's right. I am a crazy coach.) I can't believe what I have to work with. There was no junior varsity program last year and these guys are trying out for positions that they'll never make. My quarterback was the center last year and my backs are former linemen. What a mish-mash. This is so depressing. Well, I guess I'd better get ready for practice. I'm looking forward to coming home this weekend and seeing you and the kids.

Love, Dewey

August 1965

Dear Vera,

I can't believe the lack of interest in football here. I was told that Dayton is a basketball town, and that they go to the playoffs every year. After talking with a couple of mothers, I was told they don't want their sons to play football because they might get injured and not be able to play basketball. What have I done? I must have been out of my mind to come here. For two cents I'd throw in the towel and stay in Chehalis, but I guess I'm committed. Well, I love a challenge. I'm looking forward to seeing you and the kids in a couple of days.

Love, Dewey

(I cherish this letter. *WELL, I LOVE A CHALLENGE!* is the essence of Dewey Sullivan. He didn't care for writing, but that was his motto.)

◂ A BAREFOOT BOY FROM OKLAHOMA

August 1965

Dear Vera,

Barry and I had a good trip back to Dayton, and we have several dinner invitations. When some of the town moms learned we have been sleeping on the stage and going to McMinnville for meals, they invited us to dinner. We ate dinner at one home tonight and have an invitation for tomorrow also. That's better. I've talked with several moms and they encouraged me. One of them actually likes football. Things are looking up. The weather has been great and the evenings are fine for practice. Not too hot. We had 21 players on the field tonight. That's not enough to do much, but they're starting to get the idea. I have one who does a fair job at quarterback and another that will make a back. When school starts I'll see who is in the halls. Well, I'll close and get some sleep. See you soon. I miss you.

Love, Dewey

⁂

August 1965

Dear Vera,

There is an old filbert orchard by the school, and Barry has been hunting funnel-web spiders while I hold practice. He's supposed to be helping me, but I guess it's good he has something to interest him. Tonight I had the guys run to see who can carry the ball and a couple of them look like backs. I can't believe I'm here and trying to have football practice. All the other schools have two-a-day practices and most teams have at least 30 players out for football. An article in the paper said Amity has 35 players on their roster. Well, live and learn.

Love, Dewey

That was how Dayton football began for us. A lifetime ago Dewey Sullivan greeted his first football team. (Sometimes it seems as though it was a hundred years ago, and other times it seems as though it was just yesterday).

There had been no junior varsity program in 1964, and the emphasis had been on the varsity team. That team was undefeated in the regular season, and had won league. (The lesser and the younger players were discouraged from participation on the premise that they were wasting both their time and that of the coach.)

After school began, Dewey spent his spare time in the halls recruiting players. He ended the season with a squad of thirty-three -- that from the initial nineteen he had been blessed with.

The Pirates played the Amity Warriors in the first football game that Dewey coached at Dayton. The Pirates scored on the first possession with a trick play ("the swinging gate"), but lost the game by the score of 26-6. Dewey came home and said, "That was terrible. We should have scored more points. We sure have our work cut out for us." He had been excited to be coaching again, and was quite disappointed.

(But it was ten years before Dayton lost to Amity again. In 1976 Amity defeated Dayton 44-42, and Dayton was driving for a score when time ran out. The next year Dayton won by the score of 42-0. As we left the 1977 game, the Amity principal, Bill Buffum, told me, "Dayton is no better this year than they were last — they scored forty-two points both years." GOOD POINT!!)

After winning the fifth game of Dewey's first season at Dayton, the Pirates tied the sixth game and won the next two. The success of the season hinged on the final game with Willamina. In that game, Dewey called a run, but an incomplete pass was thrown on the five-yard line, and Willamina won 12-7. Once again, Dewey came home and said, "What a disappointment. We ALMOST had a winning season." (Dayton defeated Banks, Philomath and Yamhill-

Carlton and tied Sheridan 13-13, so the Pirates ended the season with a credible team and a 3-5-1 record.)

After many setbacks, trials and tribulations, the Pirate ship was righted and started sailing successfully. Although the Pirates lost the first four games of the 1965 season, the players kept the faith and eventually turned things around. George Murdock, a writer for the *McMinnville News-Register*, classified Dewey as a *Miracle Worker*. How had he done this? Who was this Dewey Sullivan?

Who was he, this man who became an icon in Oregon football history? He was a son, brother, husband, father, grandfather and coach, but most importantly, he was a Christian. He dedicated his life to God as a child, and he tried to do God's will. He was a small town coach who achieved national acclaim in the arena of sports. He loved football. He loved his family. He loved God.

He was honorable, compassionate, and trustworthy. He knew that life is transcended by eternity, and that each of us is here for only a brief moment in time. He lived each day as though it were his last, and when his time came, was ready to meet his Maker. He was at peace with himself, and he had few regrets.

Delinda Morgan, whose husband, Lance, played football for Dewey in the early '70s, thought his life noteworthy enough to be shared, so I am trying to accomplish that, but no book can do justice to this "Mountain of a Man."

Dewey was more than a football coach. He was an enigma. (A movie or a screenplay would better portray him as the caring individual he was. Actually, Caleb Kearns, quarterback for the Pirates on the 2002 championship team, is writing a screen play about Dewey.)

His story encompasses many people: former students, football players, high school friends, and coaching buddies, as well as his family. Some of the events portrayed here may not be entirely accurate, but this is about his feats on and off the field of football as best I know them. They are told as I remember, and from what Dewey reported to me. I can tell some of the amusing things that occurred in our sixty-plus years together, but I cannot tell what lurked in the innermost recesses of his being.

If you are reading this to discover the mystique of Dewey Sullivan, you will be disappointed as I can no more explain it than I can tell you what makes the earth spin on its axis. Dewey could not have told you how he did it, but by the grace of God he succeeded.

He came from school one day, and told me that his high school principal said, "You have an amazing influence over young people." That statement puzzled Dewey. He either did not believe it, or he did not see it. He did not abuse that influence, and he tried to be of service both to God and man, doing what he thought best for all.

Dewey's career began in Silt, Colorado where he was one of the boys. (With his first team, he enjoyed the pranks his players pulled. He had a fantastic sense of humor and encouraged others in "tomfoolery.")

He became the "Enforcer" at Meeker, Colorado, where he brooked no nonsense. (One mother stated that he was too militaristic.) But, the "real" Dewey Sullivan emerged at Dayton as the refined, gentle, compassionate man he really was. He lived that role fully, but realized his image was one of distinction rather than reality. He became a combination of fun-loving -- a kid at heart, and no-nonsense. He loved life, and he loved young people.

Each of us has a role to play here on earth, but some of us use our talents to better advantage than others. Dewey had the talent to be a coach and teacher and he used that talent wisely. How blessed he was.

I wish I had written this book while Dewey was living, but we were too busy having fun -- too busy living, to take time for such ventures. (Besides, I have exposed him to the world, and he would not have appreciated being uncovered. He would not have wanted people to know him as the teddy bear he was. But he could have given me many humorous episodes other than what I have noted.) We are not talking about Dewey's records, about his wins or his awards. We are talking about how he is remembered, about his legacy.

CHAPTER 4

What Really Happened

Baseball may be America's pastime, but the ratings for the World Series aren't much compared to those for the Super Bowl. Football and football history is a big part of American society, culture and economics. Professional football players and coaches receive huge contracts and salaries. A great college coach can receive over a million dollars a year. On the other hand, high school football coaches are usually high school teachers, and are paid high school teachers' salaries.

A high school football coach at Dayton would be fortunate to receive four thousand dollars a year. But Dewey Sullivan didn't coach for the money. He loved sports, and he especially loved football. He had the skill, personality and drive to be a college level football coach, making loads of money. He knew this, but he chose to live and work in a small town in an obscure state, "Northwest of Nowhere -- Oregon!"

This was a conscious choice . . . for definite reasons. From the time he coached his first high school football game he felt that was his calling, and it became his passion. He loved coaching high school kids, and he fell in love with football.

Once the contract for Dayton High School was signed, we were ready to put down roots. Little did we know what the future held for us. When Dewey went to City Hall to pay the water deposit Audrey

Zentner, the City Clerk, asked, "Should my son play football? Last year the coach told him he was wasting his time — that he will never be a football player." Dewey asked, "Does he like football?" Audrey said, "He loves it." Dewey said, "Get him out for the team. We need him and we'll make him a football player." Dewey often came home at night and said, "Football practice has been over for an hour, and Mike Zentner is still on the field hitting the dummies."

Before Mike's football career at Dayton ended he lost his class ring on the football field. It was kicked up in a field goal or extra point attempt about twenty-five years later. Mike had an illustrious career, and won All-League honors in the Yawama League. After graduation, he played football at Lewis and Clark College, and received All-Northwest Conference honors there.

Mike named one of his boys for Dewey, and Dewey wondered why anyone would name a son, "Dewey" (however, I like the name). We attended most of the Lewis and Clark games in which Mike played, and his dad, Lloyd Zentner, often laughed, "All I have to do is start the car to go to a game, and Dewey and his two sons promptly go to sleep."

The first two years at Dayton, part of Dewey's football responsibility was to do the team laundry. (Maybe he was team manager as well as coach?) We lived across the street from the high school, and weekends were spent traipsing back and forth between our home and the dressing room to put loads of laundry into either the washer or the dryer.

After two years of that hassle, Dewey tired of doing the laundry, and he did not care if some of the items did not return to the dressing room. He started sending the gear home with the players for them or their moms to wash. (The mothers probably didn't like the new way of doing things, but I welcomed it.)

Coaching at Dayton was not easy, but Dewey persevered against many odds. One year he did not have a paid assistant, but was fortunate to have help from Gary Cox, a student teacher from nearby Linfield College. An assistant had been hired, but the fellow had never played football, and knew little about it.

That coach came to our house the second night of practice and said, "Dewey I hate to say it, but those kids know more about football than I do. I don't think I can be of much help to you. I think I should resign." (The assistant had been hired as the band teacher, and all summer his predecessor had kidded him about the coaching position and what was expected.)

If he accepted the resignation, Dewey realized that he would be left to coach alone, but he said, "Well, if you really believe that we will be better off without you, go ahead and resign. We'll make do somehow." That left Dewey with no assistant.

When school started, Gary came on the scene and said, "I would like to help with football if you can use me." "Can I use you?? I would love to have you help." He was welcomed with open arms. WHEW!! Dewey breathed a huge sigh of relief.

Dewey and Gary worked well together and became good friends. They coached the team together during the daily practices, and Dewey coached the games on Friday nights while Gary scouted the upcoming opposition. Philomath was ranked fourth in state (a big deal to us then)! When Gary returned after scouting them, he reported, "They're really good."

In the Dayton/Philomath game, the middle linebacker blasted through the center, and sent Bill Stoller, the Dayton quarterback, head-over-heels. But that did not deter Bill, and he went on to have one of the best games of his career.

After the Philomath game Dewey and some players were standing around the school parking lot. When Gary returned from scouting Yamhill-Carlton, the next week's opponent, he pulled into the lot, and asked, "What was the score?" Dewey said, "44-0." Gary replied, "Well, that's not too bad." Dewey said, "Hey, we won." Gary said, "No way!" Some of the players stood around the school courtyard. He pointed at them, and said, "Ask them." Gary asked, "Who won and what was the score?" They said, "We won! And the score was 44-0!" (That victory was one of Dewey's proudest.)

Earl McKinney, the Dayton basketball coach, walked off the field with Dewey after the game, and said, "Do you realize you cost that coach his job tonight?" Dewey said, "No, why is that?" Earl said, "Well, I talked with several of their Booster Club members during the game, and they were furious. They said the coach appeared at their meeting last night, and told them the junior varsity would play most of the game – that it was just to be a tune-up game." Dewey felt badly because the coach lost his job after that season, and the Dayton game was likely a factor.

CHAPTER 5

Under the Lights

During his early years at Dayton, Dewey met with several school board members concerning the employment of football players. He wanted to cooperate with the local farmers, so as a compromise, he scheduled evening practices rather than daily doubles (two-a-day practices).

The players told Dewey they needed to work, so he tried to appease the community. With evening practices, the players could work as well as play football. (Dayton wanted a winning football team, but also wanted the players to work and attend as few practices as possible.)

You can go to any football game at any level in any city or town, and hear criticism of the coach, whether the team wins or loses. There are always sidelines coaches who second-guess the play calling. When Dayton lost the first four games Dewey coached, his strategies were questioned.

A board member drove into the parking lot one afternoon during practice, called his wife on his car phone (before the advent of cell phones), and told her, "Get on the phone, and alert the other school board members. Sullivan is still on the field, and it's after five o'clock." (That was grounds for dismissal??)

Another afternoon, the superintendent came to the field, and said, "Dewey it's after five o'clock, and you're still practicing (as though he didn't know it). Practice is to be over by five." Dewey looked at him and said, "I realize that, but if it's a problem, you should just fire me." The subject was changed to the upcoming game and was not touched on again.

Dewey came from an in-service session one year, and said, "I was told I need to be at school tonight to meet with parents about registration for classes, etc. I told the principal I would not be there. I told him that I have practice at five o'clock each evening, and that is my way of working around the farm labor problem. I know I am insubordinate, but I have done this for eight years and it has worked fine." He stewed over the problem for about an hour, and then the phone rang. It was the principal. Dewey was excused from the meeting. WHEW!!

Before new lights were installed on the football field in 1992, it was suggested that Dayton play afternoon games instead of evening ones. A student aide came to Dewey's classroom, and asked, "What time do you want your Saturday afternoon games to be played?" He responded, "We're not playing Saturday games. The games will be played on Friday nights as usual."

Dewey mentioned the controversy to several supporters, who approached the superintendent and talked with him about it. The installation of new lights was begun within a matter of weeks.

There were two football schedules that year. One schedule had games on Friday nights, and the other showed games on Saturday afternoons. (Dewey took classes in Administration at Western State College, and the class was told that the School Board is the most powerful entity in the United States. He agreed. He thrived on controversy – he did not like it, but it gave him reason to excel.)

One year when the Pirates were in the playoffs, they were assigned a time to practice on the turf where the Saturday game was to be played. The superintendent refused to let the team practice during school hours. The opposing team was allowed to practice on the turf, but Dayton waited until school was dismissed, and then practiced on the Dayton field.

One of the assistant coaches called to reason with the

superintendent, and the connection was severed, so the protest went unheard. Dewey did not care because he did not like to take practice time for travel, but the principle still stood. Shouldn't it be an even playing field? Shouldn't Dayton have the same consideration as that given other teams?

Several years ago Dewey went to football practice at the usual time, and when darkness approached, went to turn on the lights. He found they had been padlocked to keep them off! (Evidently a patron of the District had protested about the electricity being used.)

Dewey was furious when he came home that night. He fumed and fumed. He said, " Dadgummit! For almost forty years I have had evening practices so the players can work during the day. I'm not ready to retire, or I would have taken bolt cutters and cut that sucker off. I would love to stir something up, but I would like to keep my job for a few more years.

"As a matter of respect, it would have been nice if I had gotten a phone call to ask if we could practice earlier. I have been open to compromise and I have tried to work with the community, but they didn't have the courtesy to let me know there was a problem."

After that fiasco, he scheduled practices in the afternoon to satisfy those in the community who complained. (Of course, he originally scheduled practices to accommodate the farming community. You cannot please everyone.) His premise was that the administration should have told him that a change was necessary. He would have adjusted willingly.

Dewey had not been kept in the loop. In the twenty-first century, had anyone heard of telephones, of the simple act of communication, of courtesy in keeping people informed? After all, it was no longer the *Dark Ages*, or the days of the *Pony Express*. How hard would it have been to pick up the phone and say, "Dewey, I'm sorry, but there has been a complaint about the amount of electricity being used. Can you schedule practice for earlier in the day?" The next day the sun rose as usual, and football went on. The season was a success.

Dewey was usually quick with his responses, but several times was too late with quips he wished he had used. A school board member once called and asked, "Dewey, would you look around at practice tonight to see who is working for me, and then take it easy on them?" Dewey hung up the phone, and said, "Oh my gosh, I wish I had thought to ask him to look around at work today, and take it easy on the guys who are out for the football team. I really blew that one."

In the 1970s, the Dayton coaches mounted a campaign to get coaching salaries increased (one of their directives was to determine how the salaries for Dayton coaches compared with the salaries for other coaches in the league). It was learned that the girls' basketball coach at Amity was paid more than Earl McKinney, the highly respected Dayton boys' basketball coach. (That was before *Title Nine*, and the rise of girls' athletics into the sports arena.)

The information was shared at the next Board meeting, and the Chairman flatly told the committee, "We pay you what we think you're worth." (He could have couched it in less harsh terms such as, "We pay you what we can. We would like to pay you more, but that's the best we can do.") Dewey didn't coach for the money, but needless to say, many of the other coaches at Dayton left the fold in the next few years. (A little respect would also have been welcome.)

But Dewey had supporters as well as detractors. One of those supporters recently told me, "Whenever we got a new superintendent either male or female, I went in and told him or her, "Don't you mess with our football coach." (Of course, that may have thrown down the gauntlet as to whether the dog is wagging the tail, or the tail is wagging the dog.) Dewey did not abuse the influence he had in the community or with his players, but he knew that a power struggle was a possibility.

And several years ago, I learned that one school board member considered it to his credit to have been on the board when Dewey was hired. (You could have fooled me. I didn't know that any of the school board members considered Dewey a credit.)

One superintendent told Dewey, "Good luck! When your teams do well, it makes me look good. Football success lends itself to good administration." (However, that assessment was not shared by some of his successors who tried to put obstacles before the success of the program. It should not have been a competition.)

Even after he had proven himself, Dewey was doubted. His teams were successful. But in recent years, someone went into *Putt's Market*, the local grocery, to hear comments that were less than glowing, and to give pointers on what plays should have been called.

And it was reported that the School Board wanted to know when the *Old Man* was going to step down, that change was needed. You cannot please everyone, and Dewey realized there were people at his heels, but he managed to succeed against adversity.

Dewey planned to go to the *Grand Island Store*, another local establishment, some Saturday morning to learn how the Friday night game should have been played. His understanding was that he could pick up some good insights on the previous night's game (which Dayton might have won by forty or more points). Supposedly, much constructive criticism was espoused there.

And he enjoyed the book, *Friday Night Lights*, because he said it was so typical of small, (or maybe large town football), or maybe just football in general. He particularly liked the part about the *For Sale* signs that mysteriously appeared on the coach's lawn after a defeat.

He also enjoyed the movie, *Radio*, with the barbershop quarterbacks telling the coach what he should have done. Dewey had critics, but with 352 victories in 438 games, he did not let it bother him. (Actually, I believe that the newspaper, *USA Today*, has his record as 361-102-2. That is pretty accurate. He did not want to claim the losses his teams suffered in Colorado, just so he could acknowledge the wins in Oregon, but it is public record.)

But despite the *Putt's Market Chorus*, the *Grand Island Choir*, and the *School Board Band*, Dewey persevered, and stayed true to himself and the Pirates. He brought fame to the small town of Dayton. Dayton is now known for its football program, and is synonymous with small town football success. (Often when we go to a football game elsewhere, and wear a *Dayton Football* sweatshirt, someone will say, "Oh, you're from Dayton. That's where Dewey Sullivan used to coach.")

CHAPTER **6**

A Barefoot Boy From Oklahoma

But wait. I digress. This is the beginning. This is where Dewey Sullivan's life began. It is the story of his life, of his love, of his legacy. Once upon a time . . . back in the dark days of the Great Depression of the '30s . . . back before the days of television, computers or the Internet, Dewey Sullivan was born.

Early on the morning of May 6, 1935, in a small house in the tiny town of Geary, Oklahoma, a doctor slapped the back of a new-born baby, and Dewey Sullivan entered the world. A baby's lusty cry was heard, and Dewey joined his parents and two older brothers.

He was born Deward Thomas Sullivan to Willis and Josephine Sullivan, and was the third child in a family of six children. His father was a farm laborer, and his mother was a homemaker. His oldest brother, Windle, was three and his brother, Winfred (Lefty), two when he was born.

Before Windle was born, his mom and dad met an older gentleman on the street. That man told his mother, "You'll never be free from your children from this time on." His mother often repeated that statement. (She discovered that to be prophetic, as any parent does who truly loves his or her children. A parent lives through each child's anguish and celebration. You can't help the love you have for your children. It's an irresistible impulse woven into the fabric of your life. You are upset with their disobedience, but you hate the need for punishment. You cry inside at their sorrows and you rejoice openly at their successes.)

◄ A BAREFOOT BOY FROM OKLAHOMA

Dewey's father was born in *Indian Territory*, now the *State of Oklahoma*. He was the oldest of ten children. Dewey's grandmother was part Cherokee (or Choctaw), but his grandfather did not register his children on the *Dawes Rolls*, so the lineage is distorted. His mother was born on a farm in Arkansas in 1911, the sixth of seven children. Her father died when she was twelve, so they sold the family farm, and moved to Geary, Oklahoma, where employment was more readily available.

When his mother was nineteen, she attended a church picnic where she met Dewey's father. Dewey's mother said, "My heart skipped a beat because he was the most handsome man ever . . . He was with another girl at the church picnic, but he took me home that night. It was love at first sight for both of us. We were married the following May. We both knew we had found the right one." (Dewey's father was smitten, and when he left that picnic, he told his parents he had met the girl he intended to marry.)

Misery was rampant, and millions were unemployed during the *Depression*. There was a huge gap between the classes. There were the "haves" and the "have-nots," but mostly the "have-nots." The Sullivans belonged to the "have-nots." They were frugal, and raised six children on subsistence wages, but did not go without the necessities of life. Dewey's mother was a homemaker, and she knew the value of a dollar. His father valued education, and he wanted his children to go to college, which they all did.

The Sullivan family was poor, but not needy, and there was food on the table and clothes to wear. One year they were selected to receive one of the holiday food baskets. (That basket was given by a club each year and consisted of fruit and homemade things.) Dewey was too young to remember that incident, but Windle told of his embarrassment at learning his family was considered needy.

The Dust Bowl and the Great Depression of the '30s and '40s caused the *Okies* and the *Arkies* to move to California, Colorado, or wherever employment could be found. When Dewey was a baby, his Aunt Helen, who lived in Uvalde, Texas, wrote his father a letter and told him he could get employment there, so the family moved. (His aunt had two children the same ages as Windle and Lefty.)

A BAREFOOT BOY FROM OKLAHOMA

Windle said, "My parents moved from Geary, Oklahoma to Yancey, Texas in a Model-T Ford with three children and sixty dollars in their pockets." Dewey's youngest brother, Norman, was born in Texas, and was followed a couple of years later by his oldest sister, Sharon.

Dewey's mom cut the kids' hair and made their clothes, and his dad was the family dentist. If anyone had a loose tooth when Mr. Sullivan left for work (he worked for the WPA, and left on Sunday evening and returned on Friday), he warned that if it were still hanging when he returned on Friday evening, he would pull it. (That threat was usually enough to initiate action!)

(Dewey's beginnings as a poor boy shaped his future. He empathized with those less fortunate, and was an advocate for equality and fairness. He enjoyed Steinbeck's Grapes of Wrath, as he identified with the travails of the Joad family.)

◄ A BAREFOOT BOY FROM OKLAHOMA

The Sullivans shopped at the two stores in Yancey. Windle said, " What I considered different about that town was that no railroad went through it. We had to go to Uvalde or another nearby town to see a train." Dewey's cousin Merle was fanatic about trains, and ran down the railroad tracks each time a train went by.

(Dewey also loved trains and liked the romance of the old steam engines, but considered the sound of the train whistle melancholy. He often told me how much he enjoyed seeing trains go by. It made him want to say "good-bye," and to go somewhere. He loved to travel.)

Windle told me, "When Joe Louis (the *Brown Bomber*) met Max Schmeling in a boxing match in 1938, my dad wanted to listen to it on the radio, but we did not have a radio. Lefty and I walked with him about two and one-half miles to a grocery store in Uvalde, so we could hear the fight on the radio." (Dewey was three, and was too young to walk with his father and brothers, so he was left at home.)

The radio was the only venue for learning the outcome of that fight, unless you were willing to wait until the following day to read the account in the newspaper, or until the next weekend to see it on the newsreels at the movies. Mr. Sullivan did not subscribe to the newspaper, and he did not go to the movies, so the radio was his chosen means of communication.

The match was a rematch of the June 19, 1936 match held in Yankee Stadium where Schmeling knocked Louis out in the twelfth round. (Schmeling had been the European champion and the world heavyweight champion from 1930 until 1932.) Much publicity was involved with the 1938 return bout, so their father's interest was piqued.

Windle said, "The second match was over in little more than two minutes with Louis winning in a knockout. My dad was excited that an American won the crown." (The Nazis ordered the commentary cut off, because Schmeling's cries of pain were audible after Louis hit him with a right to the back and broke two vertebrae.)

(Several years ago, Dewey read in *The Oregonian*, that Joe

Louis went through the Portland International Airport unrecognized. Louis was a broken man, even though he had been prominent in the world arena of boxing. Dewey said, "I wish I had known he was going to be in Oregon. I would have gone to Portland to see him. I would have loved to see the legendary *Brown Bomber*.")

CHAPTER 7

Way Back When

When the family moved to Texas, Mr. Sullivan worked first in the school cafeteria, and later for the Works Project Administration (WPA). While he worked for the WPA, he searched for steady employment. When he learned that work was available near Fowler, Colorado, he loaded his family and all their earthly possessions into their blue, 1926 Buick and a two-wheel trailer and made the move to Fowler where Jonell, their youngest child, was born.

They rented a house about two and one-half miles from town near the Elder School, which was commonly known as *Number Six.* That school served grades one through eight, and Dewey began his education there. The family did not have electricity in that house, but after a few months, Windle used some of the hard-earned money he made in the fields, and had it turned on. (The house was wired, but a monthly electric bill was an extravagance they managed to do without until Windle intervened.) The family lived there until they moved into the "old yellow house" in the Boone School District in 1946.

Lefty went barefooted on his first day of school at *Number Six.* He had shoes, but in Texas it was a common practice to go without. The kids laughed at Lefty for going shoeless, so he wore shoes after that incident.

Windle said, "I had the dubious 'distinction' of being designated child-minder for Lefty and Dewey. My mission was to keep up with them. Dewey was not too bad, but Lefty was a handful. There was an apple tree, and I was told to keep them from eating green apples. That was hard to do. It was a hopeless cause. Besides there were two of them and there was only one of me. And what they couldn't think of to get into wasn't worth mentioning. Lefty was the instigator, but Dewey was not far behind. Lefty got into everything."

Dewey wanted to be like his older brothers, but they tired of having him follow them. They didn't want a pesky little kid with them everywhere they went. He tried his best to keep up with them in their escapades, and he got into everything they did. Sometimes he kept up with them. Sometimes he could not. He was frequently left behind, and he jumped up and down as he cried in frustration.

When Dewey awoke later than usual one morning, he found Windle and Lefty gone. He hurriedly dressed, and went in hot pursuit. He caught up with them, but they did not want to be bothered with a younger brother, so they stuffed him into a burlap bag. He screamed bloody murder, and set up such a howl of protest that their mother, who was ill, had to get out of bed to rescue the victim. Three small boys were a handful. And then a fourth one came along, later to be followed by two girls.

An irrigation ditch ran by their home, and the boys often tossed their small dog, Scotty, into it to watch him swim. Their father told them, "You boys stay away from that ditch, and don't throw the dog into it. But they did not heed their father's advice. Dewey reported that Scotty was frequently dunked.

Dewey went to school with Lefty one day, and met a boy who told him, "I have rubber tractors at home." Dewey loved rubber tractors, so he was intrigued and rode home on the bus instead of walking home with Lefty as he had been told to do.

There was immediate panic when Lefty arrived at the Sullivan household minus his little brother. After many inquiries and much distress, Dewey was found at the other boy's home where the two were happily playing with tractors. He was unaware of the turmoil he had caused, but when his parents located him, he nonetheless met with dire consequences. He did not visit school again.

His childhood was warm and protected, so when the time came to enroll in school, he was reluctant. He did not want to venture far from what he knew, but he began classes at *Number Six* in 1940. He was shy and easily embarrassed, and avoided as many encounters with others as possible. He disliked being called upon for responses to questions. He was a dreamer, and his mind wandered.

He said, "What a rude awakening when I was told I had to sit at a desk and listen to someone talk. I decided I would like to become a teacher and change the way education was handled. When I had a classroom of my own, I tried to encourage my students to learn and to want to succeed."

He looked forward to the bell that signaled the dismissal of school, and was always one of the first out the door to set out on a new adventure. (He did not like the captivity of the classroom.)

One day he was embarrassed by something the teacher said, so he left the class and went home. When he got home, his mother asked, "What are you doing here before school is dismissed?" He said, "I don't like that teacher. She made fun of me." He was escorted back to school, and he didn't try that again.

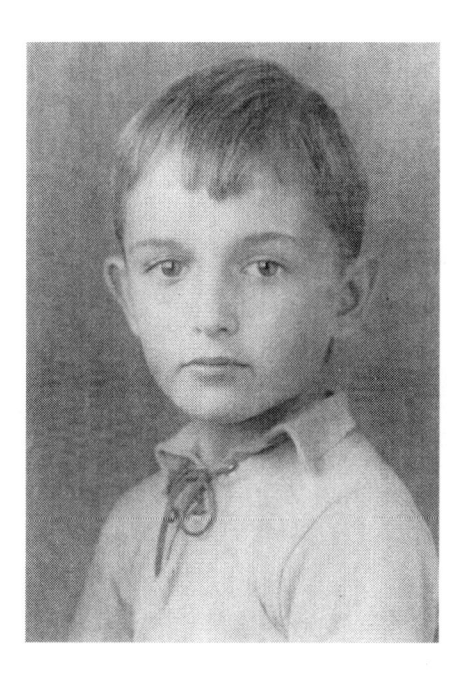

A BAREFOOT BOY FROM OKLAHOMA

The local grocer had a van and delivered groceries to the rural areas on Fridays. (Grocers made deliveries before the days of the Internet.) Flour and sugar were the items most often purchased, and the grocer treated the Sullivan children to a peppermint stick. (Sugar was rationed during World War II, so candy was special.)

The grocer once asked Dewey, "What's your name?" When Dewey refused to respond, the grocer asked, "What's the matter? The cat got your tongue?" (Dewey later told me, "I was so embarrassed. I could see a cat taking my tongue and that really bothered me.") Another time, he swallowed a lemon drop and could not get his breath. He thought he was suffocating. When he could finally say something, he gasped, "Call the 'horspistal.'"

When Sharon was four, she tried her hand at haircutting (not professionally.) She trimmed her own bangs (fortunately not someone else's), and when her parents saw the results they asked, "Who did that?" Her reply was, "'Dewud' did it." Of course, the truth eventually came out, and the bangs grew back, but it took several weeks to rectify the mistake.

Back when we watched movies in black and white -- back when kids went to matinees on Saturday afternoon -- back before the days of television and computers, Dewey Sullivan went to his first movie. He was ecstatic when he was deemed old enough to go with his two older brothers to the Saturday afternoon matinee. He was a *BIG BOY*, and he could do *BIG BOY THINGS!!*

At his first movie, he sat on the edge of his seat and marveled at the horses on the screen. He said, "I saw all those horses and could hardly wait to go out back of the theater to see them. I was so excited. I squirmed in my seat. I enjoyed the movie, but I loved the horses, and I waited anxiously for the show to end. When it was over, I raced out of the theater and around to the back to see those horses. But when I got there, they weren't there. I had seen them on the screen, but they were gone. I was so disappointed." (He learned that often what you see is not what you get.)

He liked *Hopalong Cassidy*, and *The Lone Ranger*. (He enjoyed western movies into adulthood. He disliked the way the old movies portrayed the horses running across the prairies "hell-bent-for-leather," but loved the more modern ones such as *Once Upon a Time in the West*, and *How the West Was Won*. He considered those movies more realistic.)

The price of admission for the Saturday afternoon matinees was a nickel each, and the three older children were permitted to go alone. The matinee was a serial that ran for eight or ten weeks, and each segment ended with a "cliffhanger" to entice the moviegoers to go back the following week.

The next Saturday, the movie did not start where the segment from the previous week ended, but with some footage not seen before. The anticipation through the week made the newest part doubly exciting (even though it was not continuous from week to week).

Their father told them to stay for only one show, and when their father said something, they knew he meant business. Mr. Sullivan said, "You boys come out after the first movie. Don't make me have to come inside to get you." And although they wanted to stay through several shows, they knew the punishment for not heeding his requests. Dire consequences awaited those who did not listen. When he said, "Only one show," he meant, "Only one show." No one said, "No" to Mr. Sullivan, and his sons were not going to be the first! *HE NEVER HAD TO GO INTO THE THEATER AFTER THEM!*

When Sharon was old enough to go to the movies with her brothers, her first Saturday matinee was *Tarzan*. She said, "A lion jumped toward the audience and I screamed. That startled the moviegoers, and my brothers were reluctant to take me with them again."

A neighbor lady hired Dewey and Lefty to clean the troughs she used for watering her cattle. They got into those troughs and scrubbed them before fresh water was pumped into them. The reward for their efforts was a few chunks from a peppermint stick (as mentioned earlier, sugar was rationed, so candy was a special treat). Dewey remembered that peppermint into adulthood.

A BAREFOOT BOY FROM OKLAHOMA

One of Dewey's greatest childhood disappointments was in the model airplanes that were available in cereal boxes. When he was fortunate enough to beat his brothers to the latest model, he grabbed it and ran outside, "I was excited, as I carefully started cutting the plane out according to the directions. But the balsa always split all the way across the sheet. I was so disappointed. I wanted to cry, but I couldn't wait to try again. I never saw one of those planes completed."

As a child, Dewey looked longingly into the drugstore in Fowler, where he saw an acquaintance enjoying a soda. He was envious of those who visited on a daily basis. (About four years ago he said, "I want to go the Fowler Drug Store for a soda or shake." The next time we were in Colorado, we visited Fowler, only to learn that the store had closed.)

Windle said, "While we lived near *Number Six*, I saved enough money from working in the fields to purchase a used bike. It took a while to save the money, but when I had enough, Dad and I hitchhiked to La Junta, where I found one I could afford. On the way home one of our neighbors met us, and gave us a ride. I had that bike until Dad got up early one morning, and rode it to Fowler to catch the bus to go to work. After that he took the bike, and I walked."

Dewey reported, "One night someone left that bike on the porch, and when Dad left for work the next morning, he fell over it, and there was 'Heck' to pay. We didn't do that again – after that experience, the bike was safely parked out of the way."

James Sims invited the Sullivan children to picnics and birthday parties at the church in Fowler. Dewey loved those activities. They contributed to his love of sports, and he became actively involved in anything athletic. He loved the pick-up games of kick-ball and basketball, and although he was shy, he became a leader.

Chester Dunsmoor, was the bus driver for the *Number Six School*, and was also the janitor and general handyman. (Chester was an icon in the Fowler area.) On weekends, he coached softball for a local town team, and inspired many in their love of athletics. They lived near the school, so all the Sullivan boys were able to go to the games on Sunday. Chester let them catch and shag balls for him.

Softball and basketball were the sports played. And even though it was a grade school, the kids traveled by bus to other schools to compete. At the end of each season, there were tournaments. Dewey was considerably younger than the other participants, but he was allowed to ride the bus to those games.

Several of the people that Chester worked with became excellent athletes. Windle said, "We felt that we owed him a lot, because he coached us, and taught us sportsmanship. He took us to games and tournaments in our grade school years. We also got to play basketball against the Fowler freshman team — which was a big deal to us!"

The family lived near Fowler for several years, before Dewey's father decided to look for housing closer to his work so he would not have so far to commute. When Chester learned of that, he told Mr. Sullivan that he had a house for them if they would stay in the Fowler School System. Dewey's mom wanted to accept the offer (she welcomed the thought of a place for her own cows and chickens), but Mr. Sullivan decided to move to the "old yellow house," as it was closer to the Pueblo Ordnance Depot.

CHAPTER 8

Before Indoor Plumbing

When the Sullivan family left Fowler, they moved into the "old yellow house," on Highway 50 between Fowler and Boone. That house was in the Boone School District, on the prairie in the middle of nowhere. Migrants, vagrants, hobos or tramps (whatever terminology you wish to use) visited them there. The hobos were provided a warm meal, and Dewey's father let them sleep in the barn. Sharon said, "It was rumored that, if a hobo got a good meal at a house, something was left to indicate that the residents were kind to people on the move."

Al Tilton said, "The house that the Sullivans moved into really was the 'Sullivan House.' An earlier family of Sullivans had lived there, and it was named for them. No one had lived in that house for some time, until one morning, the school bus stopped and a troop of children got onto the bus. They were like stair steps as they boarded."

The Sullivans rented the "Sullivan House" from Charley Dalton. Charley had the proviso that a room be reserved for him, so he could stay there whenever he wanted. His room was locked to keep the Sullivan kids out. The kids had heard a story of a murder there, so they were intrigued, and wondered what was behind the closed door.

One night the lightning streaked across the prairie sky, and flashed in an awesome display. The landscape was illuminated, and deafening booms of thunder were heard. The wind blew, and the old house creaked in response. A chunk of plaster fell with a crash in Dewey's parents' bedroom. Was the house haunted? Dewey's imagination ran wild. "It was scary and exciting. As I huddled with my brothers, I expected a ghost to appear. A door creaked, and the hinges screeched in protest. I was certain someone was in the house. I didn't sleep that night."

Back before the days of refrigeration in the Sullivan household, there was a screened-in porch at the back of the house where meat was hung to keep cool. The house was well built with a cellar beneath it. Double doors led to the cellar, and one morning a large rattlesnake was coiled there. Dewey's mom dispatched it, but in later life, Dewey would have taken it to the prairie to meander on its own.

Charley Dalton had some impressive horses, and the boys were told not to ride them. (However, that would have been asking a lot of young boys.) As he was on his way to the river one day, Dewey found an old bridle, complete with reins. He said, "Wow! A real bridle." (He was accustomed to playing with a "make-believe" bridle made from string, so to have the real thing was beyond his wildest dreams.)

He was excited because he knew where the perfect horse was for an adventure, and he hurried back to the corral where the horses were kept. He had a favorite horse that he had envisioned riding, and he caught it. He did not obey Charley's edict, and he got the bridle on after a struggle. He took off at a slow canter across the prairie shouting, "Giddyap." He said, "I could have been locked up for horse-rustling." Lefty and Windle also loved riding the horses.

The Sullivan family had chickens, and used them both for food and for the eggs produced. One of the chores assigned the children was to gather the eggs daily. They purchased three cows, and named one of them Lucy. Dewey and Lefty were responsible for bringing the cows to the barn to be milked. Windle said, "We sometimes rode one of the cows as we brought them in." The cows grazed and worked their way to the Arkansas River (about two and one-half miles away), and when the boys went after them, they saw quail and pheasants.

Lefty milked the cows and he and Dewey churned the cream into butter. The churn was a canning jar with a lid. The jar was shaken until the butter and buttermilk separated. (Dewey showed me how to do that when we went to a dairy near our home in Dayton for fresh milk.) Freshly churned butter was always on the menu in the Sullivan household. There was a large garden, and Windle helped his mother with the gardening.

As Dewey headed home one evening, he heard a rustle. He looked around to see where it came from, and heard another rustle. Then he heard a *RATTLE!!* He said, "I heard a rustle. Then I heard a rattle, and I was scared to death. I took a couple of steps and heard another rattle. I knew what that rattle meant. It meant a *RATTLESNAKE.*

"It was dusk and I couldn't see clearly, but I know there were at least four rattlers. I cautiously picked my way between them (he must have been near a den), and headed home. When I cleared the area and could see no more snakes, I raced like mad. That put the fear in me -- *BIG TIME!!!*"

One day he found a fuzzy black and white kitten (black with a white stripe down its back). He was excited, as he picked it up and hurried home to ask his mother, "Mom, can I keep him?" As soon as she saw the kitten she shrieked, "Eek! A skunk! Deward, you take that thing back where you found it, and don't ever bring one of those home with you again!" (That skunk must have been de-scented. He contemplated hiding it and keeping it as a pet, but he knew he could experience extreme punishment if he were discovered.)

He was disappointed, but he did as he was told. The lesson learned that day was, "Always leave black cats with white stripes down their backs to their own devices." His mother stressed that lesson.

He came from school one afternoon, and found that his dog, Scotty, had been poisoned. That was devastating to a young boy who was close to his little companion. He was saddened by his loss, and from that time, detested the use of poison for animal control. He loved animals, and when he was on the plains, he and Scotty had been inseparable.

Back when the bathroom was outdoors -- back when we used the Montgomery
Ward or Sears Roebuck catalog instead of Charmin -- back when water was either pumped from the well or brought up in a bucket, bath night and laundry day were weekly, rather than daily rituals.

There was no indoor plumbing, and hot water was not available at the turn of a faucet. Drinking water was pumped from a well, and then brought into the house to be kept in a bucket in the kitchen. An enamel dipper was used for drinking by all in the household.

Water was collected in barrels as the rain ran off the eaves. (Rainwater was considered soft, and was used for shampooing, bathing, etc.) No automatic washers or dryers were in the household.

Monday was laundry day . . . Friday was baking day . . . Saturday night was bath night. On Monday, a large pot of pinto beans was placed on the wood/coal stove to simmer throughout the day while the clothes were being washed. (Children from many families were kept from school to assist in the laundry chores, but education was of such importance in the Sullivan household, it did not happen there.)

The water for washing the clothes was pumped from the well outside, and heated on a pot-bellied stove in the house. It was then carried back outside, and poured into a galvanized tub. (That was before the advent of a washing machine in the Sullivan household.)

The clothes were sorted by color and by the degree of dirt. The whites were washed first, then the lighter colored items, progressing to the darker ones, and ending with those most heavily stained. A large, hand-held plunger was used for moving the clothes up and down in the wash water, and the dirtiest items were rubbed on a scrub board to get the dirt out. When that process was completed, a broomstick was used to lift the items from the hot water, and they were twisted to get most of the water from them.

The clean items were placed in a galvanized tub in which there was cool, clean water for rinsing. After the soap was rinsed from the clothing, the items were again twisted to get as much water from them as possible. They were then placed in a basket to be carried to the clothesline to be hung to dry.

Friday was baking day for Dewey's mother. She was prone to migraine headaches, and often did not feel well enough to get out of bed on a daily basis, but she always (at least almost always) baked on Friday. It was a necessity, and enough bread was baked to last the family through the next week. Early on Friday morning, she set the large bowl of yeast dough to rise so it could be formed into loaves, rolls and cinnamon rolls in the afternoon. Then she put the pinto beans on the back of the range to simmer, while she tended her baking chores.

Jonell said, "When the school bus pulled up in front of our house on Friday afternoon, we could smell the enticing aroma of the hot, freshly baked bread, and it made our mouths water." Freshly churned butter was ready to be put on the bread, and a friend often accompanied Dewey from school to share the bounty. I'm sure everyone on the bus wanted to get out at the Sullivan residence to sample the wares.

Saturday night was bath night, and again the water was heated on the pot-bellied stove, and carried to an oblong galvanized tub in what was referred to as the "bathroom." The family used the same water, and the designation for who bathed first was made according to age. (In our time of daily bathing, this is drastic, but much less water was consumed, and they were certainly more energy efficient.) It was definitely communal living.

Back when we had our shoes re-soled or re-heeled several times before passing them on to the next person in the family . . . back when one pair of shoes lasted through an entire year . . . the family shoes were polished on Saturday night. Each person who was old enough did his or her own, and then helped with the others. The polish was a wax applied with a rag, or from a bottle of liquid with a dauber on it. The shoes were polished, and then buffed to a high sheen before being placed on a paper near the door for final drying. (No wash-and-wear shoes in those days – no Nikes or Adidas.) The shoe shining was done in preparation for church on Sunday, and for the activities of the next week.

When the weather was warm, the Sullivans (and most other local residents) went to Fowler on Saturday night for shopping and conversing. The local farmers congregated in front of the various stores, and shared the events of the week.

Dewey's Uncle John lived in Fowler, and he gave his three kids and the Sullivan kids a small amount of change with which they bought hard candy. Candy was a luxury, and had to be shared among them all the next week. Dewey said, "We all looked forward to buying that candy."

In the summertime, Mrs. Sullivan packed a lunch, and went to the fields to pick crops. At the tender age of five, Dewey joined his brothers and his mother and they picked corn and cucumbers until sundown. Mr. Sullivan joined them when he came from the P.O.D. The corn and cucumbers were tossed into a wagon pulled by horses. Dewey said, "When we began picking, it was depressing to hear the sounds of the cucumbers or corn echoing from the bottom of the wagon as they landed. When we could no longer hear that sound, we were so happy." (The sounds became more muted as the wagon filled, and indicated that the job was almost finished.)

Windle said, "One time a car with California license plates stopped and took pictures of us picking. We felt quite important." (California was a dream destination in their minds during the '40s and '50s, and they thought those people were movie stars. But more than likely, the people in the car thought they were just a bunch of Okies.)

They planted tomatoes in the spring, and had to practically crawl along the rows as the young plants were put in the ground before tamping the earth around them. As the season progressed, they hoed the crops, and then picked them when they ripened. Dewey was not a farmer or a gardener, and he disliked working in the fields, but he worked alongside his mom and brothers.

His mother was given a calf that had been rejected by its mother, so she nursed it to health, and kept it in the house for several days while it recuperated. The kids named the calf, Butch. Dewey enjoyed butting heads with Butch, but his mother discouraged him from doing so, as she did not want Butch to be aggressive. The children all mourned when Butch was taken away.

Dewey loved banana pudding. He stealthily got into the bowl when he found that his mother had made one. He took several bites of it, and then smoothed the top over so his mother would not know. After several such tests, the level of the pudding in the bowl was decidedly lower. (It wasn't until he was older that he figured out how his mother could tell of his activities by the depth of the pudding in the bowl.)

A BAREFOOT BOY FROM OKLAHOMA

One day Dewey listened to the radio and heard an ad for a harmonica from Del Rio, Texas. He fell for the sales pitch, and was excited about the possibility of making music. He was assured he could easily learn to play, so he ordered one. It arrived, and he was frustrated as it was not as easy as he had been led to believe. He did not become proficient at playing the harmonica, and no great future in music awaited him.

Dewey was raised in a home rooted and grounded in love. He revered his Native American heritage, and envisioned himself riding bareback on an Indian pony across the plains counting coup on the white man. He said, "I loved running across the open spaces of the prairie, and I pretended to be an Indian brave." (When he went to a western movie, he often said, "Why don't the Indians ever get to win?)

His boyhood idol was Jim Thorpe, and he enjoyed reading about Jim's prowess in athletics. (Dewey's love of reading began with his interest in Thorpe and other sports figures.) He was also proud of his Irish/American lineage, and he referred to John L. Sullivan of boxing fame as a relative.

(When we moved to Dayton, Dewey befriended several Native American families – the Butlers, the Georges, the Lenos and others from Willamina and other local areas. He was a blood brother, though not through a ritual. The Confederated Tribes of Grand Ronde presented a beautiful wool Pendleton blanket to our family when Dewey died, and Jerry George gave our family a second one at the 2008 *Dewey Sullivan Memorial Golf Tournament* which is now the *Dewey Sullivan Classic*.)

CHAPTER **9**

Sixty Years to Tomorrow

This is not Dewey's beginning, but it is where I first became acquainted with him. I knew him for sixty years, loved him for more than fifty-five, and was married to him for fifty-three. He was my hero, my best friend, and my sweetheart and I miss him terribly (almost three years after his death).

On the outskirts of nowhere . . . on the desolate, wind-swept plains of eastern Colorado . . . midway between Pueblo and Fowler sits the small town of Boone. That is where I met Dewey Sullivan. He started school at Boone in the middle of our sixth grade year.

It was a different world. It was a different time. The year was 1945, and it signaled the end of World War II. Everyone rejoiced that the War was over. The servicemen returned, and things picked up at home. People married in record numbers, and the "Baby Boom Generation" was born.

Boone was, and still is an outpost. The town is so small it is not shown on most maps. There is a "City Limits" sign at each end of town, and there is little in between. There is no traffic signal. In 1945 there were three blocks in the downtown area. On those three blocks sat two cafes, two grocery stores, an automotive garage, a barber shop, two gas stations, a church, VFW Hall, post office, pool hall, lumberyard, beanery, hotel, and a frozen food locker, all on the two sides of the street that runs through Boone. (The frozen food locker

A BAREFOOT BOY FROM OKLAHOMA

was popular in the '40s and '50s, as most people did not have home freezers. Many rented lockers for their frozen food items, and some bought half a beef to be stored.) The hotel was a two-story structure used mainly as a rooming house (although an occasional tourist might have stopped by). Brown was the predominant color of the landscape, but the backdrop of the Rocky Mountains provided beauty.

The population of Boone was less than three hundred in 1945, and is about the same today. Everyone knew everyone else. From the early 1900s until 1960, there was a school there. The Bell Bean Company and the lumberyard were the two largest enterprises in the town of Boone. However, most residents worked at the Colorado Fuel and Iron in Pueblo, or the Pueblo Ordnance Depot just outside Pueblo.

One street still runs through the center of Boone, and more than sixty years later, there are no traffic signals. The trains run through the center of town, and the sounds of the train whistle are nostalgic. There is a post office. The school was demolished in 1964. An elementary school was built sometime in the 1960s and served the community for several years, but is now used for some sort of migrant activities.

The Sullivans came from Fowler, Colorado, and my family came from Oklahoma. Dewey's father found employment at the Pueblo Ordnance Depot for his first steady job. Up until the 1940s, he stayed on the move from job to job in order to keep a roof over his family, and he often worked at more than one job at the same time.

My family moved because my mother secured a position as the second grade teacher at Boone Elementary School. We had a steady income at last. She originally accepted the position of third grade teacher, but then realized she would have my brother in her class, so she switched to the second grade. Larry Fillmore told me, "Your mother taught three generations of Fillmores at Boone." (My father was older and disabled, and it was difficult for him to find work on a steady basis, so our move was made in order for my parents to support our family.)

We moved into that harsh environment in September of 1945, and that winter was our first in Boone. There were blizzard conditions, and the snow blew into six-foot drifts. School was cancelled for a week, and the students who lived north of Boone were taken home in "weasels" (some sort of Army vehicle with tracks). Coming from Oklahoma, we had never seen so much snow, or experienced such conditions, so my family found it interesting.

With the snow that blew during the winter, and the dust that blew in the spring, I was at a loss. What were my parents thinking? As I recall my early days in Boone, I can still feel the grit of dirt and sand. As a shy, young girl, it took me months to become accustomed to my new surroundings.

We rented a one-bedroom house, and my brother slept in the same bedroom as my parents. I was privileged, because I had a fold-down couch in the living room to myself. (We went to an auction in Pueblo, and purchased the necessities of life.)

With only two kids in our family, we did not need the larger space required by the Sullivan family. We had a coal-burning stove with a reservoir on the side for heating water. That water was used for washing dishes, bathing, shampooing, etc., and the range was used for cooking as well as heating.

Saturdays were spent in Pueblo, where we did the family laundry at a laundromat, and where we got ice for the icebox. We had an outdoor toilet (an "outhouse," a "privy," a "two-holer," whatever), and the house was sited on gravel – no lawns for us.

Dewey entered our classroom in 1946, midway through the school year. That day was a day much like any other during my first five months at Boone, but there was something different about it. Into my life walked this young man who would have a monumental impact on my life.

A BAREFOOT BOY FROM OKLAHOMA

We learned that his name was Deward Sullivan, and that he came from Fowler about twenty miles east of Boone. He sauntered across the stage of my life, and sixty-three years later, I remember that day. There was a bright spot. Little did I know then what his arrival would mean to me – how our lives would intertwine. I was unaware of the repercussions his life would have on mine.

We often discussed how different things might have been had he not moved from Fowler to Boone. His premise was that we would have met and joined our lives, but I was not so certain; however, God does lead.

As a shy, retiring girl of ten, I did not pay much attention to boys, but this boy was noteworthy, even to a young girl with my inexperience. There was an aura about him. (It was not the "love-at-first-sight" event many have asked about. After all, we were only in the sixth grade. But I remember his first day of school at Boone.) My seat was near the front of the classroom, and he was assigned a seat near the back.

We welcomed the Sullivan family, much as any small school would welcome a new family. It did not take long for Dewey to be assimilated into the group. He fit in well with our class, and we were happy to see someone new. Most of the girls were agog as he was nice-looking. He was one of the first selected when we went to the playground for a pickup game of dodge ball. The popular girls clustered around him. I stayed in the background, and tried not to be noticed.

Before the beginning of our eighth grade year, my parents rented a house across the railroad tracks. I was introduced to the convenience of an indoor bathroom and running water (my first experience with both). The bathroom was located inside the back door, and was quite cramped with a tub, stool and sink in a very small space. My brother had a bedroom to the right of the bathroom. My parents' bedroom was next to mine, and we lived in the "lap of luxury," with three bedrooms for the four of us.

We used an icebox for a couple of years, until we upgraded to a *Kelvinator* refrigerator with the motor on top. (I can still see that antique in my mind.) Both the icebox and the refrigerator were purchased used.

My grandfather (my mother's father) resided in Pueblo, and that, along with a steady income, contributed to my parents' decision to move to Boone. During my eighth grade year of school he had a stroke, and his second wife deserted him. He was moved into my brother's bedroom, and stayed with us until his death. At noon each day, my mother went from her classroom at Boone Elementary School to our home across the tracks to feed and care for him.

The Sullivan family lived in "The Sullivan House" on the prairie for several years, before Dewey's father purchased a house in Boone and they moved to town. According to Windle, "There were not many houses for sale in Boone after World War II, at least none that my father could afford, but he found one across the tracks for sale for $2,000.

"My dad calculated how much money he could save by my brothers and sisters and me walking home for lunch rather than eating in the school cafeteria (lunches then were probably thirteen cents), and the money saved made a big difference in his decision to buy the house – that, and the fact that he was closer to the P.O.D."

It was a more relaxed time. We did not have the convenience of automatic this and automatic that. We had fun and we enjoyed life. We ate our meals as a family. We talked. Sometimes I think we have lost the art of communication, of the written word, of talking to each other face-to-face.

In this fast-paced world everyone is rushing around looking for a better and faster way of doing things, and there is no time for being a family. Computers have speeded things up, but it seems there is more to do and less time in which to do it. But in the '50s we enjoyed family time and we did things together.

The "Sullivan House" is no longer standing. The ravages of time have taken it away, but the foundation still stands. Several times, Dewey, Jonell and I visited where the house once stood. They had many happy memories of their years spent there, and they liked to visit the location.

We have a Boone reunion every three years. Dewey's brother, Lefty, helped organize the first reunion in 1972. Those reunions were held every five years until 2002, when it was decided to have them every three years. Eventually, there will be no more Boone reunions, because there will be no more Boone alums.

Dewey and Norman enjoyed the Boone reunions. Before Norman died in 2004, he said, "The Boone reunion is coming up next year. I wish it were this year – I'm ready right now" (He died two weeks later.)

CHAPTER **10**

Boone — An Oasis in the Desert

When the Sullivan family moved into Boone, they had electricity. Dewey's mom acquired her first electric washing machine, and she no longer scrubbed items on the scrub board. Instead of twisting the clothes to get the water from them, her washer had a wringer to help with her chores.

And she was treated to her first electric refrigerator, a *Frigidaire*. She was proud of that purchase. (That refrigerator was long lasting, and Sharon used it after their parents moved to Oregon more than forty years later.) The washing machine and the refrigerator were the first major appliances that Mrs. Sullivan had. And – hallelujah – there was a radio in the home.

Each fall, Dewey and his brothers, along with many of their classmates, spent weeks harvesting the pinto beans. The harvest was in September and October, and Larry Fillmore said, "We usually missed the first six weeks of school because of that harvest." (The four Sullivan boys worked for the Gilleys, the Asbridges, the Wrights and the Bowmans.)

The workers were housed in a garage, and they rose before sunrise to the announcement, "Too bad you're poor boys and have to go to work." (Dewey dreaded that call and was reluctant to get out of bed.) The beans were shocked and stacked, and then placed on wagons to be put through the threshing machine.

The early mornings were not bad, but by mid-day with the sun beating down relentlessly, it became almost unbearable. They were treated well, and they looked forward to "chow time." Windle said, "There were some really good cooks in those families we worked for." Breakfast and dinner were eaten at the main house, and lunches were packed and taken to the fields to be eaten at midday.

Dewey told of one worker who growled at another when the food was passed, "Don't take it all." He also laughed about Mr. Gilley (the man for whom they worked), telling one of his sons, "Hush up, 'Rocks' or I'll hit you up side of the head with a 'tarmater.'" (Mr. Sullivan left home around the age of twelve to join the threshing crews moving around the Oklahoma area. He wanted better for his sons, so he insisted they get an education.)

One family had two homes, a nice brick affair north of Boone, and a comfortable one in Boone. Jonell cleaned house for them, and occasionally stayed north of Boone with the family during the summer. When we visited Colorado several years ago, Dewey turned to me and asked, "How would you like to buy that house and move back to Boone?" When we returned to Oregon he told his mother about his plan, and she told his brother, "Lefty, I think Dewey has lost his mind. He thinks he would like to move back to Boone. Can you believe he would consider leaving Oregon for Boone?" (She loved Oregon.)

When I was in high school, I had a job cleaning for Ruth Shockley, and was paid fifty cents an hour to dust, vacuum, etc. Clarence Shockley was the depot agent for the Santa Fe Railroad, and always drove a DeSoto. (It's strange what I remember.) Several times I was paid with clothing from the Shockley's daughter, Dorothy, rather than money. She lived in Colorado Springs, and must have had a decent-paying job because she had nice clothes.

One night a Boone resident was in the VFW Hall (the local "watering hole"), and Norman and a couple of friends lifted his car and placed it on cinder blocks (or blocks of wood). They then hid behind a building to watch. When the gentleman came out and started the car, he placed it into gear, but the car stayed where it was. He got out, looked around, then got back into the car, shifted gears and again revved it up. In the meantime, the guys had gotten in back of the car, and pushed it off the blocks when he hit the gas. Needless to say, he and his car hit the ground running.

None of the Sullivan boys smoked, but when they were young, their father did. Windle said, "When I was in the fourth grade, our dad called us in to talk to us. He told us that he would quit smoking himself as an example to us. He wadded his cigarette pack up and threw it away. He never smoked again."

Dewey went to Al Tilton's house one day to ride horses. He said, "We went to the corral where Al kicked around in the dried manure until he located one bridle. After knocking the manure from the bridle he found another bridle and two saddles, and we were ready to go. We were just a couple of 'hayseeds' out for an afternoon ride."

When Al got on his horse, it bucked a couple of times and Al came down hard. He split his hand on the metal of the saddle horn. Blood was everywhere! The leather had long since "given up the ghost," and the horn was bare metal. Al said, "Man, this is a dumb horse. He doesn't know who he's dealing with. He thinks he can buck me off." After cleaning up the mess and bandaging Al's hand they re-mounted, and had a fun afternoon of riding.

One evening about sundown, Al, Dewey and Lefty gathered camping gear and took off for the night. They cantered across the prairie, and suddenly the horses took a jump and sailed over something. Before they settled for the night, Lefty decided he was thirsty and went back for water. When he returned he said, "I came to this big canyon about three feet across. That's what the horses jumped over back there. It's a good thing they sensed that, or we would have been in big trouble." The next day they marveled at their close encounter.

As we grew up in Boone, Pueblo was the "Big City" to us. Colorado Springs was "large," but Denver was "huge." The first time I visited Denver was during my eighth grade year. I won the Pueblo County Spelling Bee, and went to Denver to compete. I was a small town girl in awe of so many large buildings and so many people. I did not win the State Spelling Bee – a couple of the words I missed were "quay," which I spelled "key," and "victuals," which I spelled "vittles," in my naivete.

The Korean War began five years after the end of World War II. In the early morning hours of June 25, 1950 North Korea launched an attack on South Korea and for three years the conflict raged. From 1950 until 1953 the United States joined the United Nations forces in Korea to take a stand against what was deemed to be a threat to democracy worldwide. The Korean War ended as we graduated, or Dewey would have enlisted in the service. (Windle, along with several Boone classmates, joined the Navy Reserves, and they drove to Pueblo on a weekly basis for Reserve activities.)

BOONE - AN OASIS IN THE DESERT

An uneasy peace returned by means of a negotiated settlement in 1953, and a million and half American veterans came home to a peacetime world of families, homes and jobs and a country reluctant to view the Korean War as a war that would never be forgotten.

Boone was, and still is, on the outskirts of Pueblo -- a town with its own personality. We grew up there, and I look back upon our experiences with great fondness. The '50s were a great time to grow up. We enjoyed many things that today's young people miss. We used our imaginations. We did not have computers, the Internet, or even television. We attended movies in Pueblo, either at the indoor theater or the drive-in, (where a carload got in for one dollar – at least on certain nights).

Desolate is a kind way of describing the plains of eastern Colorado. The land is dry and barren and tumbleweeds abound. Alkali turns the ground white. Boone, in the '30s, '40s and '50s, relied heavily on the growing of pinto beans on farms north of town. Acres of those beans grew there, and could be seen for miles. The cultivation of the beans meant plowing up the landscape, and that contributed to the Dust Bowl conditions. The topsoil blew in great clouds of dust across the prairies.

The land is now in a land bank *(The Conservation Reserve Program)*, and is no longer plowed. Grass now grows where pinto beans once grew, but when we attended school in Boone in the '40s and '50s, there were massive dust storms. The wind still blows, but dirt does not.

The landscape between Boone and Pueblo may be dry and desolate, but the experiences we shared were without compare. We had so much fun. There was always something to do. We were never bored, and we did not go looking elsewhere for excitement. It was all found in our small, secure environment.

Boone was an "oasis" in the middle of the desert, and it became our sanctuary. The landscape has changed, but the tradition and pride of the Boone Terriers lives on in many of us.

In the '40s and the '50s, the Colorado Fuel and Iron and the Pueblo Ordnance Depot were the two largest employers in the area.

A BAREFOOT BOY FROM OKLAHOMA

Steel no longer rules, although Pueblo is still an industrial city. I guess you could say we came from dirt, beans and steel.

The dirt blowing around Boone, the beans growing north of Boone, and the steel produced in Pueblo defined who we were and who we became. *WE WERE BOONE!!*

CHAPTER 11

Boone School

The Boone School District Number 29 was established in 1880, and the high school was built in 1921. The last class to graduate from Boone was the class of 1960, and the school building was demolished in 1964. The class pictures from that long-ago time are now housed in the train depot across the railroad tracks. The Class of 1953 is there with the others.

The Boone School was a two-story building with a basement. Dewey and I attended the sixth grade there. The sixth, seventh and eighth grades, the gymnasium, the cafeteria and the band room were located in the basement. You had to climb up concrete steps to the main floor to enter the school, or down more concrete steps to the basement. There was a coal furnace in the basement, and a truck loaded with coal regularly pulled into the school courtyard. It dumped its load into the area built for storing it. Coal dust coated everything.

A hot water radiator was located on the first floor of the building, and was used for heat. Similar radiators were found throughout the school building. Each morning, before school, the high school boys clustered around the first floor radiator (to watch the girls as they arrived). As a freshman, I remember how intimidated I was when I had to pass that group of boys. The high school classes were held on the second floor, the elementary classes on the first, and the

A BAREFOOT BOY FROM OKLAHOMA

junior high classes in the basement. There was a fire escape at the back of the top story of the school.

Fire drills were held periodically, and occasionally the boys made their "escape" down that fire escape. Norman Stice said, "It was fun sliding down the large pipe similar to a ride in an amusement park. If you were lucky enough to be first or near first to slide down, you could help catch the people behind you. As I recall, it got slicker and faster with each person sliding down. There was also the opportunity to see some unusual sights, especially when the girls were wearing dresses." (Most of our classmates went down that escape, but I did not do so until I was a senior. I don't know how I avoided it through those fire drills, but I did.)

Windle recently had a phone call from Frank Bauman, a former classmate. Frank said, "We were all poor. We just didn't know we were poor, because everyone was." He said, "Dewey didn't make a lot of fuss and did his thing. He loved his sports, but was primarily a basketball player, so it surprised me that he became a football coach. Our football team wasn't the greatest in the world."

Another classmate, Vern Wolf, was quoted, "I always thought Dewey was into basketball. Football for us was pretty rough because all we played on was dirt. We didn't have grass or anything like that, so we got pretty roughed up. And -- we weren't too hot." Frank and Vern agreed that, when Dewey died his loss would be felt, not only in Oregon, but throughout Colorado as well.

Norman Stice said, "It was not unusual for some of the students who lived in Boone (most did not) to practice basketball after school, until the janitor would invite us to go home because he was finished with his work, and was locking the school for the day."

Our seventh grade teacher, Esther Mae Roberts, helped Dewey learn to value education. She was a jock herself, and we had softball games, etc. during recess. For the first time, Dewey did not mind going to school. He was shy and did not like to be the focal point of attention, so Esther Mae helped immensely.

Our football and basketball coach, Don Chambers, was Dewey's role model. Don played basketball in college, and Dewey admired him. They talked on the phone several times in the 1990s, and when Dewey told Don of his trips to Africa, etc., Don remarked, "You never cease to amaze me."

Basketball was Dewey's sport in high school, and he was named to the All-State team his senior year. The Boone Terriers won league that year, and went to the *BIG CITY OF DENVER* for the basketball tournament. I was a cheerleader, and we stayed at the YWCA, and were in awe of the big city atmosphere. We were well chaperoned, and had a wonderful time. What a great experience for small-town kids.

The Boone Terriers did not win a football game while we were in high school. They were much better in basketball. Football was played on a tack burr-infested gravel field in Boone, not the best of conditions. We had no team our junior year and only had twenty players for eleven man football our senior year.

Norman Stice, stated, "I remember the tack burrs on our football field. After each play, the opposing team would have to stop and pick the tack burrs from their hands, and the Boone players would simply rub their hands together to get rid of the burrs (we were accustomed to playing under those conditions).

◄ A BAREFOOT BOY FROM OKLAHOMA

Our football team struggled, and we had a horrible field on which to play.

"We did not have enough players to play eleven-man football. As I recall, we barely had enough players to play six-man football. I remember wearing the old style, leather football helmets." (Despite his high school experience, Dewey grew to love the game of football and found challenges in it. Football became his passion.)

James Dean was the teenage idol in the '50s, and the boys tried to be like him. They rolled up the sleeves on their t-shirts and walked with a swagger. Smoking was widely accepted, and movies showed the stars smoking. Dewey did not smoke, but many of our classmates did. The image projected was that of the typical "bad boy."

At the beginning of our junior year, Dewey wore bell-bottom pants from the Army surplus store in Pueblo. (He usually wore shrink-to-fit Levis, but that year he had bell-bottoms.) He looked super!! The '50s were great, and we had so much fun. We really thought we were grown up.

At the theater, we watched the movies and newsreels in black and white. 3-D movies were popular, and we saw *House of Wax* with Vincent Price. Africa was of special interest to Dewey, so he particularly liked *B'wana Devil*. (*B'wana Devil* was offered several years ago on *DirectTV*, so we subscribed. He was disappointed when it aired. It was not at all as he remembered.)

Before the junior-senior prom and banquet our senior year, Dewey and I demonstrated fine dining for the student body (I'm not certain why). Our English teacher, Miss Beswick, was a true lady and worked with us on etiquette. We learned that the soup-spoon should be moved away from you instead of toward you; however, Emily Post would not have given us any stars for our demonstration.

A BAREFOOT BOY FROM OKLAHOMA

Before the beginning of our junior year of high school, Dewey's friend, Garnet Wright moved to Boone from Denver. Garnet was accustomed to classes of more than two hundred fifty. At Boone, a class of twenty students was considered large, so Garnet was unprepared for our graduating class of nine.

Garnet said, "When we came into Boone, we came over a small hill and there sat the town of *BOONE!*" (Boone -- what a shock for a young man from Denver.) He said, "I can remember the highway – it was full of chuckholes. At that time, it was hard to drive over thirty-five miles per hour. We came over a hill, and there it was: *BOONE, COLORADO.* I thought it was the end of the world.

"I did not consider Boone a town. The highway was the only paved street in town – all the others were dirt . . . I stayed inside my home in Boone for the first week (I was so depressed). I didn't want to venture out at all. But near the end of that first week, my mom came in one morning and told me there were a couple of young men outside who wanted to see me. I went outdoors and met Dewey, who became my best friend. From that day on, the town of Boone started to look better to me. We did several things together the rest of the summer. Whenever we could get a ride, we would go to Pueblo. That was where everyone went to have fun. We couldn't do much because we didn't have much money. When school started in September, Dewey showed me around."

(Dewey and Garnet lived about three blocks apart and became almost inseparable. They had many adventures together -- athletic events – football and basketball games, and several plays).

One Saturday night, I had a date to go to a drive-in movie in Pueblo. I was with Jim Davidson, and we double-dated with the twosome of Dewey and a girl named Marthena. Jim and I were together in the front seat and Dewey and Marthena were in the back. Halfway through the movie, we changed places (Dewey and I became a pair) and Marthena and Jim were together. (We must have considered each other more compatible. I don't know why we changed places, but we did.) That was our first "date."

BOONE SCHOOL

Later, while on a school outing at a skating rink, Dewey and I kissed for the first time. That kiss was like a warm breath of spring on a cold winter's day, or a ray of sunlight on a cloudy day. I blushed. The kiss was tentative, but then bells and whistles sounded. *(A kiss is just a kiss — yeah, right!!)* When his lips found mine, I stopped thinking. I could only feel. I floated on air. (Something had changed — everything had changed!)

It lasted for only moments, but it was for a lifetime — a lifetime to be filled with love and companionship! Happiness bubbled up within me like a spring. My heart was beating so loudly, I was certain he could hear. My world spun out of control, and I fell in love. I knew then that I would follow him to the ends of the earth (and I almost did). Our journey began with a kiss. Our journey ended with a kiss.

One evening, when Dewey came to pick me up for a date, I was enjoying mashed potatoes and gravy. He later told me that he was shocked at how much I ate, and he teased me about the amount of food I consumed. (I don't know why he didn't hightail it out of there when he had the chance.)

Before our senior year, we went to Carlsbad Caverns with the youth group from the Boone Baptist Church. Both Dewey's mother and my mom accompanied us as chaperones. Dewey and I became a twosome, and were inseparable. We swam in a nearby lake, and Dewey grabbed my swim cap, donned it, and jumped from the tower into the lake. He surfaced with his hair sticking out the hole he made in the top of it. I really laughed about that, even though I had to buy a new cap. He looked so funny.

We were out in the sun for hours. I got badly sunburned, and was miserable for days after our return. (I burned more readily than he did. I guess it was his Native American heritage that saw him through. He tanned beautifully.)

When we returned, Dewey got a job at the icehouse, and he loaded blocks of ice weighing three hundred pounds. He slid the ice up a ramp to be loaded into bunkers atop refrigerator cars. It was hard, backbreaking, muscle-building work, but was in a cool

◄ A BAREFOOT BOY FROM OKLAHOMA

environment. Garnet Wright's parents had moved to Pueblo, and Dewey stayed with them while he worked there.

Mr. Sullivan was frequently sent on field trips for the P.O.D., so he was not home to supervise his sons' activities. At night, Dewey and Norman often pushed the family car out of the driveway onto the street so they could drive away without their mother being aware they were gone. The gas tank usually registered *EMPTY* when the car was returned.

During our junior year of high school Dewey's cousin, Bill Evans, lived with the family and registered at Boone High School as a sophomore. He attended school for nine weeks, but his grades did not warrant further time in the household. He moved on, but while he lived with them, he insisted they return the car to the driveway with at least half a tank of gas.

Back when the car dealerships covered their showroom windows to keep the public curious about the next year's model, you had

◄ 66

to wait until the day of the "unveiling" to see the newest models. Mr. Sullivan went shopping for a car at the Ford lot in 1951. The salesman offered him terms on a purchase. With that offer, Dewey's dad said, "Let's get out of here. He thinks we can't afford that car." (He never bought anything he could not pay cash for.) He went to the Chevy lot, and purchased a '51 Chevy (the car we eloped in two years later).

During our senior year, our social studies teacher dubbed Dewey, "Dew Drop." That nickname stuck until he graduated. (He became known as "Dewey" during his third year of college. He did not like the name "Deward," as it was often transposed to "Edward." He tired of telling people, "No, my name is not 'Edward' . . . it is 'Deward.'" As though he didn't know his own name. He was happy to finally have a name that people could relate to.)

Ward Vining, our high school principal, was a graduate of the University of Colorado, and during our senior year of high school, he took Dewey on a recruiting trip to visit the Buffalos and to meet the football team. Dewey stood on the sidelines, and enjoyed the game. He attended several C.U. games that fall, and considered attending CU and trying football on a walk-on basis.

I had been awarded a National Merit Scholarship that provided books, tuition, room and board to be used at any college, and I had decided to attend the University of Colorado. But Dewey and I were in love, so we chose marriage and work over football and college.

In later years, Dewey told his classes, "You get married because you have to -- because you have found your other half. You get married to become complete, and because you want that special someone in your life – that her happiness is more important than yours." (We were fortunate to find that sort of relationship at such a young age and things worked out for us, but that is most often not the case. They called it "puppy love.")

The Boone gym was turned into a roller skating rink after we graduated. Sharon tried to do the *Bunny Hop* one night, and fell and broke her right wrist. The doctor put a cast on her arm that extended from her armpit to just above her fingers. When it was time to have the cast removed, Dewey took her to the doctor.

The doctor told Sharon that it had not healed properly and that it needed to be re-set. She moaned in the back seat on the way home. Dewey turned to her and said, "You're really lucky this did not happen to you during the pioneer days, because if it had, you would, most likely, have had your arm cut off above the wrist, and the wound cauterized with a branding iron so you would not bleed to death." She was so upset, she cried the rest of the way to Boone.

We took steps toward growing up, but when the time came for us to graduate, we hated to part with our comfortable environment. It had become our "security blanket." However, as all good things must, our years at Boone High School came to an end. We graduated and moved on. We maintained contact with some of our classmates, and lost track of others. Several have left this life, and others are still hitting the high spots. Friendships were forged that have lasted more than sixty years.

The '50s were summertime, hula-hoops and penny loafers -- flattops and ducktail haircuts – twenty cent per gallon gasoline and three cent postage stamps -- bobby socks and rock and roll. It was the time of poodle skirts and crew-cuts. We watched Red Skelton and Milton Berle on television – we watched vaudeville – we watched almost anything just to be watching television. *I Love Lucy* with Lucille Ball and Desi Arnaz, and *The Honeymooners* with Jackie Gleason were popular.

It was a decade of change. There were more and more household appliances. Married women joined the work force. The sounds of the Big Band Era were replaced by Roy Orbison. The war in Korea began and ended. Joseph McCarthy started the Communist scare, and Elvis Presley twisted his torso to fame. Gary Cooper appeared in *High Noon*, and Alan Ladd in *Shane*, and the Class of 1953 was ready to take on the world. We had everything but money! *WE HAD IT ALL!!*

CHAPTER **12**

Hugs from Heaven

During our junior year of high school, Jimmy Davidson suggested that Dewey and I, and he and his girlfriend, run off, get married and move to Missouri. (Jim had been in our class at Boone, but withdrew as a freshman.) Jim said, "Jobs are easy to find in Missouri, and we could build a couple of houses."

But that did not really appeal to Dewey (I cannot imagine why -- to be encumbered with a wife when he was sixteen or seventeen years of age). Going to work on a regular basis did not interest him either. He had higher aspirations. It was a good thing we did not try it at that time. It was hard enough when he was eighteen, and I was seventeen.

The year was 1953, and Dewey and I graduated from Boone High School in May. Our class was an eager class of nine students, and we were ready to go out into the *BIG, WIDE WORLD!!* The summer after our graduation was filled with excitement and wonder. We were ready to take on life (or so we thought). We were unaware of what adulthood entailed, but Dewey and I were in love.

While we were dating, we occasionally had the luxury of borrowing my parents' car. When we did, we often went to Pueblo for a movie and a hamburger and malt. And when Dewey's father was not using his car, we sometimes had use of it. With no telephone in either of our homes, we usually had pre-arranged dates. If we had not made a date in advance, Dewey often stopped by my house to ask me to either go to Pueblo, or to go for a walk. When we did not have transportation, we just walked around town.

Under the cloak of night, on a beautiful August evening in 1953, Dewey came by my home. We did not have a car that night, so we strolled hand-in-hand to the Boone School. The sun had slipped behind the horizon, and darkness pressed in. Crickets chirped in the background, and stars twinkled in the sky.

The scent of fresh-mown grass hung in the air. I breathed in the fresh evening air, and let the peace of the evening enfold me. Overhead the crescent moon tipped lazily in the star-studded sky, and falling stars dashed across the canopy of the heavens. Dewey and I sat on the lawn and talked. (We were the only two people in the world!)

After several minutes, he shyly said, "Why don't we drive to Raton and get married?" (My heart went "ka-thump," and skipped a beat. My hands trembled, but he couldn't see. My wildest dream had come true.) I didn't give him time to re-think his question. I said, "Yes, let's!" (The stars fell on Colorado that night! I was in love and the prospect was exciting. What a night! We were engaged! We promised each other forever and made plans to elope. We were just two teenagers in love.)

Dewey's question was tentative, but with that, our future was determined. We sealed our engagement with a kiss, and set the course for our lives. We talked for a while and discussed our future together. We held hands as we walked back to my house. (Love was in the air!) I slept very little that night. When I opened the drapes the next morning, sunshine tiptoed silently across the room. I floated on "Cloud Nine" all day.

Dewey later told me, "I didn't want to get married at such a young age, but I knew that what we had was too special to leave to chance, to the chance that we might be separated by time and relationships, and I didn't want that to happen. I had to marry you. I planned to go to college and play football, and then do some traveling before settling down."

We did not have an actual plan for our elopement, but we selected the date as August 8. The days dragged by on weary feet. It seemed to take forever, but the day finally arrived. Two days after Dewey's proposal, I stayed overnight with a friend who lived about thirty-five miles from Boone. When Dewey stopped at my home to pick me up, he was told I was in Rocky Ford. He had borrowed his father's '51 Chevy so he drove to Rocky Ford to get me. We were ready for our great adventure.

When he arrived at my friend's house, he came to the door and asked, "Are you ready?" (Was I ready? I was *READY!!*)

I wore a sleeveless dress and red sandals, and Dewey wore jeans. That was hardly wedding attire, but we were ready. We drove to Raton, New Mexico, and said our vows before a Justice of the Peace, with two strangers as witnesses.

We legally became man and wife, and were excited and in awe of our status as "newly-weds." ("Now, what do we do? What is the next step? Where do we go from here?" We did not have a clue what the future held.)

We did not share the information of our elopement in later years, because we realized the pitfalls involved with early marriages. We did not want people to think we were advocates of teenage marriage (which we were not). We definitely had struggles, and we knew we were the exception to the rule.

CHAPTER **13**

May I Have This Dance? (For the Rest of My Life?)

The day after our marriage, I left with my family for a two-week trip to California. *(WHAT A HONEYMOON!!)* My friend, Ann Chandler Carruth, accompanied us, and I told her we were married. Dewey told his mother, and she said we should tell people we were married, in the event I should become pregnant (which I did after three months of marriage).

Neither of us had a job. We had no car, but we were married. It took a while for reality to set in. We did not realize how foolish we were to start marriage under such conditions, but maybe that was a blessing. We were excited, and ready for a challenge.

We kept our marriage secret for a month. We knew the marriage certificate would be sent in the mail, so Dewey asked Norman to go to the post office on a daily basis to retrieve it before anyone became aware of what we had done.

While I was on our "honeymoon," Dewey purchased a 1942 Plymouth for $350. It was a former Army car, and was painted black (a very poor paint job – it looked like it was hand-painted), but he was proud of it. He finally had his own "wheels," and he drove it around to show his buddies.

After I returned from my trip, he came by my home, and showed it to me. It was his first major purchase, and he was excited. He once captured a small snake, and put it into the glove compartment (I'm not really certain why). The snake escaped into the car (or maybe out of it, as it was never found), but I refused to ride with him until I knew the snake was no longer in the car.

After my "honeymoon," I rented a room at the YWCA in Pueblo, and got a position at Bell Telephone. We then told my parents what we had done. To say they were not happy is an understatement, but they coped and we kissed and made up.

We were young and naïve and had no idea what we were doing, but we succeeded against the odds. Garnet Wright said, "Dewey and I went to Pueblo to apply for a job. I looked over his shoulder and saw he had marked: 'Married' where marital status was questioned. I nudged him and said, 'What's that about?'" Dewey grinned his slow grin and said, "Vera and I drove to Raton and got married." Garnet was surprised, but kept our secret.

Dewey picked me up from work one afternoon, and said, "I have a surprise for you. Wait until you see it." He drove across the Arkansas River, and showed me an apartment. It was a darling little unit and I loved it immediately. We set up housekeeping there a week later. It was a two-car garage, which had been converted into a duplex. Our bedroom was upstairs, with a bathroom and kitchenette on the ground floor. The rent was fifty dollars a month, and one of his buddies said, "That's a lot of money to pay for rent. Will you be able to handle it?" (But we did fine for the first eight months of our married life.)

It was exciting to have a place of our own. We moved in, and were happy to establish our own home. We did not lock our door, so my father occasionally stopped by and left steak or some other delicacy. Our own apartment . . . eggs sizzling in the pan . . . bacon frying in the morning. (Oh, what happy memories.)

Dewey was not a shopper, but went shopping one day and ordered four pounds of bologna. He told me, "I ordered four pounds of bologna, and the butcher started slicing. He sliced, and sliced, and sliced. I looked around to see who had ordered so much. I figured someone must have a really big family. When he handed the bundle to me, I couldn't believe it was mine. I didn't want to tell you what I had done, so I invited Garnet to lunch. I hoped we could eat enough that it wouldn't be such a noticeable stack."

Garnet said, "One day before lunch, Dewey came by the car lot where I worked. We talked for a while, and then he asked if I had eaten lunch and I told him 'no,' so he asked me to go to his house and have lunch with him. There in the 'fridge' was all this lunchmeat. I took one look and laughed. He said he went to the store and the clerk asked how much he wanted. Not realizing how much four pounds of bologna would be, he asked for that much. It was a big stack. Dewey said we had to eat as much as we could before Vera came home." (Of course, how can you hide a huge package of bologna?)

But Dewey liked bologna sandwiches. Whether we went on cross-country trips to Colorado and Kansas to visit relatives, or to National Science Foundation summer sessions, we often stopped at a grocery to purchase white bread and bologna (very nutritious). That made a quick and inexpensive meal for the six of us.

(Several years ago Dewey said, "I would like to purchase an old station wagon and take a trip with our kids. We could stop along the way for white bread and bologna." He had fond memories of our travels. I believe Candy was willing, but our other three were not, and I know I wasn't.)

Our early days of marriage were a lark. We were best friends, and were usually in each other's company. We had many adventures together. We went to movies. We visited friends. We enjoyed sodas at the soda fountain near our home. We went to the zoo. (Before our marriage, we lived in Boone, and had to drive to Pueblo for entertainment. We had not lived in close proximity to movies, etc., so when we married and moved to Pueblo, a new world beckoned and we reveled in it.)

CHAPTER **14**

Parenthood — We're Having a Baby

Our early days of marriage were fairly carefree, but then we embarked on our next BIG ADVENTURE: PARENTHOOD!! After three months of marriage, we were pregnant. We started down the "Road of No Return," and our lives were forever changed. Pregnancy did not inhibit us, and we looked forward to it, as we had marriage and our other experiences. We realized that with "our" pregnancy, our lives would undergo a drastic change. We knew that finances would suffer, and our time together would be shared with a third individual. But we were undaunted, naïve perhaps.

Dewey worked at a factory near Pueblo for the first year of our marriage. He and Windle made barrels from sheets of steel, and the bottoms were crimped and fastened to the barrel. Windle said, "Sometimes those bottoms were launched (like Frisbees), and sailed across the warehouse. We had to be ready to dodge. The work was dangerous, and I still have scars on my arms from those encounters."

I worked for Bell Telephone in Pueblo until five months before our first child, Candy, was born. Bell Telephone did not allow pregnant women to work when pregnancy became evident (discrimination?). So, whereas we were accustomed to having two incomes, we were reduced to one. We moved to Boone to live with my parents, and lived there until Candy was three months old. (Before we became pregnant, Dewey's father advised us to save my salary, and to use Dewey's to live on. That was good advice and helped us through many financial struggles.)

I drove the '42 Plymouth to my job, and Dewey carpooled with Windle. On one of our days off, we ran errands, but didn't put gas in the car (the gas gauge was broken so when I drove I kept the tank topped off). Dewey did not pay attention to such trivialities (our son, Brent, is similar and has often run out of gas). The next day I ran out of gas near where Dewey was employed. In my high heels and skirt, and in my early pregnant state, I tottered toward the barrel factory to get his assistance.

I was in time to see Dewey and Windle take off for Boone. I waited until they got there, and then called and had them come back (about ten or fifteen miles) to bring gas. I was late to work that day (the only time while I worked there). I was not a "happy camper," and never let him forget that episode in our lives together.

My pregnancy went well, and in the early morning hours of

PARENTHOOD - WE'RE HAVING A BABY

August 12, 1954, I was awakened by sharp pangs. That warned us that the birth of our first child was near. My mother rode with us to the hospital in Pueblo, and I lay in the back seat. It felt as if Dewey hit every pothole on the road. It was very uncomfortable.

When I was admitted, the doctor was not in attendance, so I was given ether to slow the birth. A baby's cries were heard at eight o'clock a.m., and Candy entered the world.

Tears of happiness welled in my eyes as I held her in my arms, and I innocently asked Dewey, "Do you like her?" He said, "Of course, I like her, Silly." He thought that was hilarious and loved telling on me. How naïve I was. (Of course, he liked her and was proud of her.)

After living with my parents for eight months (five months before Candy's birth and three months after), we rented a house one block from my parents' home for twelve dollars a month. Candy was a colicky baby, and awakened frequently during the night, so my parents appreciated having their home to themselves once again. But they loved having Candy there for that short period of time.

When we moved into that house, Garnet Wright moved in with us, and paid us five dollars a month for the "privilege." (Was it a "privilege," Garnet? It was probably more like living in a rooming house than a "privilege.") The house was big and drafty, and Dewey had weights upstairs. He and Garnet lifted those weights with much clanging and clanking.

We were married for fifteen months and Candy was three months old, when my father, who was a carpenter, suggested we build our own house. We liked his suggestion, so with the help of our families, we succeeded in building a nice, small two-bedroom house, with one-bath. We found a lot in Boone midway between where Dewey's parents lived and my parents' home. (Actually, the town of Boone was probably for sale, but we settled on that particular lot and started planning our home.)

The excitement was incredible. The plan we chose had a large picture window in the front, and my father installed hardwood flooring in the living room, and laid it around the perimeter of the

◄ A BAREFOOT BOY FROM OKLAHOMA

room, instead of in a straight line. It met in the center in a diamond pattern, and we were proud of his handiwork. (He had done a similar job in Oklahoma, and was intrigued by it.)

We shopped for the best buys on the lumber and materials needed, and we purchased mahogany siding for the exterior. While we worked on our house, Lefty said there were "too many chiefs and not enough Indians." We borrowed $1,200 from Dewey's parents for the lumber, and I went to work at the Pueblo Ordnance Depot to help pay off the loan. Ed and Meribeth Wagner purchased the house in 1958, and have fixed it up nicely. It is still beautiful.

Garnet moved with us when we moved into our own home, and he continued to give us a small amount monthly. He worked at a car dealership in Pueblo, and brought us two console radios that had been used as trade for cars. (I wish we had kept those radios.) Garnet lived with us until he and Norma married in June of 1955.

We were ecstatic. We loved our new home -- our very first house, and we luxuriated in our surroundings. For cooking, we used a kerosene stove with two burners (similar to a camp stove). That

◄ 80

PARENTHOOD - WE'RE HAVING A BABY

stove smoked if it were not properly adjusted, so we later upgraded to a gas range.

Lefty lived across the street, and Candy was enamored with his son, Willis. One day she saw him, and "hot-footed" it across the street as fast as her little legs would carry her. Dewey was in hot pursuit. He ran out of his shoes to "rescue" her. There was no traffic, but he did not want her to make a habit of crossing the street without looking.

My father doted on Candy. She was the *APPLE OF HIS EYE*. He was older (almost fifty), when I was born, and that made him more devoted to children. When we prepared to go somewhere he said, "Why don't you leave her here with us?" He loved caring for her, and he got a lot of pleasure from baby-sitting. (Candy was a little more than two years old when he died. He would have enjoyed watching her develop and grow. He also enjoyed Barry, but they did not become well acquainted as he died on Barry's first birthday.)

One night we went with Garnet north of Boone, and left Candy with my parents. Garnet's battery was low, and when we went down into a dip, the car died. We were not certain how far it was to the nearest house, so we huddled in the car with no blankets (Dewey and I were together in the back and Garnet was by himself in the front).

We spent an uncomfortable night. It was so cold. Dewey and I cuddled, but poor Garnet shivered alone. We were happy we had not taken Norma, his fiancée, with us. If she had been stranded overnight, her father would have been furious. The temperature was around thirty degrees (that was in Colorado in January). The next morning we walked to habitation (almost one and a half miles), and were relieved to get the assistance of the farmer whose house we went to.

When Candy was five months old, I got a job at the Pueblo Ordnance Depot (the P.O.D.). Soon after I began work there, we discovered we were going to be blessed with a second addition to our family. I worked at the P.O.D. until Barry was born on October

19, 1955. With his birth, we welcomed a baby boy into our home and were elated. The Sullivan name would be carried on for another generation.

The dust blew so hard one afternoon while I worked at the P.O.D. that we were dismissed from work, and sent to the buses to return home. Visibility was so poor the buses were unable to leave the parking lot, so we sat in the dust for almost two hours. The dust sifted through the windows and cracks, and got into our eyes and ears. We heard the incessant thrumming of the sand and dirt hitting the sides of the bus. There was a collective sigh of relief when we were allowed to leave.

My parents had taken Candy to Pueblo that day, and on their return trip to Boone, they were involved in an accident caused by the blowing sand. Several years ago Dewey and I saw the movie, *The Last Picture Show,* and it reminded us of Boone because of the dust. Dewey told Norman, "You need to see that movie. It reminds me of Boone."

When Dewey came from work one day, he brought two greyhound puppies home with him. He had adopted them at the dog pound in Pueblo, and was so proud. They were from racing stock, but not of quality good enough for the track. When his mom learned of his venture (misadventure?), she said, "Vera, I know Dewey doesn't have any sense, but I thought you did." (I guess I didn't!) We later adopted two more greyhounds, and took them out on the prairie just to see them run -- they could flat-out fly!

Al and Vera Tilton had a daughter Candy's age, and we often did things together. We visited them one Sunday afternoon, and there was a large mud puddle at the entrance to their house (it was a quite rural property). Dewey drove through the puddle, and our car became mired to the axles. We had to have a tractor pull us out. "No mountain too high, no river too deep." Dewey was ready for a challenge.

Mr. Sullivan had several 'coon hounds, and he frequently went 'coon hunting at night. Dewey sometimes went along on those excursions. His father allowed the dogs to tree the raccoons, but

PARENTHOOD - WE'RE HAVING A BABY

not harm them. I guess it was to hear the dogs bark "treed." Once Dewey lost one of those hounds in the canyons south of Boone. He returned several times over the next few days, but was not successful in locating that hound. His father was not happy about the loss of his dog.

Dewey worked at the barrel factory for a year after our marriage, and then he went to work at the Colorado Fuel and Iron (now Oregon Steel). (It was known that the married men needed the work, so they were given the worst jobs at the CF&I.)

Dewey worked in the coke plant, the tube mill, and other locations. (Coke plants are now outlawed in the United States.) With that job, he decided he did not want to work at the CF&I the rest of his life.

After two years of marriage, and with a second child on the way, I asked Dewey, "Would like to go to college? I think we can manage it." *(WHAT WAS I THINKING?)* We were debt-free and I was looking for a new adventure (adventure??).

Dewey disliked his jobs at the CF&I, so the idea of leaving there met with his approval. He did not pause, but replied, "Yes, I've always wanted to be a coach." He did not say he wanted to be a teacher. He said he wanted to be a coach. He worked at the CF&I until he began his studies at Pueblo College, and he also worked there the last summer before he went to Gunnison.

We had no idea what our decision would entail, but we embarked on the course. I view it as a "life-changing decision" -- the best decision we, as a couple, made during our marriage. That seemingly insignificant question changed the course of our lives. It was like a snowball gathering speed as it sped downhill toward its destination.

CHAPTER **15**

Don't Look Back

While Dewey was in high school, he had decided he wanted to be a coach. He admired Don Chambers, and considered him a role model. But when we married in 1953, he put his dream on hold. When I asked if he wanted to go to college, it all fell into place.

He began his studies at Pueblo Junior College (now Colorado State University, Pueblo) in 1955. He drove the school bus for the Boone School District, and commuted to Pueblo after his morning route. Each evening when Candy heard the crunch of tires on gravel, she ran out to get on the bus. She was excited and screamed, "Daddy's home!" She was intrigued, as most two-year-olds would be, and she loved that bus. It was a big deal to her.

Dewey tried out for football at Pueblo College, and made the team, but was run-down from his employment at CF&I. He became ill during the second week of practice, and missed several days. He believed in commitment, and felt he let the team (the other players and the coach) down by missing so many practices, so he did not go back. However, he participated in track his freshman year, and he was impressed when his team visited the newly-opened Air Force Academy for a competition.

He came home and studied religiously at night. It was a struggle because Candy and Barry were distractions, and he loved entertaining them. He played with them as his schedule allowed, but he still had homework to do. (He remained forever a kid at heart and he enjoyed working with children.)

The summer between his freshman and sophomore years at Pueblo College, Dewey got a position with Phillips Petroleum of Bartlesville, Oklahoma. He, along with another fellow, was designated to stake out potential sites for drilling for oil. The favorite prank the two of them played, was to put the stakes into the middle of a red ant hill. That was no fun for the drillers who did not appreciate their humor.

Dewey was meticulous in getting his coursework done, so he would not have to take extra time to get his degree. Each term he studied the schedule and took only the necessary courses, nothing frivolous. In art appreciation, it was discovered he had an artistic bent, and his English teacher was impressed with his writing abilities. He had a knack for expressing himself, and for getting the gist of what the author was trying to impart. He had a succinct way of communicating. He was a man of few words, but when he said something, it had meaning.

I started work at the Boone School in 1956, and worked there until May of 1957. Dewey's mom babysat Candy and Barry and doted on them. Barry was little more than a year old when we discovered we were again pregnant. *(IT MUST HAVE BEEN THE WATER.)*

During the early days of my third pregnancy, the doctor thought I was possibly pregnant with twins. I was excited when he suggested it might be a multiple birth. I could hardly wait to tell Dewey. (How naïve could I have been?)

Actually, I should have looked at a single birth as a good thing, especially considering our financial situation, and the fact that Dewey had another two years of study before he received his degree.

When I went for an exam about three months into my pregnancy, my doctor sent me to another doctor for an x-ray to determine if I might be pregnant with more than one child. (That was before the days of ultrasounds. An x-ray? The doctor did not have an x-ray machine in his office.) The x-ray revealed only one baby.

Ten days before I gave birth to the twins, I was sent for a second x-ray. By that time I was so large, the doctor thought I might be expecting triplets instead of *JUST* twins. The x-ray showed that I was going to have twins (not triplets).

The possibility of having twins sounded like fun during my second month of pregnancy, but to learn ten days before they were born, that we were having twins, was too much to handle. I was huge and tired. I broke down and cried in exasperation. I did not know what we were going to do. Candy was twenty-six months old and Barry was one, and WE WERE HAVING TWINS!!

I went to the car, and tearfully told Dewey, "We're going to have twins. How will we handle two babies at once?" I don't know how he maintained his composure, but he did. He was great. He was proud of Candy and Barry and was pleased to learn he was to be the father of twins (although he knew what a financial drain their birth would be).

Dewey said, "We'll manage. God knows what He is doing, and He wouldn't give us more than we can handle. We'll be okay. I'm sure things will work out." (We hurriedly selected names and gathered clothes. I was in a state of shock for several days.)

Twins, Brent and Brenda, were born July 1. *(DOUBLE TROUBLE!)* The birth of two babies definitely proved to be a strain on our finances. Our doctor's fee for a single delivery was one hundred dollars, and was increased to two hundred dollars for twins. The doctor had never delivered triplets, so before their birth, he agreed to deliver triplets for no charge (rather than the three hundred dollar fee as would have been pro-rated.)

We did not have health insurance to help with the bills. Since we had twins, we had to pay two hundred dollars, but that was cheaper than having a third child. A third baby would have meant more of everything, and the expenses would have been multiplied more than they already were. (Five children with the oldest less than three?? Four was enough!)

The doctor wanted me to stay flat on my back for ten days after Candy's birth, but he went on vacation the day after her delivery, and the nurses got me on my feet the third day. I was discharged after five days, rather than the prescribed ten. I stayed in the hospital for one night after Barry was born, and for two nights after the birth of the twins. I guess two babies warranted an extra day!

Candy was born in Pueblo, and the other three were born in Rocky Ford. (Our grandson, Zack, accompanied us to Colorado in 2001, so we took him to Rocky Ford. When he saw the town where his father was born he stated, " I thought it was 'Rocky Fort.'")

A friend came to see the twins, and she jokingly asked, "May I have one of them? You have two babies, and I don't have any. You don't need two." Candy replied, "Yes, Mommy can just get some more." (Dewey often teased me saying, "You remind me of a mother duck with four ducklings following behind.")

We had rented our house in Boone, and were caring for a house in Pueblo when the twins were born. They slept in dresser drawers as we did not have a crib or cribs. Jonell stayed with us from the time they were born until we moved to Gunnison in September. When I heard a baby cry, I tried to get there as fast as possible to keep that one quiet while I fed him or her, so the other would not be wakened by the noise. During the time Jonell was with us, she helped with the twins, and especially with Candy and Barry.

Dewey, never one to deal with a diaper, was always the first to let me know that one of our children needed changing. I don't believe he ever changed a diaper, but he was good about all other aspects of raising children. He just couldn't cope with the more "mundane" things involved.

Dewey graduated from Pueblo Junior College in May of 1957. That summer was his last at the Colorado Fuel and Iron, and he was given a position as an inspector. (With his *Associate of Arts Degree*, he had a better position than he had when he first worked there.)

That summer he made a good salary, and did not have to perform the tasks he had previously been assigned. Pete Pomeleo, the basketball coach at Boone, also worked at CF&I that summer. (Teachers were often employed at the CF&I during the summer months.)

Dewey asked Pete if he felt he should quit his position and finish his degree, or if he would advise him to stay in Pueblo and work to support our now larger family of four children. (Barry was twenty-one months old, and Candy not quite three when the twins were born, so we had four children under the age of three.)

Pete said, "Dewey, if I had four children, I would stay right here and work." It was a difficult decision for Dewey to make (whether to quit his job at CF&I and go to Gunnison to finish his degree, or to keep his job in Pueblo to support our family). I do not know why Dewey asked because he did not heed Pete's advice. (Boy, am I glad that we were so naïve. If we had been aware of the trials involved in putting Dewey through college, we might never have embarked on the course.) We began our journey as a family of four and finished it as a family of six.

Dewey opted to go to Western State College in Gunnison for the completion of his undergraduate degree. Norman was already a student there, and Sharon was prepared to begin her college career at Western when Dewey did. (Dewey and Norman were juniors and Sharon was a freshman.) Dewey's decision was made – we moved to Gunnison, and the rest is history.

Even though Dewey's dream was to become a coach, he had to first become a teacher. He was not studious in high school, but he became a student in college. He bemoaned the fact that he had not made more of an effort to learn in high school. He learned to love history, medicine, sports, and of course football. He became a teacher, a leader, and inevitably, a coach. He was a football coach, a life coach, and a counselor.

With the launch of *Sputnik* by Russia in 1957, the Space Age dawned. America recognized the necessity for science education, and Dewey set out on the course to become a science teacher. *Mockingbird Hill* was replaced by Elvis singing, *You Ain't Nothin' But a Hound Dog*. The Korean War ended. Dewey graduated from Pueblo College, and life moved on. It was a season of change.

CHAPTER **16**

A Date with Destiny

The week before classes began at Western State, Dewey loaded the kids and me, along with our belongings, into the station wagon, and installed us in college housing. He then returned to Pueblo to work, and to make as much money as possible.

Dewey came to Gunnison the day before school started, and dashed into the apartment. He said, "Oh, my gosh! I've missed you guys. It's so good to see you." Candy and Barry were outside playing when he arrived, and when they saw him they squealed, "Daddy's here," but immediately returned to their activities. Dewey was disappointed to not receive a longer and warmer welcome, but he could relate to the urgency of childhood play.

WITH THAT, HE WAS READY FOR THE LAST TWO YEARS NEEDED FOR HIS DEGREE. HE STARTED CLASSES THE NEXT DAY!!

Married student housing was on a hill above the campus, and consisted of an old Army barracks. Those apartments were very drafty. Our first apartment was at the end of the complex, and the floor had fallen away from the wall in our bedroom. A twelve-inch gap allowed cold air to readily come in.

Our neighbors, Cliff and Bobbi Wise, had an apartment next to ours, and were prepared to move at the end of the term. Cliff was to graduate, and they urged me to call Housing and get their apartment. I called and the move was given the okay, but not by the Housing Director, so we circumvented the customary process.

The College was not happy about our change of residence, but we were more comfortable. The second apartment was warmer and larger, and had a carpet on the floor. The former residents left an old pie safe in the kitchen for flour, etc. I wish we had kept that safe, but we did not appreciate such things then.

The apartments were furnished and there was a bunk bed in the kids' bedroom. Brent and Brenda slept on the top of that bed while we lived in the first apartment. When we moved into the second apartment we had a single bed on which they slept as well as a bunk bed for Candy and Barry. We placed a board at the front of that bed to keep them from falling off. We later purchased a used crib for them to sleep in.

During the winter in Gunnison, the snow was plowed to the center of the street, and was piled in six to eight foot banks to allow traffic to go down both sides. The intersections were plowed for cross traffic, and the center bank made it impossible to see cars going in the opposite direction.

Our first winter in Gunnison was an experience. I saw more snow than I ever had before. (My niece, Amy Ferran, and her family now reside there, and after spending several years in Albuquerque, New Mexico, like living there very much. In February of 2008, Amy reported that more than sixty-four inches of snow had accumulated in less than two months.)

Winter temperatures in Gunnison reach forty or fifty degrees below zero, and oil heaters were used for heat. Each day Dewey pumped the kerosene for our heater and carried it to our apartment. We had a rack for drying clothes, and I hung the items on the clothesline outdoors and let them freeze (they were as stiff as boards), before I brought them inside to dry. I was happy to leave after two winters there.

We visited Crested Butte, an old mining town, and were intrigued (it was almost a ghost town). The snow in winter was so deep it was difficult to get to the street from the ground floor. The homes had two stories, and there was a tall pole in the center of town. Lines from the top story of each house were attached to that pole by a pulley. The clothes were strung on those lines, and then pulled toward the pole where they were left to freeze and dry. Snow blanketed the ground, and only a shoveled pathway led to the street. Hanging clothes from the first floor was impossible.

We envisioned Crested Butte as a resort area. I told Dewey, "After you graduate we should come back, and buy some property here. It looks like a great place for a ski resort." The next time that thought came to us was about fifteen years later, when we saw a Disney movie that starred Fred MacMurray. It was filmed on location in Crested Butte (by then a ski resort), but we never had the money to invest there anyway.

Barry had a penchant for wandering off alone that dated back to his toddler days. The lure of the outdoors was too much for him. He was often on a lark of his own, destination undetermined. One morning in Boone, he scooted a chair over to the screen door, and unfastened the hook, so he could "escape." We were asleep, so when I awakened and found him gone, I panicked. I roused Dewey and said, "Barry's gone. He unlatched the screen door and is out in the neighborhood." We found him a short time later (fortunately for us the town of Boone is small, so he did not go far).

Another time he sat on a red ant den, and cried for a long time. (I had a terrible time getting all the ants out of his diaper.) When he played outdoors with the other children, he was prone to leave, so I had to check on him frequently.

When we moved to Gunnison, he joined the other kids in the complex to play outside. I spent a great deal of time pursuing him in his adventures. I couldn't keep him indoors when the weather was nice, so I had to frequently check on his whereabouts.

During our second week in Gunnison, the Athletic Director found him wandering unattended several blocks from our home. (Married student housing was on a hill and the classrooms were in a valley.) As Sharon returned from class, she met the A.D. who held Barry in his arms. Fortunately for us, but unfortunately for her, Sharon recognized him. He was not "potty-trained" (house-broken), and he reeked to high heaven.

Sharon was embarrassed to admit she knew him, and hated to claim him as her nephew, but claim him she had to. (She should have issued a disclaimer.) She said, "I couldn't believe it – the little rascal – what an embarrassment – to have the A.D. find him like that, and then to have to admit that, not only did I know him, but that we were related." (Where was his mother??)

Once I tracked him by his footprints in the snow. I found him and our dog headed toward the water reservoir in back of our apartment. I do not know where they would have gone, had I not found them when I did.

And a former Boone classmate brought Barry and Brent to our apartment one evening. We had invited that fellow to dinner, and on the way, he found them several blocks from our home.

Another time, Barry and two companions started on a cross-country trek, but one of the three wet his pants, and turned back (smart child). That time we had the police searching for him and his "partner in crime." They had gone at least a mile before they were apprehended.

We were fortunate someone always returned him to us (possibly because of the odor – who wants a stinky child?). (His grandfather and his father also liked to see how green the grass was on the other side of the fence, so he followed in their footsteps – I guess it was in his "genes.")

Brent got aspirin from the glove compartment of our car one day (that was the last time I left aspirin in the glove compartment), and persuaded Brenda to "celebrate" with him (celebrate what I'm not certain). He told her it was candy. She did not like the taste of his "candy," so she only ingested a couple, but Brent had an overdose.

We awakened the next morning to find him delusional. We took him to the doctor who said, "If this is sunstroke it's the purest case I've ever seen." Candy said, "He took aspirin yesterday." With that information, the doctor told us, "He's in acidosis. We need to get fluids into him immediately." When we took him home, he saw frogs on the ceiling and whales in the bathtub. We were fortunate he recovered. (Again – where was his mother?)

We struggled financially, but the struggles are recalled with amusement. One summer, Dewey "splurged" on a set of "new tires." He purchased those tires (retreads) from the local junkyard. To initiate his "new" tires, we went camping at Lake City near Gunnison. While setting up camp, we realized that we had a flat on one of his "new" tires. He looked at the tire and said, "Oh, gosh darn it! We have a flat. Well, I guess it can wait until morning."

The next morning we awoke to two flats. Our spare tire still had air in it, so Dewey put it on the car, and started rolling the other tire down the road. A "Good Samaritan" gave him a ride, and helped him with the tire situation. On Monday, he went back to his retailer (the junkyard), to get more "new" tires (or to trade his previous purchase back in. I am not sure). I am just thankful our tires today do not come from the junkyard.

Renting our house in Boone proved to be an unfortunate experience -- we had trouble collecting the rent, and we needed the money -- so we sold it when the opportunity arose. We sold that house for $5,000 in 1958, and that helped with the expenses we encountered in the completion of Dewey's college education.

We got our first television -- back when television was not broadcast 24/7 -- back when we watched the "test pattern" just to say we watched "tv." It was a black and white set, and we got it when the people who rented our house in Boone couldn't pay the rent. We took that set instead of the rent payment one month. We needed money far more than we needed a television, but we settled for what we could get.

The summer of 1958 was special. We were in need of a different car, so a friend took Dewey to the car auction in Denver, where he was successful on his bid for a 1957 Ford station wagon. That car was like new, and Dewey purchased it for $1,400. It was a two-door station wagon and a classic. (Part of the money from the sale of our house was used for that purchase, and the rest went toward living expenses. But even with the money from the sale, we still lacked many things.)

After seeing our car, Dewey's father decided to try the auction, so he asked Dewey and Windle, "Do you suppose you can get me a good deal like that?" They were more than happy to oblige, so they went to Denver, and Windle selected a nice-looking Cadillac. Dewey said, "Dad would CERTAINLY NOT want a Cadillac. It would embarrass him to drive a luxury car. He is more a Ford or Chevy man." Windle replied, "No, he really needs that Cadillac, and he would look great driving it. He would love it." So, against Dewey's better judgment, they bid and bought the car, and their dad became the "proud" (proud??) owner of a Cadillac.

When they drove into the driveway, Mr. Sullivan greeted them with, "Did you buy that car for me? It looks good, but the engine sounds awfully rough." (It turned out to be "rough.") He would have liked to hide it. It really was not his "style," but how can you hide a Cadillac? He didn't have the money to make frivolous purchases, so he had to drive it for several years, "status symbol" or not. But he was embarrassed to be the owner of a Cadillac. (Dewey had been correct.) The engine blew up on a trip to Arkansas, and his father sold it for junk. He was happy to "kiss it goodbye." His parents took the bus back to Colorado, and his father never again asked them to help him purchase a car. A lesson well learned?

We traveled over Monarch Pass often during the two years Dewey attended Western State. Monarch is over 11,000 feet in elevation and connects Gunnison and Pueblo. Driving when the roads were snow-packed required skill, and Dewey knew where the ascent became steep and he always revved the car up before we got to that point.

Someone once told him, "If you stop and put bleach on your tires, it will help you get traction." That sounded like a good idea, so we tried it (anything to help), but all it accomplished was to put more wear on our already bald "new" tires. After we stopped for the "bleach trick," Dewey could not get the car revved back up to the speed needed to get over the summit.

A DATE WITH DESTINY

We paid someone ten dollars to pull us to the top of the Pass, and we did not try that again. We could have purchased chains with the money spent, but Dewey did not like to bother with chains. I don't know where we got the ten dollars (I believe we borrowed it from my mother), but we managed.

Dewey nicknamed our 1957 Ford station wagon, *Old Betsy*, and as we tried to reach the summit of Monarch, he instructed our kids to rock back and forth to give the car momentum and to chant, "Come on *Old Betsy!* Come on *Old Betsy!* Come on *Old Betsy!*" They loved doing that, and they did it with enthusiasm.

(A story was told about two college students from New York who had a flat as they drove over Monarch Pass at night. When they got out to fix the flat, they looked down and saw lights far below. They were speechless, and crawled back into their car where they remained until morning. When the sun came up the next day, they were stunned by how high they were on the mountain.)

Vacations were trips to see relatives – camping overnight – picnics in the mountains – fishing in the streams. Dewey and Norman enjoyed the summers, and often went fly-fishing. Summers in Gunnison are beautiful, but the mosquito population was prolific (at least, it was when we lived there). There were open canals, and the mosquitoes thrived in that environment. When Dewey's father came for a visit one summer, he went fishing with them. Dewey said, "When I looked down, my dad's pants looked like they were pinned to his legs by mosquitoes."

One morning, Norman's wife, Lynne came to take our four children and me to the doctor. She babysat a three-year-old girl, Debbie, and left her in the car while she ran in to get us. When we came out of our apartment, we found her car gone. Lynne said, "Oh, my goodness! Where is the car? What happened?" Then we heard a loud crash, and saw the car "parked" in the side of a classroom. (Debbie had either touched the gearshift, or the car went into gear and rolled down the hill.)

Someone saw the entire episode, and reported that the car

pulled out and backed up (as though someone were driving). It then went down into a gully, and came to rest against the classroom. There was a loud crash, and a thump, and the room shook from the impact. (Fortunately, the gully slowed the car enough that it did not go through the wall.)

Norman was a student in the class where the car "met" the classroom. The students rushed to the window to see what had happened. One said, "Sully, your car just hit the building, and a kid is driving." (Actually, I believe the building jumped in front of the car.) Debbie was unhurt, but it was a lesson in more secure driving for all of us. (That was before the days of seat belts.) It was a long time before Norman lived that incident down (if he ever did).

We met some nice, helpful people in Gunnison. A family with triplets learned we had twins, and brought us a twin stroller (that stroller and a single one had been used for the triplets). It was nicer than what we could afford (in fact, it was the only stroller we ever had the luxury of – even with four children).

And one time our black-and-white television needed repair, so Dewey took it to a repairman who only charged for the necessary parts. He said, "I know how you must be struggling to get through college." Such random acts of kindness were appreciated.

I made the girls' dresses and most of their other clothing, and I often made shirts for all four kids from the same fabric. They particularly liked shirts made from a fabric with large puppies printed on it. (Wearing clothing in a similar pattern made it easier for us to keep track of everyone.) They thought we were rich because they liked their clothes. I discovered a treasure trove of kids' wear at a church thrift store, and I found boys' white shirts in like-new condition for a quarter each.

And I learned to make our food budget stretch, and stretch, and stretch. We bought powdered milk, and kept it mixed and chilled in the refrigerator. (Candy says she remembers finding lumps of powder in it.) That was cheaper than the "real" thing, and the kids grew up on that. One of my favorite recipes was from a Betty

A DATE WITH DESTINY

Crocker cookbook and used sliced wieners baked into cornbread. A single package of hot dogs was stretched into three meals by using that recipe.

I remember waking in the night, and contemplating how many meals I had the ingredients for. One night, Dewey came home with kerosene for our stove and a "bonus." He found a frozen beef roast in the snow near where the oil was distributed. He came into the apartment and said, "Look what I found. I have no idea why it was in the snow, but here it is." We asked no questions. It was a "Godsend," and we enjoyed it for several days.

Another time we were "down and out" (totally broke), and only had cornmeal pancakes to eat. Fortunately for us, we received a welcome infusion of cash with a check for twenty dollars from my mother. That made it possible for us to do a little shopping, so we hurried to the grocery store. Our stomachs rumbled in anticipation. (And we even had money left to put gas in the car.)

One fall afternoon, Dewey and Norman took Barry to a Western State football game. It was a cool, crisp autumn day, and the game was great. Dewey wanted Barry to experience the excitement of a college game, but Barry who was three, was more interested in the band. Norman cracked up as Barry strutted around and pretended to be a drum major the entire next week. What a disappointment for Dewey!

I canned prodigiously, and we did not eat in restaurants. The summer before we moved to Gunnison, Dewey's mother and I canned pie cherries (the kind used for pies, not sweet cherries). One neighbor at Western State found them desirable, and she bought them from me for fifty cents a jar. That was another source of income (slight, but welcome). Fifty cents bought several items in the '50s.

As I was turning pancakes one morning, Dewey took the spatula from me, and flipped a couple. Brent scowled at him and said, "You not the mama." Somehow, it worked out. We were fed and clothed and lived up to the challenges, but we looked forward to the end of Dewey's college "experience."

During the time we were in Gunnison, Norman and Dewey did

odd jobs delivering propane bottles and furniture, etc. Quitting college was not an option for Dewey. (When he set out on a mission, he single-mindedly saw it through to completion.) And he knew that the CF&I beckoned.

Stubbornness was in his genes. If someone told him that he could not do something, he'd leave no stone unturned to show how wrong that person was. He'd stick his chin out and prove them wrong. That helped him in his struggle to finish college, and to become the coach he became.

With four small children it would not have been financially wise for me to work, so I was a "stay-at-home" mom and didn't contribute monetarily. I chased "rugrats," and Dewey studied. The odd jobs helped with expenses, but for the most part, we were without an income. We had only what we managed to save while he worked.

Dewey's parents had Norman and Sharon in college, so they could not help us financially. My mother helped a little, but with a teacher's salary of $2,000 year, she had her own struggles. With God's help we made it. We had a "hand-to-mouth" existence, and were on our own. We were so happy when Dewey got his degree.

(When he got his first teaching position we thought our financial struggles were over, but we found they were not. We were behind in the game of life, but we found that things are appreciated more if you have to struggle to reach your goals. We struggled both financially and emotionally.)

Those times were a source of drawing us closer together as a couple and as a family. We had fun getting through college (well, it was not actually fun; challenging is more accurate; but we coped and were together).

After checking off his intended coursework each term, Dewey graduated on schedule in March of 1959. He was the first in his family to receive his college degree, and we were proud. He began the work for his Master's Degree in the spring of 1959, and had two terms completed when he got his first teaching position.

He could have worked at CF&I during the summer between his junior and senior years, as well as the summer after he graduated.

But it would not have been cost-effective to move to Pueblo for the summer, and then back to Gunnison in the fall.

Before he graduated Dewey learned of a new program for returnees from the Korean War, as well as for other students. The National Defense Student Loan Program (NDSL), provided loans for students, and Dewey learned that, if he were to teach in a deprived area, the loan would be forgiven.

We did not pursue the loan program. *BIG MISTAKE!!* If we had applied for a loan we would have been better off financially, but that was not our style. Silt (Dewey's first teaching position) qualified for 100% forgiveness of the loans, so we would have been money ahead if we had borrowed $10,000 or even $5,000.

CHAPTER **17**

Where the Heck is Silt?

The year was 1959. Dewey registered for his last term as an undergraduate, and we experienced a feeling of jubilation, a feeling of excitement, a feeling of relief. It was rewarding to arrive near the end of the road, and to see the "light at the end of the tunnel." Dewey checked with the Teacher Placement Office daily to see where the jobs were.

In April he interviewed for the position of basketball coach at Uravan, Colorado. He was offered the position and was to become the principal or superintendent within two years. His master's degree was in Administration, but he did not want to pursue that avenue when he graduated. He wanted to be a coach. (He had grown a beard in celebration of some event, and when he was called for the interview, had a difficult time shaving it off. It amused me to watch him deal with it. It was almost like hacking brush.)

A couple of weeks after his interview at Uravan, he came home and told me, "I just visited the Teacher Placement Office, and learned of an opening for a basketball coach at Silt. If I get the job, I would have to coach football and track, but that would be okay. I don't know where Silt is, but I'm going to find out." He grabbed a map and located Silt. *SILT, COLORADO!!*

He applied for the position, and was invited for an interview over the Memorial Day weekend. (We did not have a phone, so he got messages from the Placement Office.) The interview was to be held on a Saturday, and he was so excited. We walked on air all week.

We packed a lunch the night before we were to go for the interview. We awoke early the next morning ready for our adventure. We hurriedly readied the kids for the trip, and took off. We drove through the Black Canyon of the Gunnison, and our excitement mounted after we left Grand Junction. We loved the area, the mountains, the canyons, and the river. As we drove along the highway toward Silt, we could barely contain our enthusiasm. The area was like the "Garden of Eden" to us. We had waited so long for that day to arrive.

We prayed that Dewey would get the position of basketball coach. When we drove into the town of Silt, we located the school. The building was similar to the Boone School. We were a few minutes early, so Dewey had time to look around.

The kids and I stayed in the car while he met with the superintendent of schools. Dewey was beaming when he came to the car afterward. He had been offered the position. He said, "I got the job and I get to coach! I'll be the football and the basketball coach. Oh boy!!!" To us, Silt spelled S-U-C-C-E-S-S!!

(He accepted the head football position, but he knew virtually nothing about football since his experience with football at Boone had been so dismal. He found someone knowledgeable who worked with him, and he devised an offense for six-man football. He was ready for the challenge.)

Dewey's salary was to be $4,000 for the year. $4,000!! We felt like millionaires. We could not fathom how much money that would be. At long last, we would have money to spend! *(RIGHT!!)*

We drove around Silt and the surrounding area before we headed home. We then drove to Grand Junction where we celebrated our good fortune with dinner in a restaurant, and an overnight stay in a motel.

Before we settled into the motel, we took a tour of the Colorado National Monument, and a rock went through the radiator of our station wagon. A shop put some "gunk" in it, and successfully stopped the leak. What a trip and what excitement. Dewey had a job teaching and coaching. We were ecstatic.

Nestled in the Colorado River Valley sits the small town of Silt. As in Boone, there was a *City Limits* sign at each end of the town with little in between. Silt is in a beautiful location between Rifle and Glenwood Springs, and boasts relatively mild winters. I am not certain what the population of Silt was in 1959, but the town itself was quite small. Like Boone, there was no traffic signal, and the town consisted of several blocks. There was a post office, a service station, two churches, a grocery, a City Hall, a tavern, a restaurant and one school (elementary, junior high and high school in one building).

Philip Pyles was the superintendent of the district, and he oversaw the education there. (One of his directives to Dewey was, "This is not a popularity contest." That served Dewey well in the ensuing years.)

Mark Ukele was the custodian, and he and Dewey became good friends. Dewey was hired to help Mark paint the school building during the three weeks before school started. The two of them had a lot of fun together. They went fishing on weekends, and took at least one camping trip.

Mark had a great sense of humor, and he and his wife, Esther, enjoyed our young family. The City Clerk was Elsa Pyles and her son, Ron, played football and basketball for Dewey. (When Elsa called me recently, she said, "One thing I remember that Dewey said was, 'Once a coach, always a coach.'" I translate that to, ONCE A PIRATE, ALWAYS A PIRATE.)

CHAPTER **18**

Silt — Our "Garden of Eden"

We rented a small two-bedroom house with one bath about three blocks from the school. The rent was fifty dollars a month, and the house had a wood/coal burning stove for heat. We lived there for about ten months. After an evening out, we often returned to a house filled with smoke. The floor was on a slant, and if you put a ball at the kitchen door (at the back of the house), it rolled down to the living room.

Our four children slept together on a rollaway bed (foot to foot and side by side) in one bedroom, and Dewey and I slept in the other bedroom. One day Brent and Brenda locked the bathroom door while they were inside. I went to a neighbor's home and phoned Dewey to ask him to come and help get them out. I was frightened as to what harm might come to them. (That house did not have the sort of lock that could be released from the outside.) Before Dewey arrived, they managed to unlock the door, so I met him and told him to go back.

When Dewey got paid at the end of his first month of teaching, we drove to Glenwood Springs and purchased a three-piece suit (a jacket and two pairs of pants), a couple of sport coats and two pairs of slacks. He had a corduroy jacket and a two-piece suit from his high school days, and when he started student teaching we had also purchased a sport coat at the Montgomery Ward outlet store in

Denver for nine dollars. He was definitely in need of suitable clothing. With his new purchases, it was nice for him to have a wardrobe with some variety. In 1959 and 1960, teachers were required to wear ties and white (not pastel or colored) dress shirts.

It was also nice to have a little money to spend. We put most of his things on lay-away until we could afford to get them out the next month. Some of the items needed alterations, but we were started. That purchase put a dent in the first full paycheck he had received in more than two years, and it soon became evident we were not in "hog heaven" as I had thought we would be.

As the kids and I readied for Dewey's first football game, I hurried them into our station wagon, and drove to the school. As in Boone, the games were played on a dirt field. There were no bleachers, so the spectators parked around the perimeter of the field. We honked our horns in applause when a touchdown was scored. It was truly exciting.

The Silt Pirates lost the first game that Dewey coached by the score of 33-24, but he was challenged. He came home, and said, "Dadgummit!! We were so close to scoring on that last drive. I know we can do better than that." (His enthusiasm never waned, and he was on his way to becoming a coach.)

The Pirates won the next game 25-0, and defeated Carbondale 19-6 in the third game of the season. Silt had never beaten Carbondale before, so the town of Silt was elated. In recognition of that win, the team was treated to a steak dinner at the local cafe. *(BIG TIME STUFF!!)* Dewey's first year of coaching ended in a successful season.

Silt played Newcastle twice the next year, and the Pirates won the first game. They made it into the playoffs, and as the team went to the field before the second game, I overheard one of the Silt players say, "This is just another easy game." With that I knew the Pirates were in trouble and thought, "Oh, no! This is not good." They lost that game. (Undaunted, Dewey's first experience coaching football stirred his passion for the game, and he was anxious for the next season.)

SILT - OUR "GARDEN OF EDEN"

After we had lived in Silt for several months, I found an unfinished house near our home. I told Dewey that evening, "I found a house a couple of blocks from here. I think we should look into buying it and finishing it." After dinner, we walked over and took a look at it. It had two bedrooms, one bath and a basement. Upon inquiring, we found that we could purchase it on the installment plan for $2,500 with monthly payments of fifty dollars.

(The story I heard was that the gentleman from whom we bought it had an affair with someone else's wife. He was banned from living in the city limits of Silt, so could not complete it. I do not know if that was the truth, but that was what I was told. Remember, the year was 1960. In today's world, I can't imagine being banned from living in a town because of infidelity, but it might not be a bad idea.)

The framework of the house was complete with siding, a floor and a roof, as well as a Stoker-matic furnace in the basement. The rest was ready for us to complete. We did most of the construction, and Dewey did the wiring, plumbing, etc. as well as much of the interior, but he had a carpenter do the cabinetry. He often sent me to get something, and it took a while for me and the hardware store or lumberyard to sort it out. (He knew what he wanted, but I did not.)

We worked on that house each evening. It was a load for Dewey to teach all day, do his coaching activities, and then work until ten o'clock at night. I remember his frustration one night, when he could not get a piece of sheetrock into place, and he broke it. We could ill afford the added expense, but the pressure overwhelmed him.

Before the end of his first year of teaching, we completed the construction, and moved into our own home. (That was the second house we built together, and I vowed never to work on a house with him again. I said, "I won't do this again, because if I do we'll probably get a divorce." We worked well together on most things, with the exception of building a house.)

The next winter, we frequently had railroad spikes from the coal caught in the furnace auger. When Dewey came from school, I greeted him with, "We have another spike in the auger. I guess you'll have to change clothes and go down and deal with it." (He had to remove those spikes to keep the heat functioning.)

For recreation, we took our children to the drive-in movies. I fixed popcorn, hot dogs and soda pop for dinner and snacks and we had fantastic times. Candy interpreted for the other kids when Dewey spelled out "S-H-O-W." We could not keep secrets from her, and she gleefully shared her information with the others.

The kids' features were shown first, so after their movie, we put the kids to bed in the back of the station wagon. I believe the little rascals peeked over the seat to watch such as *Summer Place*, but that is not nearly as risqué as some today.

Several times we drove to Grand Junction for a movie, a drive of ninety miles each way. The kids loved those outings, as well as our many overnight camping trips. (Of course, they slept on the return trips, so why wouldn't they enjoy it?)

Once, when we took our children for immunizations, they were given the option of getting their shots in their arms or their bottoms. Candy chose to have hers in her arm, but the others opted for theirs in their fannies. Dewey wanted to see a movie that evening, so he asked if they wanted to go with him. Everyone except Candy was too sore to sit, so she went to the movies, and I stayed home with the others. (That is one of her favorite memories of father/daughter, one-on-one time.)

Brent perched on a chair at our back door each afternoon, and watched for his father to return from school. (He stood there for half an hour or more while he waited. He was more patient at three than he was at twenty-three.) When he saw Dewey approach, he screamed, *"DADDY'S HOME! DADDY'S HOME!!"* He was so excited. It was a celebration.

One of our neighbors had an Airedale, and when Brent saw that dog, he yelled to Dewey, "Inka's dog, Daddy! Inka's dog!! (I believe, the owner's name was Linker, and he interpreted it, "Inka." Anyway, he was delighted to tell his father about it.

The next spring, Dewey ordered our own Airedale to be delivered to the train depot in Rifle, Colorado. The kids were familiar with the neighbor's dog, so they knew what to expect, and were excited to go to the depot to greet their new dog. He was a scrawny, little puppy, but they adored him. Dewey loved Airedales, and Teddy was special. He was one of a succession of several Airedales.

Near the end of our first year in Silt, Candy was invited to participate in a kindergarten at a small two-room school just outside town. She returned from her first morning, and reported, "They have a new kind of bathroom at my school – you get to go outside." She was impressed. (How far we have progressed. Her father and I had known that kind of "modern," but that was her first experience with it.)

When school let out for the summer in June of 1960, Dewey went to Gunnison to work toward the completion of his Master's Degree. We had not arranged housing for our family, so the children and I stayed in Silt. When Dewey returned at the end of the first week, he informed me that he had found a basement apartment for rent.

With that news, we packed and moved to Gunnison. (Dewey did not want to be away from his family.) We had an old wood/coal-burning range to cook on, but did not use it since it would have made the apartment too hot. We purchased an electric skillet, and I prepared our meals in it. I even baked cornbread and cakes. The cakes did not brown on top, but cooked thoroughly. The skillet served its purpose well, and the aroma was the same as baking in a regular oven.

When the summer session ended, we returned to Silt to find a letter from Dewey's father. He said they had started building a house in Fowler (about twenty miles from Boone.) We did not unpack. Dewey loaded us into the station wagon, and we drove all night to get to Boone.

We arrived in Boone to find that the foundation for the house had been laid (cinder blocks), but was not straight. Dewey surveyed the situation and helped remove the foundation (it had to be chipped out and replaced). Then he contracted someone to do it right.

We stayed with Dewey's parents while he got the house started. There was no house plan, so Dewey designed the house, and he did much of the beginning construction. He worked at a hectic pace to get as much done as possible before he had to return to Silt for the start of school and football practice.

In October we received a second letter saying the house was now enclosed, but that his parents were going to let it sit until prices came down, which was unlikely. In 1960, Silt had a week off for hunting season, so with the arrival of that letter, Dewey said, "Pack up! We're going to Fowler!"

We loaded our car, and drove to Boone for the week (of course, the kids were excited). Dewey used the time to work on the house, and again got the construction underway. Our kids loved those excursions, and the opportunity to visit their grandparents.

In December, we received a letter that stated the house was completed, but that Dewey's parents would not move until spring. It was Christmas vacation, so Dewey said, "Get ready! We're going to spend Christmas in Fowler!" We drove to Boone, only to discover that Sharon and her family had gotten there first, and the move had been completed.

When Dewey's father came from work the first night, he was disappointed to discover that he had been moved. (I wasn't. I don't care for moving, and I was not looking forward to helping.) Dewey's mother was delighted with her first new home. After thirty or more years of marriage and struggling to survive, she deserved it, and Dewey was happy for her.

The next summer, as Dewey prepared for the completion of his Master's Degree, we moved into the basement of the home of the Western State Librarian, and again used the electric skillet for preparing our meals. We spent two summers in basement apartments -- the summers of 1960 and 1961. I have many happy memories.

A neighbor with an English bulldog named "Timotheus" lived next door. Our kids called him "Timothy Bulldog," as that was easier for them to say than "Timotheus." We told them, "Stay away from that bulldog. You don't know whether he bites."

I was ironing one morning when I heard a commotion outside.

SILT - OUR "GARDEN OF EDEN"

Candy and Barry came screaming and crying into our apartment, "Timothy Bulldog has Brent down and is killing him." I quickly unplugged the iron, and rushed up the stairs and into the alley where Timothy was chained. They were right. "Timothy Bulldog" did have Brent down, and was trying to "lick" him to death.

During our second year at Silt, Art Trojan was hired as math teacher, and we became good friends with him and his family. Art and his wife, Peg, and Dewey and I accompanied the senior class on their "sneak" trip to Denver. We stayed in a hotel, and ate at *Writer's Manor*, where we were introduced to lobster (to become an all-time favorite of ours in the food arena; I do not think we had even heard of lobster before that). We had a great time on that trip.

After four years spent struggling, and living with very little money, we lacked many of the necessities of life. Our children were ready to begin their educations, and we found that Dewey's paycheck did not go as far as we would have liked or thought it would. His salary for his first year of teaching at Silt was $4,000, and was increased to $4,100 his second year. When Dewey signed his first contract and began teaching that amount sounded like a fortune (but it was not).

Salaries were increased in increments of $100 annually. Dewey received his Master's Degree in 1961, and asked for a salary of $4,300 rather than the $4,200 offered. After the years spent getting him through college, he felt he warranted an additional one hundred dollars annually. His request was refused, so he resigned, and started a new job search. We had four kids, no income and not much money, but we were together as a family.

Dewey applied at several schools, but was unsuccessful in his quest. We did not have a telephone, so we used our neighbors' phone to receive messages. (We later learned that the superintendent at one of the schools where he applied, called to offer him a position as football coach. When he could not be reached, someone else was hired.)

Before the days of "text-messaging" and cell phones, a phone was an expense we were able to forego. (Of course, it is almost impossible in 2009 to live without the luxury of a phone — that is how it is viewed. In today's high-tech world, most people have a land-line, as well as one or more cell phones.)

After two months of searching, Dewey heard of a position at the Colorado State Reformatory. We were desperate, so he applied and was hired. He was the first Recreation Director there, and he remained in that position until the fall of 1962, when he went to Meeker, Colorado as football coach and science teacher.

In August of 2006, Dewey had calls from two of the students he taught in Silt. It was always special for him to connect with his former students, and he had a good visit with both Ron Alley and Helen Ruggero Johnson. I am glad he talked with them one last time.

Dewey and Jonell visited Silt in the late 1990s for *Hey Days*, and he enjoyed visiting with many of those he had known more than forty years before. At *Hey Days*, he saw some of the players from the first teams he coached, but regretted that Jim Allen was not there. Jim lived in Las Vegas, and someone called and told him "Coach" was there. Jim said, "I would have come if I had known 'Coach' was going to be there. I'll come to Dayton for a football game this fall because I'd like to see 'Coach.'" (However, Jim died that fall, and Dewey did not see him.)

The area around Silt is becoming more commercial, but is in a wonderful location. It was a great place to live and to begin a teaching career. Dewey and I visited Silt several years ago, and the entire town had changed. The old Ukele place had been subdivided and was a small town itself (the Ukele Estates). After we left, the Silt School ceased operation. (But I learned at Dewey's induction into the *National Hall of Fame*, that classes are again being held there.)

CHAPTER **19**

"The Man"

When Dewey learned of the opening at the Colorado State Reformatory, he applied and was hired. We rented our house in Silt, and moved to Buena Vista for a fresh start. Dewey had his Master's Degree and experience, and the staff welcomed him.

Buena Vista is about thirty miles from Leadville, the "Two-Mile-High City," and we had high expectations as we again had an income. We found a nice three-bedroom, one-bath brick house, and rented it. (Before we moved from Buena Vista, we could have bought it for $9,000. We should have purchased it. It was the nicest house we had lived in.)

On his first day at the Reformatory, Dewey went into one of the cells, and closed the door to get the feeling of being incarcerated. He knew he did not want that sort of existence, but he also knew that there was a price to be paid for one's actions. (Lefty was a policeman in Pueblo, and some of the people with whom Dewey worked, were "referred" by Lefty.)

Lefty and Dewey compared notes on their mutual acquaintances, and they shared some interesting stories. Families of inmates (fathers and sons) often resided there, and the population increased when winter arrived. A warm bed and three meals daily were an enticement for those on the street.

One of Dewey's assistants was imprisoned for murder. After that fellow's discharge from the service, he went to a bar and got into an altercation with another patron. He went back to the motel where his wife and child slept, got his service revolver, and returned to the bar, where he shot the other man. That assistant was released after several years, but was an exemplary prisoner while he worked with Dewey.

Dewey was popular with the inmates, and his nickname was "The Man." (Everyone had a nickname.) He was a "stud" (his shoulders were broad and his forearms were huge). He played basketball on the local town team, and he held the keys to the gym, etc. He worked out in the weight room, and was quite "buff."

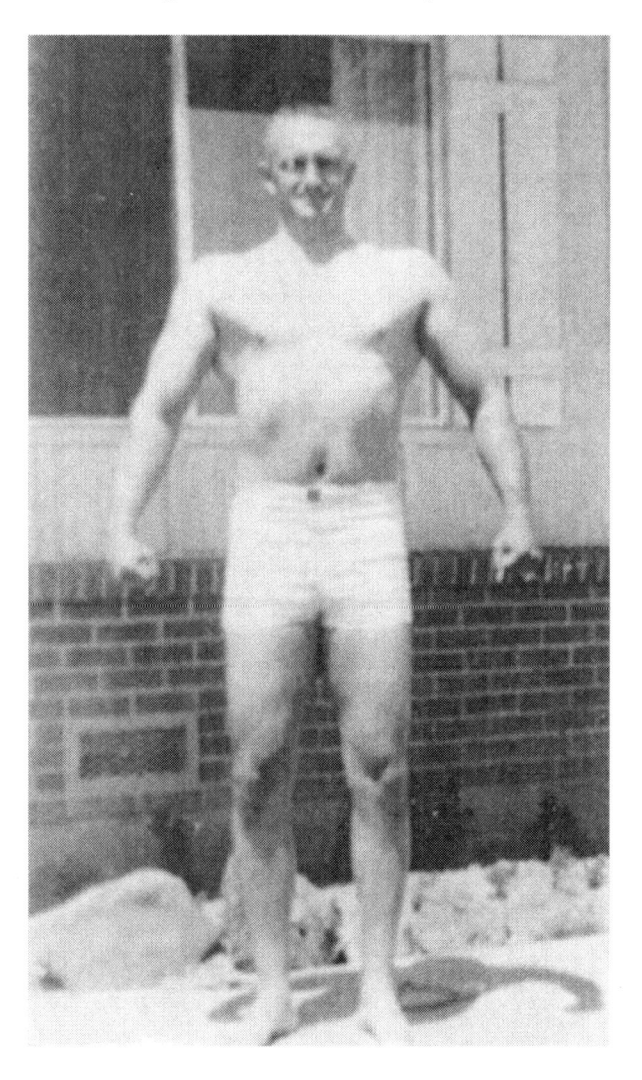

"THE MAN"

He was the coach, and he accompanied the inmates to their various athletic events, ballgames, etc. His primary assistant worked in the kitchen, as well as with recreation. When Dewey returned from games, he was served as much as he wanted of whatever was on the menu for the evening. If he wanted something other than what was served, the cook prepared it for him. He was initiated to filet mignon, etc., and he enjoyed his culinary experiences.

As Dewey looked forward to the release of one of his assistants, he was optimistic. He told everyone the gentleman was rehabilitated, and he held great expectations for his future. When Dewey told others of his hopes, someone said, "He'll be back before two weeks are up." Dewey was disappointed when they were proven correct.

There was an escape one night, and the guards went through our housing development looking for the miscreant by spotlighting between the houses. Dewey accompanied them, and came to our house to check on us. He told me, "Keep the door locked and do not open it for anyone."

He borrowed a record player from one of the inmates, and had it at our house for several months. That sparked his interest in stereo equipment, so he had the wood shop employees make a pair of stereo cabinets from a design from *Mechanics Illustrated*.

We became friends with a couple with a swimming pool. The water for the pool came from a hot spring beneath the surface of the ground, and was a comfortable temperature. During the winter months, we often went to their home and swam. (At least most of the family swam. I just relaxed). There was snow around the pool, and it was fun to be in the heated water and see your breath. That couple had a dog that "sang" in accompaniment to the piano, and our kids enjoyed hearing his renditions. They found his antics hilarious.

Dewey was not satisfied with the calmer pace afforded by working at the Reformatory, so when spring arrived, he looked once again at teaching and coaching opportunities. He wanted more of a challenge (a headache??) than that offered by the food and the attention. He came home one evening and said, "I have to get out of here. I'm going to get fat and lazy." He learned of an opening at Meeker High School, applied and was offered the position of football coach, so we prepared to pull up stakes and move again.

Dewey could have made more money had he stayed at the Reformatory, but he had developed a love for working with high school students, and for the game of football. He was ready to return to the public school arena. Happiness and contentment are of more importance than money, and Dewey's goal was to be a high school coach. But he enjoyed his time in Buena Vista, and we loved the town. He said, "We could live anywhere if we were together."

CHAPTER **20**

Meeker — A Learning Experience

Dewey jumped at the opportunity to coach football at Meeker, and at the salary of $6,000 annually. ($6,000!! WOW!!) It was supposedly a step-up from Silt and the Reformatory, and he was excited. But Meeker was not a "fit" for Dewey. After the Reformatory, he became the "warden" and took the opposite tack from Silt. He was no longer "one-of-the-boys." One mother stated he was too "militaristic." He later mellowed, and became much (well maybe not much, but somewhat) softer.

When we visited Meeker to look for housing, we had an amusing experience. The high school principal was a former high school English teacher, and accompanied us to look at several rental properties. One house was unlocked, and he took us for a tour through it. Fortunately (or maybe unfortunately), the owners were not at home. When we called about renting the house, we were told it was not a rental. At least we weren't arrested for going through someone's home. We were embarrassed. (I am glad no one ever made that mistake at our home.)

At one stop, a can or a bottle rolled from our car, and the principal's question was, "Shall we 'surreptitiously' let it lie?" I remember his exact words, and I am still amused (only a former English teacher could have used those words).

We met Rich and Beriece Castle and their four children, and

◀ A BAREFOOT BOY FROM OKLAHOMA

became good friends. Dewey was the head football, assistant basketball and head baseball coach. (He preferred the faster pace of football and/or basketball to the challenge offered by baseball. He had not coached or played baseball, but was successful coaching it at Meeker.) Rich was the head basketball, assistant football and head track coach, and he and Dewey worked well together.

The Castles arrived in Meeker several weeks before we did, and were fortunate to find a comfortable house for sale. We were not as lucky, but did locate a three-bedroom, one-bath home for rent. The house we found was not as nice as the one the Castle family found, but was across the street from the high school. Dewey walked to work and left the car for me.

The high school in Meeker is located on a small hill, and the football field is in a bowl above the school. Deer are often seen grazing there. When we moved to Meeker in 1962, the school was "state-of-the-art." It was one of the richest school districts in the State of Colorado, and had its own swimming pool.

One evening Dewey came from school and reported, "The drama class tied the teacher to his chair today and set him out in the hall while they conducted class on their own. The teacher was highly amused by that."

(Later, when Dewey started teaching at Dayton, he attended a *Small Schools* workshop. At that workshop, the biology/science facility in the Meeker High School was featured in a slide presentation. Dewey told the group, "That was my classroom and laboratory when I taught at Meeker.")

Barry said, "The biology room was a lecture room with stadium seating similar to a college classroom, and there was a human skeleton on display. The science lab was an amazing facility — particularly for a high school biology room." (As a second grader, Barry was impressed.)

The town of Meeker is self-contained, and is isolated during the winter months. We did most of our Christmas shopping from the Montgomery-Ward or Sears catalog outlets. There were two grocery stores, a theater, six churches, several taverns, a Western Auto store, and a Ford dealership. (The father of one of Dewey's football players had the Ford dealership, and that player drove one of the first Mustangs). Sheep ranching was the primary source of revenue.

Our neighbors had two daughters about the ages of our children. One of those daughters referred to Dewey as, "Mr. Coachman." Rodeo grounds were located a short distance from our home, and our kids and the neighbor kids played there in the fall and the spring.

Before we moved to Meeker, we adopted a boxer (a dog) from the Humane Society in Canon City. We soon discovered why he had been put up for adoption. He loved to chase cars and was ill-mannered. At night he slept on the couch in the living room (where he was not supposed to sleep), and he once lost one of his teeth by grabbing the tire of a grader that passed our house.

One morning he encountered a porcupine, and Dewey had to spend time clipping and extracting quills before going to school. That dog often went missing, and Dewey learned he was usually at the sheriff's house. (He eventually became the sheriff's dog, since he spent more time at his house than at ours. We considered it a good deal all around.)

The highway between Meeker and Rifle is on a migration route for deer. Many deer were hit during the winter. When we drove to Rifle in May, we kept the car windows rolled up as the stench from rotting deer carcasses was unbearable. The outside temperature was seventy degrees or warmer, and with the mild weather and no air conditioning, it was uncomfortable.

Dewey mentioned that, when the team bus encountered deer on the highway, the driver turned the bus lights off to enable the deer to clear the highway. (The lights of oncoming vehicles blinded the deer, so they were often struck.) I do not recall any collisions between the team bus and deer during Dewey's time in Meeker, but there were many between other vehicles and the wildlife.

However, I was not as fortunate. I hit a deer one evening while returning from Grand Junction. Beriece Castle and I and our combined families (the Castle four and our four), drove to Grand Junction. We met a herd of deer on the way home, and I hit one. (During our first year in Meeker we had purchased our first new car, a 1962 Studebaker station wagon, and were proud of it.) That dent was the first mar on it, so I felt terrible about the damage to the car, but I felt worse about the poor deer.

And that was not the end of my woes. One Saturday morning, I came out from grocery shopping, and found the local law-enforcement officer looking at our car. By his side stood one of Dewey's football players. That young man had hooked into the back bumper, and it was sticking straight out in back. After dealing with the paperwork, etc., I drove home.

I stood at our kitchen window and watched Dewey walk around the back of the car when he came from basketball practice. Of course, it would have been impossible to miss the way the car looked. I could not have hidden it if I had wanted to. (Maybe I should have draped a sheet over it.) After assessing the situation, Dewey came into the house and asked, "What happened? What did you do?" I told him, and he found it amusing (well, maybe not amusing, but ironic) that the accidents our car suffered were inflicted while I was the driver, never when he was driving.

Another time Beriece and I took our eight kids (again our combined families), to the hills on a sightseeing excursion. We found a young doe whose leg was caught between two strands of barbed wire, so we stopped and I got out of the car. I grasped the strands of wire, and twisted them in order to free her.

As I did so, she scraped my arm with her hoof. She dashed to safety, and Candy said Debbie Castle went to school the following day and reported that her mother released the animal. She was indignant that I did not get credit for the rescue, but I said, "The only thing that really matters is that the deer escaped to safety."

During the winter, one of our favorite Sunday afternoon activities was to take a drive to see the herds of deer. I usually put dinner in the oven to be ready upon our return. Dewey and I enjoyed the sightseeing, but our children would have preferred to stay at home to play with their friends. However, they had a competition to see who could see the most deer.

I recall counting more than two hundred deer in one herd, and we also saw many elk. As we drove from Meeker to Rifle one day, we were fortunate to see a bobcat (one of only two I have seen in their native habitat). That was especially exciting.

One spring afternoon, we took a picnic to a lake above Meeker. After lunch we skipped stones across the lake, and relaxed by the water. We headed home when it neared sundown, and Barry took our Airedale and led the procession. We arrived at our car, but Barry was nowhere to be seen.

We called and called, and then retraced our steps around the lake. But there was no Barry. We were frightened, and after several such trips, we decided to get into the car, and look for him on the way.

We met a car coming up the mountain, and inquired if they had seen a boy and a dog. We were told, "Yes, we passed a boy of nine or ten about two miles down the road, and he had a funny, fuzzy dog with him." We knew we were on the right track, but had wasted valuable time looking for him.

The two of them were found about two and one-half miles from the lake. We asked, "Where were you going? Why didn't you wait for us?" His answer was, "I was going home." (Nights in the mountains of Colorado are chilly during the spring, so we were relieved to find him. At least he had not taken off cross-country on one of his excursions.)

I spent hours making clothes for the girls' Barbie dolls for Christmas 1962, and they felt truly pampered with so much style. The next year we had my brother purchase *Patty Play Pal* dolls for them. He and his wife lived in Grand Junction, so they purchased them there, and brought them to us. We hid the dolls in a small hideaway over the closet in our bedroom. That was the only time in Candy's first eight years of life she did not know what she was getting for Christmas. She always snooped into everything, and told the other children what their presents were.

Candy usually roused everyone early on Christmas morning, and I think she was up at two a.m. that year. We shooed everyone back to bed, but after she had seen what was under the tree, her excitement was uncontained, and she tried the same thing again at about four o'clock. We got everyone settled until a more reasonable hour, and then enjoyed Christmas as a family (even if we were not well rested).

I heard voices one morning as I hung laundry on the clothesline. When I checked I found two truant children. Barry (a second grader) had persuaded Brenda (who was in kindergarten) to play hooky with him. They sat between two sheds, and were having a good visit. I chastised them for their misbehavior, then loaded them into the car and took them to school. Barry told me his teacher cried because of his performance. She thought he did not like school (or possibly her). He was saddened to see his teacher cry, so it served him right for his actions.

Brent dashed home one night after a basketball game, and called one of our friends. He said, "My dad caught a whale, and we're going to eat it for breakfast." We never learned what triggered that thought. His imagination must have worked overtime. He loved the outlandish, and enjoyed using the phone.

The Stoker-Matic furnace in our house in Meeker was in the living room, whereas in Silt it was in our basement, but it was the same type of apparatus. The first winter we lived there I ordered Dewey white canvas gloves similar to those worn by *Mickey Mouse*. He used them when he brought coal into the house.

At a faculty get-together one night, he pulled those gloves from the pocket of his sport coat. Everyone howled. *Mickey Mouse* gloves with a dress jacket?? He loved the reaction. (Maybe he was more a showman than I realized.)

We experienced extremely low temperatures during the winters in Meeker. It got down to fifty-four degrees below zero the last year we were there, and the temperature did not get above zero for two weeks straight.

After basketball practice each evening Dewey showered at the high school. As he left the building, his hair immediately froze and stood on end. The hairs in his nostrils froze and thawed – froze and thawed -- froze and thawed as he breathed. The bright side of such conditions is that the wind does not blow during the winter. If it did, the wind chill would be devastating.

During that stretch of cold weather, Dewey filled an aluminum tumbler with water and placed it on the cement floor beside the bed where our boys slept. There was a small gas heater at the entrance to their room, and the tumbler was placed near that heater. The next morning the water in the tumbler was frozen solid (even with the additional heat from the heater).

We had every available blanket and quilt piled on the beds. It was so cold you could see your breath while you sat on the couch in the living room, four feet from the Stoker-Matic furnace. I remember the invitation of that furnace, as it was the only warm place in the house – the problem was that you could not spend your entire day in close proximity to it.

I never wanted to experience winter again after Meeker. It started snowing in October, and the ground was not visible again until May. Gunnison had been bad, but I considered Meeker unbearable. (After we moved to Chehalis, Dewey often went outdoors without a coat. The Pacific Northwest winters were mild in comparison with those we experienced while in Colorado.)

After his second year at Meeker, Dewey was asked to step aside as football coach, but to remain as baseball coach and biology teacher. He wanted to coach football. (Had baseball been taken away, he would gladly have acquiesced.) He resigned on the principle that he was a football coach, so we were again without a paycheck. That failure helped form him into the coach he became. (He felt that Meeker did him a favor – his dismissal gave him something to prove. He knew he could coach football, and he refused to accept defeat.)

Beneath the snow new greenery waited for spring -- and like the winter in Meeker, we looked forward to a new beginning in our lives as Dewey looked for another position.

A BAREFOOT BOY FROM OKLAHOMA

I don't believe Meeker ever won a state championship in football, or possibly even a league title, but the teams Dewey coached at Dayton won five state titles in six appearances, and held the Oregon state record for consecutive playoff appearances with twenty-six at the time of Dewey's death. His football teams celebrated sixteen league championships, including thirteen straight titles.

CHAPTER **21**

Go West Young Man!!

We were again without a paycheck (for the principle of not accepting the turn of events). Dewey began a job search, and learned of a position in Chehalis, Washington at Green Hill School for Boys. Dewey was interviewed by telephone, and he accepted the position when it was offered.

WASHINGTON!! Dewey was excited as we prepared to make our *BIG MOVE!* He was "rooted" by his love for the familiar, but the pull of something better won his heart. (Wanderlust was in his genes.) We left the people and the things we loved, and moved to the State of Washington. When we left Colorado, we moved into "uncharted territory," but God provided for us.

Before our move to Washington we lived near our families, and could get to them within a matter of hours – when we moved to Chehalis it was a matter of days. I was not as excited about the move as Dewey was. I was a "Mama's" girl, and I enjoyed the comfort and reassurance of family. With our move we were to be a "stand-alone" family, and I was uncertain.

But it was an adventure!! We were really striking out on our own, just like Lewis & Clark. Well, maybe not exactly like Lewis and Clark, but to us it was a challenge. Dewey had lived in Oklahoma, Texas and Colorado, so he wanted to see more of the United States. He was curious. He was an adventurer, and was born one hundred and fifty years too late. (He was interested in Native American lore, and would have loved coming cross-country in a covered wagon. Since he was too late for that, he considered our move the next best thing, and he was ready for the challenge.)

There was much preparation to be done for our move. When school let out for the summer, we stored our household items and furniture in a shed at the Castle residence. We then drove to Fowler, and stayed with Dewey's parents for a few days while we got things organized.

A pickup was something Dewey had long wanted, so when he accepted the job at Green Hill, he purchased a 1954 Ford pickup (his first pickup). He loved that pickup. It was a light aqua color. After we moved to Dayton, he had it spray-painted red. He was proud of it, and it served us well for several years. (His first pickup!)

After "playing" with the pickup in Fowler for several days, we returned to Meeker to get our belongings. We stayed with the Castle family as we packed and readied for the move.

When we left Meeker, Dewey drove the pickup, and pulled a large U-Haul trailer. I drove our 1962 Studebaker station wagon with another trailer in tow. The boys rode in the pickup with Dewey, and the girls and our cat rode in the car with me.

A short distance out of Meeker, the pickup started to sputter. Dewey stopped and came back to the car and told me, "There's a problem with the pickup, but I think I can make it to Grand Junction. Follow me and I'll stop at a garage." The pickup coughed and sputtered, but we made it.

When we got to Grand Junction, he took the pickup to an automotive repair shop where a small piece of debris was found in the carburetor. After the "repair," we took off for Salt Lake City.

Things went well until we neared the city, but the grade into town was steep. With the heavy trailer in tow, the pickup brakes got hot. Dewey barely made it into town safely. He managed to stop the truck by repeatedly bumping it gently against the curb to slow it down.

He stopped by a park and got out and came to the car. He said,

"My brakes have overheated, so we are going to stay here for a while until they cool off." We spent more than hour in the park, while we waited. The episode with the brakes was frightening. It was "hair-raising" for Dewey, but our kids enjoyed the interlude (any excuse to get out and play).

It was late afternoon when we eventually left Salt Lake City. Several miles out of town, there was a fork in the road. There was some distance between our two vehicles, and Dewey took one road, and I took the other. I drove on, but Dewey went back over the route several times to try to locate me. He was unsuccessful, and after four or five such attempts, he again started along our chosen route. He stopped at a weigh station, and asked if they had seen me. He was told, "A white Studebaker station wagon with a trailer passed by about an hour and a half ago, but didn't stop." He knew he was on the right track, and he took off to find us.

Several hours passed before we got back together. We had no means of communication, and neither of us knew where the other one was. We were both frantic. I was ahead of him, and had continued on our chosen route.

When the sun dropped behind the horizon and darkness fell, I was frightened. (We were in the "Middle of Nowhere," and I was alone with the girls and our cat!!) I had not traveled alone at night far from familiar surroundings, so I pulled into a motel, and prayed for the best.

A few hours later, Dewey and the boys rapped on the door of the motel, and we were happy to see them. I thanked God! I had parked away from the front of the motel, and Dewey asked, "Why didn't you park near the highway, so your vehicle could be seen?" I said, "I didn't think of that. It should have occurred to me, but it didn't."

(And to make matters worse, I purchased traveler's checks in my name before we left Meeker, not thinking of the possibility that we might be separated. After that experience, I insisted he get half the checks in his name when we traveled, so he would have resources in the event the same thing happened again.)

Before we left Meeker that spring, Dewey had accepted a National Science Foundation fellowship at Montana State University in Bozeman, Montana. The course was for six weeks, and was to begin in mid-July, so our move from Meeker to Chehalis had to be completed by the second week in July.

We arrived at Chehalis on the Fourth of July, and had a little more than one week to find housing, and to get ready to leave for Bozeman. Dewey met both the superintendent of the school district and the principal of Green Hill School, and they were helpful as we looked for housing.

While we looked for a place to rent, we stayed in a motel, and ate one of our daily meals at a nearby buffet. Brent always loaded his plate with Ritz crackers, and Dewey told him, "Go back through the line and get something more to eat. Crackers aren't enough." (Dewey wanted him to get something with more substance and nutritional value; something that would stay with him longer than an hour.) Brent said, "But I like crackers." Our other two meals were eaten at the motel, and consisted of cereal for breakfast and white bread and bologna for the third meal (whether lunch or dinner).

At the motel one afternoon, Brent and Brenda decided to go on their own *BIG ADVENTURE*. They said, "We're running away." (I guess they were tired of our "motel existence," and they really had not wanted to leave Meeker. We offered to help them.) They left the motel, but were back within fifteen minutes. *BIG ESCAPADE!!*

As the time to depart for Bozeman neared, we had not found housing. We became desperate, and rented a dilapidated two-bedroom house. We unloaded our trailer, but did not unpack any of our boxes. We stayed in that house for two nights, and just before our scheduled departure, Dewey went back to Green Hill School. He was told, "We've found a more suitable house for you to rent." We checked on that house and rented it. We loaded the pickup and the trailer once again, and made the second move. What a relief!

The second house was two-story with three-bedrooms (one bedroom downstairs and two upstairs) and one bath. Our children had not lived in a house with an upstairs, so they were excited.

They had the upstairs bedrooms, and Dewey and I had the one downstairs. Since we had not unpacked at the first house, it was only a matter of moving boxes. A massive task awaited us. We had to unpack and arrange furniture, etc. before school started.

When we returned from Bozeman, we attended the before-the-school-year picnic for faculty members and their families. At that picnic Brenda met another girl who was in her class. After the first day of school, three of the four Sullivan kids returned home on the bus, but there was no Brenda.

(Why didn't the other three children make sure Brenda got off with them? I don't know. Candy suggested that maybe they thought we could do without a fourth child; or maybe she was willing to part with one of her siblings as she had been when they were babies.) I was frantic. We were in a new town without any acquaintances, and OUR DAUGHTER WAS MISSING!!

We did not have a telephone, so I loaded the three remaining children into the station wagon, and drove immediately to Green Hill to alert Dewey. He got into the car with us, and we went first to the elementary school, and then to the bus barn, to see if we could find our "runaway" daughter.

Luckily we located the bus driver who had driven that route, and he told us, "She got off the bus a couple of blocks after your other three did." With that information we were able to determine the family and the address where the "culprit" landed.

We got to her friend's house (not far from our home), to find her and the other girl playing happily, totally unaware of the distress she had caused. As a second grader she was "grounded" (this after playing hooky in kindergarten), but we were so relieved to have a happy ending to her saga, that she did not suffer any lasting repercussions. (Maybe she followed in her father's footsteps, as he had done the same thing before he started school.) She did not pull that stunt again. Thank heavens! (And, Barry was not even the instigator that time.)

One day we read an ad for miniature dachshund puppies, and were excited. We knew our kids would be thrilled with a new dog.

(There's something about kids and dogs!) We adopted a female, and named her Greta. When the kids saw her they were ecstatic. They dressed her in some of the doll clothes I had made for one of the girl's dolls, and entered her in a dog show. She won a prize (a t-shirt) and a ribbon. Brent was proud of her and of the ribbon she won.

One morning I heard Greta barking frantically, and went outside to investigate. A horse was coming down the street, and she put up a brave front until the horse got about twenty feet from her. Then she turned tail and ran yipping to hide under the house. How brave she was!!

We experienced our first earthquake in the spring of 1965. An earthquake? I had read accounts of earthquakes, but to experience one was frightening. Dewey said, "We sent the students outside, and we saw the ground undulating in waves. To see the ground rolling like the ocean was amazing."

(Before we moved to Chehalis, I read you should get under something in the event of an earthquake, so I grabbed Greta and crawled under our kitchen table. The two of us must have looked comical.)

The quake was brief, but did extensive damage to some of the local buildings. Falling bricks killed one man at a grain elevator near our home. I never wanted to experience an earthquake, and I do not care to do so again (although there have been several in Oregon while we lived here).

We headed to the store for something one day, and Barry took off at break-neck speed to get to the car first (a competition with the other kids?). Dewey grabbed his shirt as he dashed past. He was pulled back to the curb just as a car zoomed by. Had Dewey not gotten hold of his clothes, Barry most likely would have been killed. That car was going far too fast for a residential area. Barry said, "Dad saved my life."

Dewey was the basketball coach and biology teacher at Green Hill School for Boys, and again found himself without enough of a challenge. Football coaching had become his passion, and he dedicated himself to it. (Once he had a taste of football nothing else satisfied.) He worked with a wonderful staff at Green Hill, but longed for the excitement of high school football.

Dewey accepted the position at Dayton in May, and resigned from Green Hill with regret. When he tendered his resignation, he was offered a position as an assistant football coach at Chehalis High School. But he liked and respected his supervisor at Green Hill. He felt it would be a betrayal of the school and the principal had he taken it, so he refused and took the position at Dayton. Green Hill was a residential school, so Dewey taught until mid-August when he had to report to Dayton for football practice.

CHAPTER **22**

Dayton — Is This My Calling??

"Oh, the depths of the riches and the wisdom and knowledge of God. How unsearchable his judgments and his paths beyond tracing out. God is always speaking to us and giving us just the words we need for what He knows lies ahead."
-- Romans 11: 33-36

When Dewey learned of the opening for a football coach at Dayton, he was excited. The Pirates of Dayton had won the league title the previous fall, and Dewey thought there must be an interest in football. He applied for the position, and was invited for an interview in May.

Nestled in the beautiful Willamette Valley of Oregon, midway between Salem and Portland, is the small town of Dayton. Spring in the Willamette Valley is beautiful, with the flowers and fruit trees in bloom . . . with the dogwoods and the flowering shrubs.

We were excited as we drove from Chehalis to Dayton for the interview. The I-5 corridor is scenic, and we enjoyed the trip.
We liked the "small-town" feel of Dayton. We did not want to raise our family in a large city.

Dewey went into the high school for the interview, and was impressed with the condition of the school, that late in the school year. It looked as though everything had been freshly painted. He sensed a feeling of pride, and his first impression of the town and of the school was positive. (It said, "Home.")

The kids and I stayed in the car while Dewey met with the principal. After about an hour, he came back to the car, and told us, "The interview went well. I have to go to the superintendent's office, and talk with him. We drove the three blocks between the high school and the district office, and again waited in the car while he met with the superintendent.

When he came to the car after that interview, he said, "Well, I got the job. I get to coach football, but I will also be the wrestling coach. I told the superintendent that I can handle that, and that I am happy to accept the offer." We were excited as we drove back to Chehalis, and we talked about the possibilities. (We were young and naïve, and were not daunted by another move.)

The league title the previous year was the biggest factor in Dewey's decision to accept the offer. It wasn't until later that he realized that the 1964 football season was the first time in sixteen years that Dayton had reached that goal; the first time in sixteen years the Pirates were in the playoffs. (Had he looked at the years before that season and at the lack of interest in the football program, he would have been less likely to accept the position.)

We spent the time from May until July preparing for our move and learning as much as we could about the Willamette Valley. In July we returned to Dayton to look for housing, and spent two days in the area. We camped overnight at Maud Williamson Park, midway between Dayton and Salem.

Housing was difficult to find, but we found a three-bedroom, one-bath house on Eighth Street across from the high school and rented it. That house had two stories, and the boys' bedroom was upstairs, and the girls' bedroom was on the ground floor, next to ours.

We could not move into that house until Labor Day. Dewey needed to have football practice two weeks before school began, so he and Barry went to Dayton in late August, and stayed until the beginning of school. They slept in sleeping bags on the stage at the

DAYTON - IS THIS MY CALLING??

high school, and returned to Chehalis the weekend between the two weeks of practice (the weekend before we moved to Dayton).

When we returned to Chehalis, we found Dewey's parents parked in front of our house. Our kids squealed, "Nanny and Grandpa! Nanny and Grandpa!" We did not know they were coming, so we were surprised when we got home and found them there. They were prepared to drive back to Fowler, since they didn't know where we were. Had we returned an hour later, we would have missed them. (How is that for communication?)

We moved into our house in September, but we did not move our dining table, etc. inside until we painted what needed painting. Willamette Valley weather is usually mild in the fall, so it was pleasant to eat outdoors. After seeing us eat on the patio, the principal's daughter remarked to her mother, "Those people are really strange. They eat their meals out on the patio! They must be a bunch of 'hicks.'"

We lived in the house on Eighth Street for four years, and then we moved into a three-bedroom, two-bath home on Seventh Street. I met Benjie Hedgecock at a basketball game recently, and he asked, "Do you want to come see my new house? It's at 204 Seventh Street." I said, "That address sounds familiar." He replied, "It should. You lived there for several years, and it is known as the *Dewey Sullivan House*." (Forty years later that house has been remodeled and looks quite nice.)

In the late 1800s and the early 1900s, Dayton was the hub of trade and commerce for the Willamette Valley of Oregon, but in 1965 things had changed. Ferry Street was the main street that ran through the center of town, and there was a flashing red traffic signal at the intersection of that street and the highway that runs through town. We had moved up in the world.

Two blocks encompassed the heart of downtown Dayton, and a blockhouse from the 1800s had been moved from the Grand Ronde Agency to the park in the center of town. There was a pavilion in the park, and teachers were required to live in the Dayton School District.

The drugstore ceased operation the year before we moved. Films were no longer shown at the theater. There were three grocery stores and five churches, a beauty shop and a barbershop.

The population of Dayton was less than 1,000 in 1965. At last we arrived in a town with three *City Limits* signs. When we were first married, we had lived in Pueblo, and then in Buena Vista and Chehalis. Before we moved to Dayton, the towns we lived in for the longest periods of time had only two *City Limits* signs, one at each end of town. DAYTON HAD THREE!!

The Oregon Coast is approximately forty-five miles to the west, and Mt. Hood is about seventy miles away. Almost anything one might desire is easily accessible. Culture, music and art, as well as sporting events are available in both Portland and Salem, and the distance to either city is not far. We did not want to live in a large city, but we did like some of the advantages offered by the larger venue, so were happy to relocate to Dayton. Dayton personifies *Small Town America*.

The population of Dayton is a little more than 2,500 today. Several housing developments have been incorporated into the city limits, and a new addition has been made to the school. *The Joel Palmer House* is a gourmet restaurant featuring local mushrooms, and is frequented by "out-of-town" guests. A distinct nineteenth century atmosphere prevails.

The Howard Hughes *Spruce Goose* is housed at the Evergreen Aviation Museum about six miles from Dayton, and is a popular destination for those driving through the Willamette Valley. There is a *McDonald's* (Dewey referred to it as the "Dayton *McDonald's*," as it is so near Dayton). A Cineplex with eight screens is six miles away, and a new hospital (across from the theater and medical plaza) was built on Three-Mile Lane about ten years ago. Bill and Cathy Stoller have purchased a portion of downtown Dayton, and have plans for revitalizing the town.

There is still a pavilion in the park, but teachers are no longer required to live in the town of Dayton. There is a feeling of the 1800s in much of the architecture. The population of McMinnville was about 6,000 when we arrived in Oregon, but is now more than 31,000.

DAYTON - IS THIS MY CALLING??

From a sleepy, little rural town Dayton has grown, but it still has a quaint, colonial charm. It has changed to a more thriving community, and is in the heart of Oregon's "Wine Country." There is no industry, so it is primarily a "bedroom" community for Portland and Salem.

Strawberries were once one of the main crops, and are still grown, but wine grapes have taken on a more significant role in the economy. Pole beans were widely grown in the Willamette Valley when we moved to Dayton, but they along with strawberries, are labor-intensive and have given way to bush beans grown for the cannery. Sweet corn is raised, and much of it is used in the making of ethanol. Grass seed is an important crop. There are no longer any service stations in the town of Dayton, and residents must go to Lafayette, McMinnville or Amity for gasoline.

Farming is still prominent in the Dayton economy, and is the main source of revenue. But anyone familiar with Oregon football has heard of Dayton and of Dewey Sullivan.

CHAPTER 23

Dewey in the Classroom

"Knowledge is of two kinds – we know a subject ourselves or we know where we can find information on it."
-- Samuel Johnson

Dewey had an inquiring mind, and he asked many questions. If he did not have the answer himself, he prided himself on knowing where the information could be found. He became a teacher because he was always eager to learn.

Two student aides served in Dewey's biology classes in the '70s. Frank Stoller and Bruce Morgan strutted around school, and wore white lab coats and felt important. A shipment of frogs was delivered to the office area one day, and Frank and Bruce opened the boxes. They turned out the lights, and left the room. They returned several minutes later to find frogs hopping everywhere.

Frank told the story of making a "volcano" with a chemical that reacts violently when water is added to it. (When that is done the mixture spews high into the air much like a real volcano.) One morning Frank and Bruce mounded dirt for the "volcano," and placed the chemical in the center. They prepared to pour water onto the "volcano" from a safe distance (about six feet above their concoction), and then looked up and saw "Coach" as he approached. Dewey looked down at the "volcano" on the ground, then up at his two assistants, shook his head and walked on by. (When the water was poured on the "volcano," it spewed high into the air as intended.)

When we moved to Dayton, Dewey catered to the interest in stereos he had developed. He studied stereo systems, and graduated to more sophisticated speakers than those he had made while he worked at the Colorado State Reformatory.

(Years later, Bruce Morgan brought him *Sansui* speakers from Korea, and Brent still has those. However, Dewey coveted the *Klipschorns* speakers that Frank Stoller had, but he never acquired a pair of them.) Several years ago, Candy purchased a sub-woofer for him for Father's Day. He was proud of it, and he used it with his surround sound system.

We spent many weekends in Salem and Portland looking at stereo equipment. After much reading and studying, Dewey assembled an impressive set-up, and he loved the technical aspects of stereo systems. He derived a great deal of enjoyment from shopping for the components, and putting them into their proper alignment.

He also helped several of his students and players set up their systems. He helped Frank Stoller shop for and assemble his. One Saturday night, Frank and several of his buddies were at Frank's house enjoying his "tunes." Frank's mom, Helen Stoller, and her husband, Wilbur, returned from an evening out, and found the roof of the house practically being lifted off by the sounds of *Credence Clearwater Revival*. (Mrs. Stoller always referred to me as "Mrs. Coach.)

Mrs. Stoller heard the music (noise?) as she entered the house, and put her hands on her hips. She marched determinedly up the stairs to Frank's bedroom. Before she got to the top of the stairs, she began chastising the noisemakers with, "What on earth is going on up here? Our neighbors miles away will be calling to complain about the noise." However, when she found "Coach" sitting on the bed with the "boys," it was not so bad in her eyes. She accepted the music more readily, and she was mollified when she realized that "Coach" was involved.

DEWEY IN THE CLASSROOM

When Barry was a freshman, he was kept past time for class to be dismissed. He was consistently released late, and was tardy when he got to the next class. The second teacher had locked his classroom door when the bell rang, and Barry was locked out. He was marked "Absent."

Barry was frustrated, and after several days of that, he told Dewey what had happened. Dewey decided to talk to the teacher about it, but when Earl McKinney learned of the dilemma, he said, "Don't worry, Dewey. I'll handle it." (And he did. Barry had no more problems after that conversation.)

At a faculty meeting one morning, the Athletic Director announced that someone had been making calls to a 900 number. Dewey raised his hand and volunteered, "It was probably me. I've been making quite a few calls." Everyone looked at him in astonishment, but he said, "I've been making calls to get information in regard to the playoffs. What's the big deal?" (900 numbers. What is that?) My initial reaction was to wonder why the 900 numbers had not been blocked (I believe they have been since that incident). It was later learned that the football manager or someone else made the calls.

Dewey was often asked, "Have you made any 900 calls lately?" I think those stories are funny, but he did not. I was not supposed to share them (at least, not while he was here to know I did. He was not amused by the same things I was). Actually, it's not a bad thing to not know what 900 numbers are.

Dewey was chuckling one evening, when he came from school. One of the students in his physical education class went unexcused to the *Pirate's Den* (the small fast food restaurant across from the high school), and brought a milkshake to class. The bounty was hidden under the bleachers, but Dewey saw the process. He told his student aide that someone brought him a treat, and to go enjoy it. The aide went to the bleachers for an "early lunch," and the purchaser was left "holding the bag."

One principal told Dewey that he was a master teacher. He was recruited to mentor younger teachers, but he already did that, and did not want to take time away from his classroom. At that time substitute teachers were utilized while the regular teacher was in training. Dewey felt he was paid to be in the classroom and he dedicated himself to that premise, so he did not leave his students.

He once supervised a couple of student teachers, and noticed they were emulating him. He called them to his office, and told them they needed to develop their own style of teaching. He cultivated good relationships with those he supervised, and he had many from Linfield College, Oregon College of Education (now Western Oregon University) and George Fox University.

An Air Force retiree served as the Dayton High librarian for several years, and he often regaled the faculty with stories of his experiences and exploits. He once told a story of the aircraft he piloted that made an emergency landing on Colfax Avenue in Denver (one of the busiest streets). He said both wings were clipped off, but the plane landed safely, and not one person was injured. (INCREDIBLE!!)

Another tale he told was of being taken prisoner during the Korean War. When he recognized one of his captors, he reminded that fellow that he had played against him in the Thanksgiving Day football game in the Seattle area several years before. After recounting that incident, he was afforded more respect.

One morning, that fellow said he had been called to pilot a plane to Alaska, and on the return flight, had flown under the Astoria Bridge. He said, "I'm one of an elite group that will be called to Colorado Springs in the event of a nuclear attack. That group will propagate the United States if the population is decimated." Dewey really chuckled about that.

He also told of an encounter with the Mafia, while he was stationed at a base on the East Coast. He said, "The school principal was intimidated by the Mafia, so when I registered my daughter in school, I was told to be wary of their influence. When I met the intimidators, I took no 'guff.' One day I was instructed to meet a couple of them down on the wharf. I did so and they tried some strong-arm tactics on me. I got into their car, started it and pushed it into the Atlantic Ocean. I heard nothing more from them after that fiasco.

DEWEY IN THE CLASSROOM

Each evening Dewey had some tale of that man's bravado or experiences. Earl McKinney, the Dayton basketball coach, left the lounge when the stories got higher and deeper, but Dewey loved them and encouraged him in telling them. He appreciated the outlandish. He found those tales hilarious, and he especially enjoyed repeating them. He often laughed so hard that he cried.

Dewey had a phone call from Dwight Ediger one evening. Dwight's daughter, Michelle, was hurt about something Dewey said in class. She had evidently forgotten an assignment, and Dewey mentioned it. When he learned of her embarrassment, he apologized to her the next day in front of the class.

He was grieved when he learned of the death of a former (or current) student or player. He attended funerals for many of those who died of natural causes as well as one from murder, one from a hunting accident, one from suicide and several from traffic accidents. He mourned those losses.

He confided in me some of the distresses his players and students suffered, but I am certain there were things shared with him in confidence that he did not tell me. He carried a heavy load because he felt the pain his students endured. None of us go through life without strife, but he made it his mission to help as much as he could.

When Shelley Sonderman was killed in an auto accident on an icy road, Dewey wept when he came into my office. He felt the tragedy deeply. Her brother, Darren, was injured in the same accident, and we visited him at the hospital. Dewey felt the agony for a long time. Darren recovered enough to play in the championship game that fall, and that was a highlight for the team.

Brent reminded me recently that, in the early '70s, one of Dewey's students made a plaster cast of his head. Before we moved from the town of Dayton, the cast was dropped and it broke into smithereens. At the time I had Dewey, and although I valued the cast then, I don't have Dewey today, so I wish I still had it.

One year a new girl moved to Dayton, and after her first day of school she reported, "That Mr. Sullivan scared me to death. I have him in biology and he looks so stern." FAST FORWARD – TWO NIGHTS LATER: a friend joined the family for dinner and the young lady stated, "Guess who my favorite teacher is?" The guest said, "Mr. Sullivan." She was puzzled and asked, "How did you know?"

Dewey looked out his classroom window one afternoon, and saw a couple of his students doing something under the hood of his pickup. He finished his class, and when he went to the pickup after school, he lifted the hood and found that a smoke "bomb" had been installed. He removed it and got in and drove away. He noticed the students standing a short distance away, and they appeared disappointed that he was aware of their prank.

Once a new girl came to school, and was not readily accepted. She was absent on the third or fourth day of class, so he inquired and was told she had committed suicide the previous evening. He wondered what he might have done to ease the anguish she experienced. He was troubled to think that maybe he could have helped.

He knew how difficult it is to enter a new situation, so he tried to get his students to be more tolerant of others. He told of the young lady who told him, "I don't care," in regard to an assignment he gave her. He said, "Well, I care about you and what you do. I want you to succeed." She was surprised, but he wanted the best for his students. He loved young people.

During one in-service session, a presenter lectured on "assertive discipline." Dewey dozed off, and the presenter noticed that Dewey was nodding. He was nudged and awakened by one of his fellow teachers. When the presenter asked what he thought about the concept, his response was, "Ma'am, when kids are misbehaving in class, I just look them in the eyes . . . It works for women also." (I don't know if Dewey's response was what she was seeking, but it's what she got.) Roger Lorenzen said, "When it comes right down to it, he's all about teaching the game of life."

Once one of the students in Dewey's biology class remarked about the large numbers of animals in Africa. He told her, "Just go to New York City and you can see more humans than all the numbers of wildebeest, zebras, lions, etc. combined in Kenya. There might be a million or more animals in the Mara, but there are more humans in New York City alone."

As a sophomore, Charity Baker had Dewey as a biology teacher, and when her brother, Vince, got into high school, she said, "You're going to just *LOVE* Mr. Sullivan. He's such a nice man." Several nights later Vince came home from football practice and slammed his gear on the floor with a thud. When asked, "What's the matter, Vince?" he grumbled, *"YOUR MR. SULLIVAN IS NOT THE SWEETHEART YOU THINK HE IS!!"* (We figured Vince had received a little extra "coaching" that evening.)

Vince was a "force" on the team, and was named to the All-League Team. He made All-State honors his senior year, and played in the East-West Shrine game in Baker City in August of 1996.

As the time for his last high school football game (championship '95) neared, Vince did not want the season to end. He enjoyed the camaraderie and the fellowship. His mother had a photo of the seniors from the '95 championship team screened onto a t-shirt, and she presented it to Dewey at the awards ceremony at the end of the season. He said, "It's too important to wear, so I'll keep it as a memento."

But Dewey's hands were full as we left the celebration. He dropped the shirt in the mud, so it had to be laundered. That shirt had special meaning since it was a gesture from the heart, and he treasured it.

After Dewey's death Charity wrote, "Dewey held a special place in my heart the first day I actually met him. I started attending Dayton football games in the 7th grade because that was the thing to do on Friday nights. I had seen him at those games, but never thought our lives would intersect the way they did, but God knew.

"I met him the first day of my sophomore year in biology class – first period. He sat behind his desk which was a little elevated above the students' desks. He wore his glasses at the end of his nose and folded his arms. He made sure we knew that his class would be hard, and that not all of us would pass. What 'helped' his speech was a poster hanging to the right of him (set back on a door) with an eagle looking you dead-on (not blinking) and the caption said, 'I'm smiling.' That poster helped me believe his 'speech' because of how much Dewey and the eagle looked alike. They both scared me to death!

"The stories go on and on – stories of Vince playing football and helping to win a championship – of pies being 'lost' – 'found' – 'enjoyed' – of road trips to all of the games – of Sunday nights at my parents' home watching film."

During her high school days, Charity adopted Dewey as her "Grandpa," and we served as surrogate grandparents for her wedding when she married Matt Kuiper in Colorado Springs. The wedding was beautiful, and the reception afterward was held at the Air Force Academy.

The movie, *Napoleon Dynamite*, appealed to Dewey, and he thoroughly enjoyed it. He was intrigued and said, "That is so typically high school. I have seen much of what is portrayed in that film. I can't believe it is so well done."

When Dewey retired from teaching in 1993, he said, "I'm going to miss the kids. I never set out to coach the Pirates as long as I have. I've just gone a year at a time. I won't tolerate poor attitudes, and I would never 'beg' a bunch of sixteen- or seventeen-year-olds to play football. I have fond memories of the state championships in 1985 and 1986 and the desire is there to win again."

Dewey enjoyed his years in the classroom, but was ready for a little "down time." He continued to coach and that was enough to keep him busy. He never stopped questioning and he never stopped learning.

CHAPTER **24**

The Building of a Dynasty

When Dewey started coaching at Dayton, there were four classifications in sports: "Eight-man, 1-A, 2-A, and 3-A." The only three losing seasons of Dewey's career at Dayton were while the Pirates played at the 2-A level. (Three losing seasons at Dayton out of forty-two.) He was quoted as saying, "It was tough because we were really 1-A, but we played at the 2-A level. The OSAA told us to move down a classification, but the school board refused."

In the eighth game of the 1967 season, Dayton beat Colton 20-0 in a non-league contest. Colton finished the season by winning the state championship at the 1-A level, and Dewey's premise was that the Pirates could easily have been state champs had they been in the proper classification.

From 1965 through 1981, only one team from each league advanced to the playoffs, and it was not until 1976 that Dayton made it into the playoffs. Dayton was the smallest 2-A school in the State of Oregon (with less than two-hundred students in high school), and played against schools with populations of more than six hundred students.

The playoff participant was often determined by which team had beaten which other team (based on a point system). When Barry and Brent played from 1970 through 1974, the Pirates were co-champions of the Yawama League, and shared five consecutive league titles, but did not advance to the playoffs. They stressed to later teams, how fortunate they were to "get" to play in the playoffs.

Barry and Brent did not play tackle football until Barry was in high school and Brent in the eighth grade. Flag football was the only game in town. Yellow flags were attached to their hips with *Velcro*, and if a player pulled his opponent's flag, that player was "tackled."

Dewey was instrumental in getting tackle football accepted into the curriculum at Dayton, and he helped start the *Dayton Little Guy* football program. He and Dave Cook, with the assistance of Ann Hop from Dayton and a gentleman from Gaston, presented the *Little Guy* program to the Dayton Booster Club. Ann became one of the initial directors of the program, and signed loan papers at the bank to enable the group to purchase the necessary gear.

In 2007 we contributed $1,000 from the *Dewey Sullivan Memorial Golf Tourney* (now the *Dewey Sullivan Classic*) to the *Dayton Little Guy* program, as that is where the interest in football begins. The program is far different today than when it began, but everything changes. Three local schools were involved in the beginning, but today almost every school in the area has several teams.

During Dewey's tenure, several people were involved in filming Dayton games, but Dwight Ediger and Verlyn Baker spent the most time. Brian Smith also helped on several occasions. Jack Edwards, Stu Stewart and several others filmed before that time. Dewey appreciated their expertise.

He realized how fortunate he was to have the quality demonstrated by those photographers. In one exchange, he received a tape that began with about fifteen minutes of treetops and cheerleaders. He and Max Wall chuckled about that, and Max said, "Good luck, Dewey. You're going to get a lot of help from that tape. It really shows what your opponent is going to do."

The filming of Dayton games on 16mm became a reality in the late '60s, and the games were recorded on cartridges, processed and put on reels to be shown on old projectors. Dewey went to the Booster Club each fall, and asked for funds for purchasing and developing the films. After the games, we took the films to one of the television stations in Portland, and waited while they were processed. But occasionally we took the film to the bus depot in McMinnville where it was shipped to Portland for processing.

When the films were sent to Portland, they were not returned until Sunday evening. Since Dewey liked to have the film to look at during the weekend, we most often delivered the films ourselves. With the advent of videotapes, it was an entirely new ballgame, and he came from the game to watch and assess what had transpired the night of the action.

On Sunday evenings, Dewey and the assistant coaches met at our home, or the home of one of the other coaches. We had a potluck while the fellows watched films. Back in the early days of video recorders . . . back before wireless recorders . . . back before *DVDs*, Dewey purchased his first video recorder. We used his coaching salary to purchase that recorder (a wired remote). We were so proud of our purchase, and were excited to have moved into the twentieth century. Karina Lorenzen was two, so we had to watch her carefully, as she often tripped over the cord for the remote. What a revolution has been seen with the change from wired remotes to wireless recorders and then to digital recordings.

To serve on the chain gang at Dayton (running the down markers for games), is almost a lifetime commitment. With the success of the football program, it became an honor to serve. Jeff Willard, Mike Henry and Forrest Jacks have served for many years, and Kenny Albright volunteered until he became too ill to move the markers. For many years, the voice of the Pirates has been Jim Connelly assisted by Wayne Herring. Those two make an outstanding color broadcast team.

Dewey coached track on a volunteer basis in 1966 and 1967. He received no pay, but did it so the school would not drop the sport. Track returned to the salary schedule in 1968 and Dewey coached until 1971, when Hal Tanaka took over the reins of the program.

Dewey also coached wrestling from 1965 until 1982. After

A BAREFOOT BOY FROM OKLAHOMA

wrestling practice, he got onto the mat and challenged his wrestlers to take him on. Barry likened it to an elephant with monkeys jumping around. One of Dewey's favorite wrestling stories was of the wrestler who came to him at the state tournament and reported there was a large family involved in the tourney. Dewey asked, "What family is that?" He was told there were a lot of "Bye" brothers. (In the first rounds of the tournament, many wrestlers draw a "bye," so that wrestler interpreted it as the surname of the wrestler.) Dewey came home chuckling.

Jim Pratt won the heavyweight championship in wrestling his junior year, and the movie, *Rocky*, was a box office hit. Before the championship match, the team went to that movie and it served as inspiration for Jim's success.

In 1965, Dayton, along with the schools of Amity, Sheridan, Willamina, Sherwood, Yamhill-Carlton, Philomath, Banks and Nestucca, were in the Yawama League. After the disastrous 1981 season (0-9), the move to the 1-A classification was mandated by the OSAA.

The year was 1982, and it was the beginning of a dynasty. The Pirates had been reclassified into the 1-A class, which meant they competed against schools similar in size to Dayton. From that time until Dewey died in 2006, the Pirates made an annual appearance in the Oregon football playoffs.

The Yawama League became the West Valley League, and wrestling schedules changed. Matches were held on weekends, and meant no family time for coaches. Dewey resigned as wrestling coach in 1983.

While Dayton was in the West Valley League, sixteen league championships in football were won, and the Pirates finished second nine times. (Dayton teams made playoff appearances for thirty years while Dewey was the head coach.) The Pirates had fourteen undefeated regular seasons. They played in six championship games, and won five state titles. At the time of Dewey's death, the Pirates held the state record for most consecutive playoff appearances with twenty-five. He definitely paved the way for success in football at Dayton. (From mediocrity to acclaim!)

CHAPTER **25**

The Forty-Year Reign

Roger Lorenzen played football four years at Dayton, and then assisted Dewey before he moved to Amity as Athletic Director and football coach. Dayton defeated Amity during Roger's second year of coaching, and when they talked after the game, Dewey told Roger, "You know you're like a son to me Roger, but sometimes dads have to spank their kids." After Dewey's death Roger wrote *The Forty-Year Reign* (see below):

> THE FORTY-YEAR REIGN
>
> *I stare out my window, and through all my pain*
> *An end of an era, a forty-year reign*
> *He gave everything that money 'caint buy*
>
> *Chorus:*
>
> *His family surrounds him, while he slips away*
> *Fulfilling his wishes, to ease all the pain*
> *Warm tears from heaven flow once again'*
> *The end of an era, a forty-year reign*
> *His precious family holds four and his bride*
> *All others felt welcome – they let 'em inside*

One large impression, through his chosen game
Rewards of a good life – his forty-year reign

(Repeat the Chorus)

While we pray for answers, a legend moves on
In this game of life – no doubt that he won
Living without him, just won't be the same
We'll always remember, his forty-year reign

(Repeat the Chorus)

Warm rain's a fallin,' and there goes the pain,
Granting his wishes, God welcomes him home
Thank God for memories, and through His sweet name
The promise of heaven, an eternal reign.

(Written by Roger Lorenzen, In Memory of "Coach" Dewey Sullivan, November 13, 2006 and reprinted with permission)

Dave Bowlin played that song on the guitar, and sang it at Dewey's celebration of life. (He has also recorded a compact disc.) Dave played football at Dayton, and Roger told me, "Dave usually had a thirty-two ounce container of *Mountain Dew* with him. One day I told him that stuff would kill him, and he replied, 'Nope, I'm just doin' it for the 'Dew.'"

Dayton was scheduled to play Salem Academy in 1991, and a newspaper reporter called and asked, "Do you realize you're on the horizon of winning your 200th football game?" Dewey was astonished and replied, "Heck no. Are you kidding? That's a lot of football games. When did I win the 100th game? That must have been a long time ago if I'm approaching 200 wins. I don't think I'm old enough to have coached that many games." (He was unaware of that milestone until the media picked up on it.)

Jason Herring, the team manager, scheduled a celebration at a pizza parlor in Salem, following the game. When Dewey learned of that he said, "What if we don't win?" He did not want to prepare a celebration if the outcome was uncertain. *(A bird in the hand is worth two in the bush.)* Dayton won the game 38-15, and there were many at the celebration.

(Dwight Ediger filmed that game. He had a serious farm accident that summer, and his determination to return for the Salem Academy game was remarkable. He wanted to film the game denoting the milestone that was Dewey's 200th victory.)

The game that marked Dewey's 300th victory was played at Nestucca High School in Cloverdale in November of 2000. *The McMinnville News-Register* had a weekly countdown denoting each victory, so the 300th win was an "occasion." For that game, Stevie Whited had reproductions of Dewey's face put on sticks for the fans to hold up.

Rob Umbenhower, the assistant coach (now the Dayton head football coach) did not ride the bus to the game, but intended to ride home with the team. The Dayton locker room was broken into during the game, and Rob stayed afterwards to talk with the authorities.

With all the "hoopla" that went on, Dewey did not realize Rob intended to ride the bus home (or forgot since Rob had not ridden to the game with them). He took off on the bus with the team to go to the celebration. Halfway through dinner, a sheriff's deputy escorted Rob into the restaurant, and a loud "Hurrah" arose from the crowd. Rob was "ruffled," but the players loved it. They dubbed him, *Barney Fife*, and teased him unmercifully.

The Pirates defeated Yamhill-Carlton 34-8 in 1971, and the next week their opponents were the Banks Braves who were ranked #2 in state. Many Dayton fans did not consider the Pirates had a chance of winning the game, so opted to skip the contest. Those who attended the game came back elated as the Pirates upset the Braves by a score of 7-0. Dewey said, "That win rates as one of the best since I've been at Dayton." (Two Pirate first half scores and one touchdown in the second half were called back, but Dayton still won.) Dewey said, "Our kids put up an excellent effort against a good football team. Before the game, we were really high and very wild. The score could have been 20-0; we should have scored more, but we missed some golden opportunities."

Barry was the quarterback, and was injured at the end of that game. Dewey told him to kneel on the ball, but he was tackled. He sustained a shoulder injury, and was sidelined for two weeks. We took him to the doctor the morning after the game (Saturday), and it was determined his shoulder blade was chipped. The doctor stated that his season was over, but at breakfast a couple of weeks later, Barry said his shoulder felt better. Dewey again took him to the doctor, and an *x-ray* showed that he was healed. The doctor was amazed at his rapid recovery.

Barry missed two games, but was back for the conclusion of the season. After losing two games, the Pirates were out of the playoff hunt. The 1971 season ended when Yamhill-Carlton lost to Gladstone 16-8 in the title game. Since Dayton had defeated Y-C,

Dewey felt the Pirates were close to a championship, had it not been for injuries, and if Dayton had been properly classified 1-A.

Russ Walker, the first Dayton Booster Club president, was an indefatigable Pirate fan. When Y-C advanced to the championship game that year, Russ was interested in the outcome. (He wanted to see how Y-C compared to the eventual champs.) One of the Yamhill-Carlton coaches told Dewey that Russ appeared there, and rode the rooter bus so he could see the title game.

Before Dayton played Woodburn in 1972, a reporter from the local Woodburn paper came unannounced to our home in Dayton for an interview. Woodburn had a good football team, and was ranked in the state polls. (Gary Johnson, who later played for the *Seattle Seahawks* was on that team.) One of the questions asked was, "How do you plan to stop the Bulldogs — they are huge?" Dewey's reply was, "I guess we'll just do what we always do." The reporter told Dewey he would like another interview after the game (thinking Woodburn would be victorious). Dewey agreed to the second interview, but after Dayton won the game 34-14, the reporter did not return.

A player moved to Dayton from California in 1972, and Dewey was delighted to welcome a young man with so much potential. He looked like a "sumo" wrestler, and the team dubbed him "Fujiyama" or "Fuj" for short. Dewey fitted him out in Pirate uniform, but his shoulders were so thick that there were no shoulder pads large enough to fit him. The largest ones sat atop his shoulders, and only his nose and eyes were visible (resembling a comic football player.)

The team went through the agility drill where the coach stands in front of the players and quickly moves the ball from right to left, then left to right before placing it over his head. "Fuj" moved from right to left okay, and then left to right, but then he tried to get the ball when it was put over Dewey's head. He jumped up and down like a frog, and Dewey backed to get away from him. The team cracked up. (It went "thunk, thunk" then "thunk, thunk, thunk" instead of "thunk, thunk," and then "run on by.") Dewey became exasperated by "Fuj's" antics, and yelled, "Stop! Stop! Now, watch how to do this correctly."

When Dewey came home that evening, he was still chuckling. He came in and said, "Oh, my aching toes. The funniest thing happened at practice tonight. We had a transfer from California, and he looks like a football player, but what a "greenhorn." We did the drill where I hold the football, and have the team go right and then left and then run on by.

"This young man did the right and left movements okay, but then he tried to get the ball from me when I placed it over my head. He stomped on my toes before he got the message. It was so funny that we all cracked up. My toes may never recover, but it was worth the pain. I haven't seen anything that funny for years."

"Fuj's" position was on the line on defense, and his mission was to disrupt the offense of the opposing team. He crashed through the line, and scattered his opponents. Before each play he was instructed, "We're on defense, 'Fuj' – we're on defense.'"

In the final game of "Fuj's" career, Dewey let him play fullback. Dayton defeated Clatskanie 49-12 and "Fuj" scored. That spoiled him for defense. He loved the fullback position, and would gladly have moved to offense had he been given the chance. He talked about it at school all the next week.

The Pirates defeated Cascade by the score of 24-0 in 1973. The next summer one of the Cascade coaches came to my office at Linfield College, and stated, "Dayton surprised us last season, but it won't happen again."

(But it did. Dayton won the game the next year 22-14. The margin was not as wide as in the first game, but it was a victory nonetheless.) The two wins by Dayton in 1973 and in 1974 were non-league victories; however, when it really counted (in the fall of 1980), Cascade defeated the Pirates 34-22. That game was in the quarterfinal round of the playoffs, and the Cougars won the state championship two weeks later.

When Dayton lost to Cascade, Dewey was disappointed. The Pirates had handily dominated their opponents all season. He said,

THE FORTY-YEAR REIGN

"That was my last chance at a state title. I'll never get a team that good again." Several coaches called to ask if he were giving up football. (He said he should have given it up for a year, since the Pirates did not win any games in 1981, and had a record of 0-9.)

Before the Pirates played the Regis Rams in the semifinal game of the playoffs in 1996, Dayton was invited to appear on television after the game. That game was played at Civic Stadium in Portland, and Dewey's comment about being on television was, "I don't like that idea. How embarrassing it will be to appear on television if we don't win."

The Pirates won 63-44 in a real "shoot-out," and for several years, that game held the state record for most points scored in a playoff contest. On a reverse, Regis didn't realize Mike Cushman had the ball, and he rambled down the sideline for a sixty-eight yard touchdown. The television announcer said, "See ya! Wouldn't wanna be ya!" Mike had an outstanding game, and the interviewer stated that Mike should be worn out by the amount of running he did.

For the championship the next week, Dayton met Weston-McEwen. After the Pirates held the TigerScots to seven yards rushing on thirty-three attempts, Dewey's assessment was, "Everyone said we couldn't play defense when we gave up forty-four points Regis last week, but we knew we were a good defensive team. Who said we had a weak defense?"

Several years ago the Tigers of Yamhill-Carlton were the underdogs in their first playoff game in twenty-one years. The game was played at Linfield College the night before Dayton's Saturday afternoon game. Dewey attended, and as the teams went onto the field, leaned over the rail and inquired, "Where's Morgan?" The team looked up and hesitantly replied, "Right here." Dewey said, "Go get them!" He gave the team a "thumb's up." Cole's teammates asked, "How do you know Dewey Sullivan?" Cole explained, "My dad played for him in high school, so I have known him for a long time." Cole later said, "I feel the victory was due in part to the fact that Dewey was in the stands and was pulling for us. That energized us."

Max Wall had a green bus dubbed, "The Autzen Express." That bus was decked in green and gold (the colors of the University of Oregon Ducks who play their home games at Autzen Stadium). The first time Dewey met Max to go to a Duck game he said, "Do I really get to go to the game in this kind of style?"

Dewey rode that bus several times while Dante Rosario played at Oregon. Max had recliners and a video recorder set up, and he and Dewey watched game tapes on the way to the games. When they arrived at the stadium, Denise Wall fixed breakfast burritos for the crew, and Dewey enjoyed the experience (the food, the camaraderie and the games). He also enjoyed the time afterward, while they waited for the crowds to subside. A lot of football lore and knowledge was tossed around there.

Max called Dewey several years ago, and told him a new player had moved into the Monroe School District. Max asked the young man, "Are you tough?" The reply was, "I'm damn tough." Later, whenever Dewey and Max talked, Dewey chuckled when he asked, "How's 'Damn Tough'?" Dewey loved that story. And, after "Damn

THE FORTY-YEAR REIGN

Tough's" final season, Max reported that he really was, "Damn Tough."

Dewey once scouted a game between Santiam-Christian and Willamina, both West-Valley League opponents of the Pirates. When a play did not go as planned, a fan asked, "Dewey, what play would you have called?" He replied, "I would have called that same play." (He did not criticize the coaches who opposed him.)

Several years ago, the Sisters School District called Dewey for a recommendation for Bob Macauley. Dewey said, "Take him. I want him out of the WVL. He's too good a coach, and I'm tired of trying to defend against his strategies." When Bob was hired, Dewey told him, "I feel I can take credit for you getting that job."

The Pirates won league the year that Scott Walker moved to Dayton. At the conclusion of the final league game Scott jumped up and down in excitement, and was so exuberant that several team members looked at him in puzzlement. They asked, "What's wrong?" He told them, "We've just won league. Aren't you excited?" The reply was, "What's the big deal? We always do." (Of course, that was not true, but it had become an expectation for Dayton to win league. How jaded we become with winning.)

In 1984 Santiam-Christian defeated the Pirates, and the two teams were co-champions of the West Valley League. When Dayton lost to Gaston in 1989, it was the first league loss suffered by Dayton since 1984, and the Pirates did not lose another league game for five years.

Dayton had an undefeated regular season in 1990, and again won the league championship. But the Pirates lost to Vale 22-20 in the semi-final round of the playoffs. The Pirates finished that season with a record of 11-1.

Two years later, the Pirates lost to Vale 26-20 in the quarterfinal game. That game was played at Vale in near blizzard conditions. There were no dressing room facilities to accommodate the Dayton players, and they were forced to sit on the bus at halftime. The Pirates led 20-0 at the half, but two questionable second half calls (one an out-of-bounds Vale pass that was ruled in-bounds, and the

A BAREFOOT BOY FROM OKLAHOMA

other also a pass), determined the outcome of the game. Vale won the state title two weeks later.

The team was snow-bound after that loss, and spent the night in a motel in Baker City. It was a glum group that watched the game tape. It would have been a wonderful celebration if the film had been of a victory. At the state wrestling tournament the next spring, one of the Vale coaches told Dewey the Pirates got the short end of the stick on those calls. (Dewey agreed with him!)

Heppner bagged the *BIG PRIZE* the next year. I ordered a sweatshirt with Heppner recognized as the championship team, but Dewey's players did not appreciate my humor -- I guess it was like rubbing salt into a wound.

A play went particularly bad at practice one afternoon, and it looked like a "human haystack." After the second such fiasco Dewey called the team to the side and asked, "What in the world happened there?" One of the players said, "Well, 'Coach' if so-and-so had done this, it would have worked.'" Dewey looked at him, and started singing, *I Don't Believe In If Anymore*. (Roger Whitaker made that song famous in the '70s, but of course, the kids `in the '90s had not heard of Roger Whitaker or that song.)

Dewey said, "You guys go home tonight, get on your computers and come back tomorrow so we can sing *I Don't Believe In If Anymore.*" (His sense of humor was almost without compare. He particularly enjoyed Jordan May ending practice with, "Supper's on the table, Coach. Mom's waiting.")

Dewey once called Brian Cruickshank, the Dayton quarterback, to the sidelines during a game, and went over strategy with him. Brian's mother, Barb, was the official team photographer, and she saw the turmoil. After the game she asked Brian what Dewey said, and was told, "What the 'blankety-blank' were you doing?" Barb wanted more specifics, and again asked, "What did Dewey say?" Brian's reply was once more, "What the 'blankety-blank' were you doing?" The third time she said, "No, I mean what did Dewey say? What did he REALLY say?" And again the answer was, "What the 'blankety-blank' were you doing?"

One afternoon at practice, Dewey heard Jeff Stahl muttering to himself. Dewey called Jeff aside and said, "Stahl, we don't bad-mouth our team members." Jeff replied, "But, Coach, I'm not bad-mouthing the team." Dewey said, "Yes, you are. You are bad-mouthing Jeff Stahl, and he's part of the team."

As the playoffs neared one year, a trip to Nyssa was on the slate. The night before we left, Jeff's father, Fred, came into the restaurant for the team meal. He said, "Why do we have to travel to Nyssa?" I said, "Fred, we don't have to go there . . . *WE GET TO GO THERE*. There are several hundred teams and a thousand or more players around the State of Oregon who would love to have the privilege of playing in the playoffs. They would love to drive to the game. We are fortunate." Fred said, "Of course. You're right! It will be a fun trip."

The summer before his senior year, Jeff participated in rodeo as a bull rider. Dewey asked Fred to discourage him from such professionalism until his senior football season ('99 season) was over. But Fred said, "It's his life." Jeff broke his tailbone near the end of that summer. The bone healed, but was still sensitive when football practice started. Jeff played through the season with the injury, but re-injured it the week before the championship. After the title game, his dad said, "So you wanted to be a cowboy?"

CHAPTER **26**

Dayton's "Knute Rockne"

In the final league game in 1995, Dayton met the Greyhounds of Gaston. Corey Sutton carried nine times for seventy-six yards and four touchdowns, and Jeremy Wilson and Mike Cushman each scored twice.

The next week, the Pirates played Knappa in the first round of the playoffs. They won that game by the score of 57-14. That victory gave Dewey his 250th victory with the Pirates, and put him three wins away from a tie for third place on the all-time win list for Oregon.

⤙ A BAREFOOT BOY FROM OKLAHOMA

Dewey said, "I'm just trying to celebrate the 250th win. This is one of the better teams I've coached. The kids have been doing a good job, and I'm just glad we won."

The Pirates entered the quarterfinal game averaging fifty-three points a game, and defeated the sixth ranked Wolverines of Santiam 50-12. Dayton won without attempting a pass, and the Santiam coach said, "They controlled our line." Dewey pointed out that the offensive line had a hand in Corey Sutton's performance.

When the Pirates met Lost River for the title it was the tenth anniversary of the 1985 championship. Dewey said, "I'm like a little kid right now. I'm excited . . . This is the ultimate game, the dream that all kids have. There's that chance to win that first prize."

The movie, *Rudy*, was a box office hit, and the famous Knute Rockne speech was aired. Corey Sutton said, "I thought 'Coach' has to do that for us, and maybe I could talk him into it. The next day I saw 'Coach,' and told him about the movie and the speech. Being the wise coach that he was, he was very familiar with this big speech. I then said, 'you gotta' do that for us.' Coach replied, 'Let's get to the big game, and I'll do it.'"

Dayton went through the season undefeated and won the league title. The Pirates played in the championship game, and before the game, Corey nudged Dewey and said, "Remember you promised." After all the players were dressed and ready Corey said, "'Coach' walks out of the team room and quickly returns with a chair. He puts it down and steps up with both feet. He then begins, 'Men, we're going inside, we're going outside . . . inside . . . outside. And, when we get them on the run, we're gonna keep 'em on the run. We're gonna hit 'em on the right . . . we're gonna hit 'em on the left, and we're not going to pass unless their secondary comes up too close. But, don't forget, men, we're gonna get 'em on the run, and we're gonna go, go, go, go! And we aren't going to stop until we cross that line!'"

Corey said, "I think 'Coach' must have been more nervous about that speech than about the game. He had been in hundreds of games, but a speech like this was outside his comfort zone. Anyone who has been in Dayton's locker room pre-game or played for Dewey knows he doesn't yell out loud rah-rah speeches. He goes over assignments, and breaks down x's and o's on the chalkboard. The entire locker room blew up with yells, screams and excitement. The speech took seconds, but the effect on our team morale was amazing. 'Coach' had just prepared his team like another legendary coach, and he knew it would work. Nobody could believe that he had just done this. Only three or four other people in the room knew it was coming.

"After the game I heard that a few people thought that the team was much too relaxed for the game. They thought that was not the way to prepare our team. One of the coaches asked, 'What is he doing? Doesn't he know we have a game to play? Has he lost it?'" To that question, one of the players replied, "Coach promised if we got to the final game." Corey later said, "I am sure if 'Coach' was complimented on the pre-game antics he would just turn it into a compliment for Coach Rockne. So, thank you Coach Sullivan, and thanks to Coach Rockne."

A former Dayton player, Roger Hildebrandt, reported, "I was impressed as Dewey led the team onto the field that day. The players followed him as in 'follow the leader' and did their warm-ups. Corey Sutton scored four touchdowns, and set the ball on the goal line each time. The team was business-like and professional. They were individuals working toward a common goal. I was impressed with the discipline and determination they demonstrated — by the spirit they exemplified as they went to the field, and as they played the game."

Roger called Dewey before that game, and asked, "Dewey, can you pass just once?" (But the execution was effective without passing. Of course Dewey was often criticized for not using more of a passing attack — it was said that his offense was boring.)

Roger was the quarterback on the '64 league championship team, and his son, Jon, was a special friend of Dewey's. Dewey tried unsuccessfully to get Jon to play football, but his game was basketball. Jon is skilled at basketball and has recorded several digital recordings on ball handling. Dewey said, "You should be a *Harlem Globetrotter*. You are so good at handling the basketball."

After Dayton won the title game 42-6, Dewey said, "This is an awesome team. I can finally say that. I didn't want to say that until the end of the season." The Lost River coach said, "The Pirates are from another world. They probably should be playing at the 3-A level. They are that good. They play almost perfectly."

DAYTON'S "KNUTE ROCKNE"

After the title game, Dayton player, Jesse Everett, said, "It's the happiest day and the saddest day of my career. The happiest day because we won the state championship. The saddest day because football season is over. This is a family." Corey Sutton said, "I've learned a lot. How to work together as a team in order to reach a goal."

Dewey was a perfectionist, and he insisted each play be run until it was done correctly, even if it took multiple times. He was meticulous in trying to get each detail perfect. Most coaches give up and move on after one or two attempts, but Dewey wanted it done correctly. He felt that if something was worth doing, it was worth doing right.

Corey Sutton (who was later named "Little All American" at Western Oregon University) said, "Most coaches go out and run one-hundred plays one time. Dewey runs each play one hundred times. It's great because the community knows what he's going to do. From seventh grade on through high school you're running the same offense. He's had some great athletes, but a lot of coaches with great athletes never do anything with them. He coaches everybody to do their jobs."

Corey said, "I consider 'Coach' to be one of the biggest influences in my life as well as a best friend. He has taught me that being a genuinely good person is, above all, the most important quality a person can have. If I were to explain in one sentence what I learned from 'Coach' it would be, 'life is about giving more than you take.'"

It became a tradition for the Pirates to run sprints after each game, and those sprints were run according to the number of games left to be played during that season. The tradition was started one year at the Kennedy Jamboree when the lines for the chicken barbecue were long. The players decided to run sprints while they waited for the chicken. (The Kennedy barbecue was one of Dewey's favorite venues because he loved the chicken, and he enjoyed talking with the other coaches.)

According to the tradition, the team ran sprints corresponding to the number of games that remained in the season. After the Jamboree, the team ran thirteen sprints, (thirteen games to the championship), and the number dropped each week until the championship round. If the Pirates won the semi-final game, one sprint was run as only one game remained in the season. Dewey chuckled as he said, "I guess early on when we ran twelve sprints some people said the coach must be really upset with the kids."

One time Dewey tried to get the coaches from two schools together to analyze a game film. As he talked on the phone, I stood in the background, and told him it would not be a good idea, as two of the coaches were league rivals. He did not understand that concept, as he was always willing to dissect football films with anyone interested. (He was naïve in that he thought everyone got along well together. He had rivals, but he did not consider any of them "bitter.") His meeting did not happen.

I often came from work to find him going over films with J.R. Torres, a former Dayton player, when he was the head football coach at Amity. He also spent hours watching films with John Kuppenbender and Randy Traeger from JFK. He liked sharing his football knowledge, and he questioned his strategies with others. He probed for insights and was inquisitive. He loved "talking" football.

When J.R. and Greg Baker were in the third grade, they volunteered as managers for the football team. Greg came to Dewey before practice started that fall, and introduced J.R. as his assistant. There were many humorous incidents while they were the managers, and their team was the first under Dewey to make it to the playoffs. I remember one time they told Dewey that something they had done was "pure college style." They loved Dayton football.

One year Dewey took the junior varsity team to Newport, so the younger coaches could go home to their families. The team saw whales as they neared Newport, and that made the trip exciting. (Rod Losier student taught with Dewey in the early '90s, and was the junior varsity coach at Newport. He was an assistant to Gene Morrow, the long-time Newport coach, who was also at the game. Gene was second on the Oregon wins list at the time.) Rod greeted

Dewey, and said, "Two football legends on the field at the same time."

Dewey had a memorable evening (of course, it was football). He recalled Gene Morrow saying, "Time is your enemy." In later years Dewey agreed with that. And at the last, he too, just ran out of time. As Andy Rooney said, "Life is like a roll of toilet tissue. The closer it gets to the end, the faster it goes." (Most of us can't wait to grow up, and when we do, we wish we were younger.)

For Dewey, football was the "only game in town." He loved the excitement, the thrill of the game, the strategy. He loved watching football, but loved coaching it even more. The intrigue of devising plays and watching them unfold kept him interested in what had just happened, what was likely to happen, or what was meant to happen.

Dewey's offense stressed the subtlety of illusion, and of keeping the defense always wary. His quarterbacks were masters of disguise. (There were instances when a play was whistled "dead" because the official lost track of where the ball was.) The thing Dewey had that many coaches lack is love. He loved kids, and he loved the game of football. He did not coach for the glory. He coached for kids, and because he enjoyed the game.

Dewey likened football to life. He felt that many of life's lessons are learned on the football field. He was a teacher of life, and he taught perseverance and the tenet that you should never give up. He was an eternal optimist who believed the cup was half full, and that anything could be used to your advantage.

Several years ago, Jonell told me, "If Dewey were ill, or could not coach, you could take over and run the team." Ha!! I do not know a trap from a reverse. I do know the difference between a run and a pass, but that is as far as it goes. I lived around the game of football for fifty-three years, but I am still not knowledgeable about it.

Dewey often told me, "You would never make a football coach. You are too willing to give up." My response was, "I never wanted to be a football coach."

(I also did not want to be a teacher. Dewey wanted me to pursue a career in education, but I did not have the desire to do so. He regretted that I did not go to college, but I told him, "If I had truly wanted, I could have gotten a degree while I worked at Linfield.")

Dewey mentored many during his lifetime, and was also mentored by many. He was inquisitive, and he was not too proud to ask questions. He was a "football clinic in a nutshell," and was one of the most knowledgeable men ever about the game of football. He probably forgot more about football than many coaches will ever know.

CHAPTER 27

Amity/Dayton — The Big Rivalry

Dayton and Amity are about ten miles apart. A distinct rivalry has existed from the time the first game between the two schools was recorded. They met twice in 1928, and Amity won the first contest 27-0. The second game ended in a 0-0 tie. Amity dominated the rivalry until 1966, but the Pirates then held the advantage until losing to Amity 44-42 in 1976. The Pirates returned the favor in 1977 by winning 42-0.

In 1998 Amity defeated Dayton for the first time since 1976, and the intensity heated up. Dewey came home the night before *THE BIG GAME*, and told me, I don't know how we can possibly play a game on our field tomorrow night. It's a 'quagmire.' It's so muddy you can hardly walk across it."

All week the "hype" from the media had stirred everyone's interest. It was for the West Valley League title, and was the "Game of the Year." Both teams were undefeated and the locals were excited.

When the kick-off came, the stands erupted in cheers. On Dayton's first possession, Brian Cruickshank, quarterback for the Pirates, sustained a leg injury. It was feared he had a knee injury, but it was later learned that he had fractured his leg. Dewey was relieved when he learned that it was Brian's leg, rather than his knee. Dewey was certain a bone would heal faster and better than a knee.

For four quarters, the game "see-sawed" back and forth, with neither team scoring. It was played to a 0-0 tie in regulation, and went into overtime. Amity scored, and won the "Mud Bowl" game and the league title by the score of 6-0. With that victory, Amity fans said they could beat anyone and they did.

Amity won the league championship, and four weeks later won the state title. Then they won it again in 1999, 2000, and 2001 – in four years they won four consecutive state titles. The only blemish on their incredible string of victories was a 34-14 league loss to Dayton in 1999.

Dayton clinched the league title in the sixth game of the 1999 season by defeating the Warriors 34-14. When Justin Hubbard of Amity scored the first touchdown, he ran triumphantly down the Amity sideline with his hand held high. Someone asked Dewey, "Did that make you mad?" Dewey replied, "No, I thought it was great." (Not that Amity had scored first, but that Justin was so excited and showed so much emotion. Dewey loved that emotion.)

Dayton won that game and the league title. The revenge was sweet, but it didn't last long. The two teams met for the state championship seven weeks later, and the Pirates lost. Before Monroe met Amity in the playoffs, Max Wall told Dewey he likened trying to catch Justin Hubbard to trying to catch a chicken in a pen. Just when you thought you had him he would fly right by you. Dewey agreed with that analogy.

The Pirates played Sherman County the week before the championship, and nine Dayton starting positions were lost due to injury. (Dayton players play on both offense and defense, as do players from most small schools.) When Dayton and Amity met for the title, the Dayton squad was decimated.

After the Sherman County debacle Dewey shifted players around, and was still optimistic until the day before the *BIG GAME*. Then, in practice, one of the players broke his ankle. Dewey said, "I can't believe it! Of all the rotten luck! To have so many of our team out of commission for the championship game." He began to wonder if the Pirates really might be "snakebitten."

And if that weren't bad enough, on the day of the game, another

AMITY/DAYTON - THE BIG RIVALRY

player stepped over a bench, landed on some gear, and "blew" his ankle. After the game he showed it to me, and I was shocked. I said, "Did Dewey let you play on that ankle?" He replied, "He didn't know. I had one of the other coaches tape it because I knew he wouldn't let me play if he had known." The game was exciting, but the Pirates lost 20-12.

When the two schools met, home field advantage was desired, and special arrangements were necessary. Additional bleachers were brought to Amity, and it was "standing-room-only" (SRO) around the track encircling the field. The Dayton stadium is somewhat larger than that at Amity, but it was also packed and seating was at a premium. The crowds were seven or eight deep around the field.

Early on the day of the *BIG GAME*, (or sometimes even the night before), territories were staked out with blankets, etc. People waited in line for more than half an hour. Sometimes the first quarter of the game would be over before all were admitted. Record-breaking crowds were in attendance.

Fans from nearby towns: Newberg. McMinnville, Salem and even Portland came. It was the *GAME OF THE WEEK*, and was highly publicized in all the newspapers and on television. Both teams wanted to claim "bragging rights" for the coming year.

In 2002 Dayton lost the last regular season game to Amity. After repeatedly jumping off sides, Dewey called the team to the sideline and said, "Do you fellows realize we've made more yards for Amity than they have?" (Dayton had twenty-one off sides penalties in that game. A flag was thrown. Then another flag was thrown, and then another. It was a true "hanky-fest.")

With that victory, Amity won the league title, and played Dayton for the 2-A title four weeks later. It was a sell-out crowd, and more than five thousand people were in attendance. St. Paul and Perrydale teamed up for the 1-A championship the same afternoon. All were local teams, and Tom Welter, Executive Director for the OSAA told me he was responsible for the arrangements for the two games. (He was the Assistant to Wes Ediger, the Executive Director at the time.)

The size of the crowd overwhelmed the facility, and parking

was at a premium. Many were ticketed for parking illegally, and some cars were towed. When Wes arrived at the game and saw the confusion, the parking, etc., Tom asked him, "tongue-in-cheek," "Who's in charge here?" (Of course, Tom was!)

The championship was a rematch of the final league game, and Amity won the coin toss. The Warriors opted to kick, so the Pirates received the ball, and fumbled on the first possession. Amity recovered, and a collective groan went up from the Dayton fans. The Warrior fans went WILD!! (Was this to be more of the final league game??) But after the first three Amity attempts led to lost yardage, the Warriors were forced to punt.

When the Pirates regained possession, Dewey was asked what he wanted to run. He said, "Run that same play again, but run it right this time." He was asked, "Are you sure?" He said, "Yes," and the second attempt was successful. His strategy was questioned, but his advice was heeded, and the Pirates took the ball to the end zone for the first score. Dewey had confidence in his team and his players, and felt they could prevail. Dayton dominated the game, and won by the score of 45-20.

Earlier that season Eevin Kunze, a Dayton player, had a miraculous escape. He swung out over the gym floor on a rope suspended from the ceiling of the high school stage. The rope snagged, and Eevin fell to the hardwood. He landed on his head and was knocked unconscious. Black stuff oozed from his mouth. One of the bystanders said, "His guts are coming out." (It was later learned that he had an Oreo cookie in his mouth.) It was a miracle he did not break his neck, and be either paralyzed or killed.

An ambulance transported Eevin to the McMinnville Hospital (about seven miles away), and Dewey was called with the information that Eevin had been injured. Before Dewey went to practice that afternoon, he visited Eevin, and was relieved to find him conscious and able to talk. Eevin recovered sufficiently to play in the playoffs, and he also played in the East-West Shrine game in Baker City.

Before the 2002 championship game, Dana Lundy, whose son, Mark, was the center told Dewey, "We want to have a dinner on

AMITY/DAYTON - THE BIG RIVALRY

Sunday night to celebrate the season." (The championship game was played on Saturday afternoon, and the celebration was to be on Sunday night for all in the community who might be interested.)

Dewey's response was, "What if we don't win?" Dana replied, "That's okay. It has been a great season anyway, and we need to recognize that." But Dayton won, and there was a memorable celebration with many in attendance.

During those years, both school administrations got together and placed breakfast or some other wager as the reward for winning or the penance for losing the BIG GAME.

One year Roger Lorenzen, the Dayton High School principal, wore a blue jersey (Amity colors) to lunch with the student body of Amity High School, and was presented with a blue satin rose that signified the Warrior victory. The Pirates won the game the next year, and the Amity superintendent wore a Pirate jersey.

Jeff Flood was the football coach at Amity for nine years and the Warriors won four state championships from 1998 through 2001. He said, "Once we beat Dayton in 1998, our kids knew we could

◄ A BAREFOOT BOY FROM OKLAHOMA

beat anybody. That's because the kids respect him (Dewey) so much. It's part aura . . . it's part respect."

Flood said, "He's been the face of small-level football in Oregon for four decades and you can't look at what we do today anywhere in the playoffs, without thinking about what he's done in the past."

When Joel Magill took over the reins of the Amity program in 2002, the Amity success continued. Joel credits Dewey with the fact that he is still coaching. Dewey told him, "We need more coaches like you, coaches who love kids and work well with them. (Amity won the league title in 2008, and was undefeated in regular season play.)

From 1995 through 2003 the road to the Oregon State Football Championship really did go through the West Valley League. Dayton (West Valley League) won the championship in 1995 and 1996, Lost River (Southern Cascade League) won in 1997, Amity (West Valley League) won in 1998, 1999, 2000 and 2001 and then Dayton won in 2002 with Amity following once again with the title in 2003. What an incredible string of championships. Eight in nine years!! (It was almost a "West

Valley League State Championship" at that time. There were three Dayton titles, and five Amity championships.

CHAPTER 28

The Road to the Championship — Shades of '48

In 1985, the *Salem Statesman Journal* reported, "In the tiny farming community of Dayton Dewey Sullivan has quietly assembled what could be the state's top Class A football program . . . Dayton, a perennial powerhouse in the West Valley League, has never won a state crown under Sullivan, but has been close. When Dayton competed at the Class AA level the Pirates were beaten three times by the eventual state champs . . . Dayton was eliminated by Enterprise in the quarterfinals in 1984 and the Savages went on to take the title . . . Dayton always seems to turn out good teams despite an enrollment of 154 students."

Dewey said, "It seems like we always come up with good players. Every year we're favored, and I think that helps us psychologically. Being Number One is fun. We're always near the top."

The Pirates defeated Sheridan 28-20 in the third game of the 1985 season, and it turned out to be for the league championship. Dewey was asked, "Did you feel comfortable leading 20-0 at halftime?" He laughed and said, "You'd have to be out of your mind to feel good about a lead like that over a good team. I was worried. I knew we were playing a good team, a well-coached team."

Sheridan tied that game at the end of three quarters, and the outcome was not decided until the final seconds of play. It looked as though Dayton was "doomed," but those "pesky Pirates," with their

A BAREFOOT BOY FROM OKLAHOMA

"never-say-die" tenacity didn't give up. With twenty-five seconds left in the game, Carl Duncan recovered a Sheridan fumble, and returned it twenty-five yards for a touchdown.

Twenty-five seconds. *IT SEEMED LIKE AN ETERNITY!!* Time stood still. It was unbelievable how long it took for the game to end. Until that point, each minute sped by. Then, when the final minute was there, it took forever. When the last second ticked off the clock, the stands erupted. The final score was 28-20, and the Pirates gained the confidence to breeze through the regular season.

In the quarterfinal round of the playoffs, Dayton played Enterprise, and Chuck Corak, the Enterprise coach, said, "Dewey, this game is for the state title." (He was correct. It was the state championship game.) Dewey said, "I don't know about that . . . the championship is a long way away." The Savages had won twenty-three straight games, and were the defending state champions. (The previous year Dayton lost to Enterprise in the quarterfinal round by the score of 13-0.)

Dayton trailed 10-0 with seven minutes remaining in the game, and it looked as though the season was over. Both Enterprise scores were set up when the Pirates lost three fumbles, and had a pass intercepted. (When Enterprise kicked a field goal, one of the Dayton fans yelled down at Dewey, "That's what a field goal will do for you, Sullivan." After Dayton scored the winning touchdown, I turned and said to him, "That's what a touchdown will do for you.")

The Pirates survived the fumbles and the interception, but when Butch Jumalon got the ball, he rambled eight yards to the Enterprise thirteen-yard-line, where the ball was again fumbled. The Savages recovered, and it looked as if the game was over. But Shawn Troutman recovered a fumble on the Savage thirty-two yard line, and that led to Dayton's first score. Then Chuck Wert ran for fourteen yards, and Troutman threw a pass to Matt Owen for the two–point conversion. The score was 10-8 Enterprise, with six minutes and forty-four seconds left.

With six minutes on the clock, Troutman intercepted an Enterprise

THE ROAD TO THE CHAMPIONSHIP - SHADES OF '48

pass on the nineteen-yard line. That set up the final score of the game. Chuck Wert ran seventeen yards to the two-yard line, and Butch Jumalon took the ball into the end zone, but fumbled again. Matt Owen said, "I was blocking and saw Butch out of the corner of my eye. Suddenly the ball was just lying there. I fell on it. It was just a reaction. I thought Butch scored. Everyone was looking around, and I just fell on the ball. I got up and the referee looked at me, and then signaled the touchdown. Emotion overcame me and I started crying. I didn't know what to do. It was so great. We seniors decided this could be our last game. Everyone wanted to do it for Dayton and Coach Sullivan. He deserves a state championship. We had to stick it out. Chuck told us in the huddle we had to get going or we (the seniors) would never play again. Everyone thought about it, and we went out and did it."

Dewey told the team, "You can do it. You're not out of the game yet." The Pirates rallied from a 10-0 deficit to win the game 14-10, and scored all their points in a span of six minutes and forty-four seconds. It had been all Enterprise until the last six minutes, but the interception and the fumble recovery by Matt Owen in the end zone provided the winning score.

Dewey said, "They (Enterprise) didn't give up, but we just got higher and higher. We had that will to win in the last quarter. Something came over our kids. It was nothing the coaches did. We were disgusted by the way we were playing. The kids said, 'we're not going to let this one go.' They caught fire and decided 'we're going to win this game.' They stuck together and took off. After our scoring drive the kids felt they could do it. I thought our kids got physically stronger as the game went along. Our line just took over. It was amazing. Maybe it was all that running we do."

(The Pirates won thirty-six consecutive games and captured two state titles after that win. The thirty-six game win streak was a state record for several years, until Vale broke it with thirty-nine consecutive wins in 1992.)

The semi-final game between Dayton and Regis was played the next week on a frozen field in Stayton, and Dayton won 34-7. The

Salem Statesman Journal touted it as the *Battle of the Greybeards*. Bill McArthur, former coach at Oregon College of Education (now Western Oregon University), was the coach for Regis, but Dewey (who was fifty) took umbrage at that. He did not consider himself a "greybeard."

Dewey gave plaudits to the line when reporters came to interview before or after a game, and he tried to get them to interview members of the line rather than the backs who had scored the touchdowns. His philosophy was that the backs could do nothing without the line.

Before the Regis game, the press wanted a photo of Butch Jumalon, one of the Dayton running backs. Dewey said they could do that if they took the photo with all the seniors on the team (which they did.)

(In the first four games of the '85 season, Butch racked up 754 yards on 112 carries, and had an average rushing attempt of 6.7 yards, and an average of 188.5 yards per game. He carried the ball forty-five times for 266 yards against Sheridan, and thirty-three times when the Pirates played Colton.)

When the week of the championship game arrived, Dewey had as many of the participants from the '48 team as were around the area come to the high school, and run a few plays for the team. Coach McReynolds was in attendance as was Howard Putman and Marvin Lorenzen.

And at last . . . the Pirates "got" to practice on Thanksgiving Day! Dewey's big moment had arrived. He was delighted! He had "almost" reached the goal toward which he worked. To practice on Thanksgiving Day was the epitome of success. The CHAMPIONSHIP GAME loomed!! A short, but intense practice was the venue for the day, and then it was home for turkey and family.

Two days later, snow blanketed the ground. It was the morning of *THE BIG GAME*. When we drew the curtains to go for our walk, Dewey said, "Shades of '48!" (The 1948 championship had been played in the snow, and Dayton won that game — the first Dayton football championship.) A blast of cold air greeted us when we opened the door, and white flakes the size of silver dollars drifted

THE ROAD TO THE CHAMPIONSHIP - SHADES OF '48

slowly to earth. Dewey said, "I hope this game isn't rescheduled. Our kids are ready now. They're pumped and anxious. A delay would be bad."

After our walk, Dewey said, "I have to get to Dayton. The team will be nervous, and I need to find out what the plan is." We drove to Dayton and met the players who had congregated at a local cafe for breakfast. We were greeted by the aroma of freshly brewed coffee, and of bacon sizzling on the grill.

After breakfast, Dewey kissed me goodbye, and went to the locker room to see to last-minute preparations. He was nervous, but excited. The game was not delayed, but was played in the snow.

The players loved it. (That season was the coldest of all the seasons Dewey coached at Dayton, but was also one of the most memorable.) A caravan of cars followed the team bus out of the parking lot at the high school, and the ride to Portland was solemn, but anticipatory. The players were anxious and ready for kickoff.

Dayton defeated Neah-kah-nie 39-20 for the championship. The field was scraped at halftime, so the players and officials could see the lines. *THE EXCITEMENT OF A CHAMPIONSHIP GAME!!*

I held my breath! It took FOREVER, but when the final seconds ticked off the clock, the Dayton fans jumped up and down. The Dayton section erupted in cheers, and the players on the field were overcome with joy. Many broke into tears.

The hard work of the season had paid off and the fans were in an uproar. It had been thirty-seven years since a Dayton team accomplished what the Pirates did in 1985. The chant was, *"PIRATES – PIRATES – PIRATES!! We are the champions! We are the champions!"* *(THE FIRST OF DEWEY'S FIVE STATE CHAMPIONSHIPS!)*

The players hoisted Dewey onto their shoulders, and carried him triumphantly onto the field for the awards ceremony. A medal was placed around each player's neck and the trophy was presented to the team. The cheering went on for what seemed an eternity. Everyone looked back in triumph. What was experienced that day was to be cherished for a lifetime!

◄ A BAREFOOT BOY FROM OKLAHOMA

Marvin Lorenzen said, "I had to be here. I played in the '48 game in the snow, and this game was played in the snow." The Dayton Fire Department met the team five miles from town, and escorted the bus down the main street of "small town Dayton." There was so much snow that some cars had to be pushed up the slight incline into Dayton, but all made it. Oh what memories we have.

(For many years a sign over the dressing room door at Scio proclaimed: THE ROAD TO THE CHAMPIONSHIP GOES THROUGH DAYTON!!) With the '85 title it could be: THE ROAD TO THE CHAMPIONSHIP ENDS IN DAYTON.

In *The Congressional Record* of Thursday, December 12, 1985, Les AuCoin, Oregon Representative to the House of Representatives, noted the Pirates' victory. He said, "As the late football coach Vince Lombardi would say, 'Winning isn't the most important thing, it's the only thing.'

"Coach Lombardi was a little tough. But a group of high school footballers in my Oregon district are probably thinking the same thing right now.

"Dayton High School has captured the Oregon State Class A

◄ 184

THE ROAD TO THE CHAMPIONSHIP - SHADES OF '48

high football championship. The last time the Pirates took home the State champ cup was 21 seasons ago.

"I recently met several of these rising football stars. And I believe they represent a new breed of high school athlete. Their performance on the gridiron and in the classroom is proof that athletics and academics really do mix.

"Last week, Dayton played its best in what could only be described as an Oregon 'ice bowl.' Neither snow, subfreezing temperatures, nor the rock-hard frozen turf prevented the Pirates from sliding to victory. Vince Lombardi would have been proud.

"Neah-kah-nie High School put up a valiant fight – but Dayton persevered, and rolled 38-20, to victory. Led by Butch Jumalon and the best offensive line in Oregon Class A ball – Dayton chalked up a win that will be remembered in Yamhill County and around the State, for years to come.

"I grew up in a small town, and attended a small town high school. I know how hard it is to make the grade in statewide competition, let alone come out on top. And I know how important this victory is to the coaching staff, the parents, and especially the Dayton students who worked so hard to achieve their goal.

"Coach Dewey Sullivan and his team went 13-0 this season – that's an envious record, whether you live in Dayton, Oregon or Washington, D.C. Those of us who spend a lot of time in the Nation's Capital can only wish the Redskins could post such outstanding statistics."

Kenny Albright had two sons and two brothers on the state championship team in 1985. The press did not pick up on the uniqueness of that situation, but it was unusual and Dewey appreciated it.

The week after the championship Dewey stepped onto the basketball court, and swished a three-pointer from mid-court. Matt Owen was on the court and remarked, "A legend in his own time.

CHAPTER 29

The Road to the Championship "Ends" in Dayton

The 1985 season was "The Dream Season." But the 1986 season matched it. When the Pirates won the championship in 1985, the next year's seniors declared, "That championship belongs to last year's seniors. This year we want to win our own." In 1986, as in 1985, the league game with Sheridan was crucial, and again was the deciding game for the league championship.

In the second quarter of the game, the Pirates led 22-0. But four unanswered Sheridan touchdowns during the second, third and fourth quarters were not enough to treat the Spartans to an upset victory. Those touchdowns gave the Spartans a 28-22 lead with nine and one half minutes left in the game.

Nine and one half minutes. *FOREVER!! THE SUSPENSE WAS ALMOST UNBEARABLE!!* It's strange how long it takes for a game to end when your team is behind!

The game was played at Dayton, and I sat in front of Larry Samples, the Sheridan basketball coach. It looked as though it were "lights out" for Dayton. When the Pirates trailed 28-22, Larry told those around him, "We're going to win this game." (And they almost did.) But once again, the tenacity of those "pesky Pirates" carried them through.

Sheridan had the ball on the Dayton twenty-five yard line with nine and one half minutes remaining on the clock. The Spartans quick-kicked, and Mark Jacks caught the ball and ran it back fifteen yards. That gave the Pirates new life. On the next possession, Shawn Troutman, quarterback for the Pirates, threw to Chuck Albright who made an amazing catch. Then Tony Nelson ended the series with a touchdown run of three yards. The two-point conversion gave the Pirates a 30-28 lead. Dewey said, "We showed character. We got behind, but did not panic." The Sheridan coach, Rusty Clemons, said, "It was one great quarter of football. It was fun to watch."

After the thrill of the game with Sheridan, the Pirates handily disposed of the remaining teams on their league schedule, and waltzed into the playoffs with an unblemished record.

Four teams brought perfect league records into the playoffs. Dayton, Salem Academy, Union and Wahtonka were undefeated in league, and they all sported 9-0 records. Tyler Smith, the coach of the Corbett Cardinals, said, "Playing Dayton wakes you up real fast. They're better this year than they were last. They control the ball for six, seven, eight minutes at a time. It might almost be better to let them have a quick touchdown so you can get the ball back." (The Pirates averaged forty-three points a game in '86. Three more points than in '85.)

When the Pirates beat Wahtonka in the quarterfinal round, Buck Armstrong, the Eagles coach, said, "They just beat our butts. They were a better team than we were on this night. We were not expecting this. Dayton is a good act. I was impressed with their kids, and they are well coached."

In the first ten games of the season, the Eagles had outscored their opponents 370-2, and had not surrendered a touchdown. The two points scored against them came when the center snapped the ball over the punter's head, and the opposition scored a safety.

Armstrong said, "I thought we could contain them. We were not thinking of shutting them out. We wanted to do what they do best, to control the ball and have our defense stop them. We wanted it to be a ball control game. Well, the way I see it, it was. They kept the ball."

Dewey's game strategy was to score first and stun the Eagles

THE ROAD TO THE CHAMPIONSHIP "ENDS" IN DAYTON

since they thought they could not be scored on. It worked, and Tony Nelson had a "hey day." As Dayton rode the running skills of Nelson, the Pirates ruined the efforts of the Eagles to stop the ground game. Tony scored -- and scored -- and scored again, and Dayton won the game by the score of 44-13. The radio announcer said, "Tony Nelson did everything tonight except sell popcorn and take tickets."

Dewey said, "We wondered all week what it would be like to not have anyone score on you in ten games . . . and then give up points." It had been projected to be a hard-hitting game and it was. Nelson was the leading rusher with one hundred-sixty-five yards on thirty-five attempts. The fans went wild when the whistle ended the game.

Unlike in 1985, when the championship was played in the snow, the 1986 title game was played on a sunny afternoon. The Pirates played Salem Academy at Parker Stadium (now Reser Stadium) in Corvallis. The pump system had not worked, so water had to be pumped from the field before the game. The weather was warm, but rain had flooded the field.

After the game there was a great celebration. It was the culmination of fifteen weeks of hard work, so there was much to celebrate. Two championships in two years!! (Those "pesky Pirates" had done it again!)

CHAPTER **30**

Halls of Fame

To be inducted into a hall of fame is particularly noteworthy, and Dewey was inducted into three. He was inducted into the *Greater Pueblo Sports Hall of Fame* on November 19, 2003, the *Oregon Sports Hall of Fame* on September 25, 2007 and the *National Federation of High School Sports Hall of Fame* on July 7, 2008.

To be selected for the hall of fame honor the first time an individual is nominated is unusual, but Dewey was chosen on the first nomination each time. Often two or three nominations are entertained before the nominee is selected for induction.

Boone classmates, Vern Wolf and Leonard Martinez nominated Dewey for induction into the *Greater Pueblo Hall of Fame* (Pueblo, Colorado). Dewey appreciated the nomination. That ceremony was during football season, so he considered not attending. But he felt so honored to be selected, that we flew to Denver on Wednesday morning for the ceremony. The Pirates were in the playoffs, so when I made our reservations, I made them for a one-night stay. (We stayed Wednesday night, and then we left early Thursday morning.)

The Pirates lost in the quarterfinal round of the playoffs the previous Saturday, so the season was over, but we did not know that when I made the reservations. Had we known, we would have stayed, and watched a game or two in Colorado. That *Hall of Fame* ceremony was beautiful, and we knew many in attendance. There were at least thirty people from Boone there. Lauren Dunsmoor, granddaughter of Chester Dunsmoor from Fowler, was the female recipient of the *Brian Macartney Award* for student athletes.

When Dewey and I returned to Oregon, Norman called the *McMinnville News-Register* to inform them of the induction. Dewey was called for an interview, and he told the reporter that Norman had the information wrong. He said that it was someone else. (He didn't want publicity about the induction.)

Ten years before he was inducted, Dewey was privileged to attend the *Oregon Sports Hall of Fame* banquet. A corporate sponsor reserved a table for ten for each state championship team in 1996. Dayton won the title in football in '95, so a table for ten was reserved for Dewey and nine others. Corey Sutton and Vince Baker were in La Grande practicing for the Shrine game, so Jerry Sutton and Dewey attended and took eight players to the dinner.

When Dewey came home from that dinner, he said, "Oh, my gosh! That would be so embarrassing to have to stand in front of a group that large and be interviewed. I don't think I could ever do it."

(But Dewey didn't have to do it.) I accepted the award when he was inducted in 2007. Roger Lorenzen sat with me on stage, and I was interviewed by Bill Shonley of Portland fame. (I do not like media coverage, but am getting more familiar with it.) That ceremony was emotional, and I have a wonderful memory.

Jeff Bornac nominated Dewey for the *Oregon Sports Hall of Fame*, and when he got the call that Dewey was to be inducted, we were pleased. It is a great honor to be selected, and more than sixty people from Dayton were present for the ceremony.

Steve Walker from the OSAA called me in January of 2008 to tell me that the OSAA was nominating Dewey for the *National Federation of High Schools Sports Hall of Fame*. I considered it an honor for Dewey to even be considered. And when Bruce Howard called to tell me that he had been selected I was very proud. A *NATIONAL HALL OF FAME! WOW!*

HALLS OF FAME

(When Dewey was inducted into The National Hall of Fame, he joined such sports notables as: Jesse Owens, Dan Gable, Jack Nicklaus, Arnold Palmer, Paul Hornung, Billy Mills, Jackie Joyner-Kersee, Tom Landry, John Wooden, Jackie Robinson, Larry Bird, Mel Renfro, and Steve Prefontaine, among others.)

Candy, Brenda, and Jonell accompanied me to Washington, D.C. My interview was taped two days before the presentation, so I didn't have as much of the "fear factor" as I did the first time. When Tom Welter, Executive Director of the OSAA, placed the medal (similar to those in the Olympics) around my neck, he whispered to me, "You can smile." I giggled at that, and it eased my tension.

The induction ceremony was beautiful and awe-inspiring. Each inductee (in Dewey's case . . . me . . . entered the stage through a mist much like a cloud), and was introduced on stage, before being escorted to the floor of the ballroom. The interviews were displayed on the screen, before each person was called back to the stage and presented with a beautiful trophy.

Warren Mitchell, a coach at Limon, Colorado, was one of the inductees in Washington, D.C. Limon is to Colorado small-town football what Dayton is to Oregon small-town football.

Dewey had been curious about Limon for a long time, so after the Boone reunion in 1997, Jonell took him and Norman to see the school and the town. He was duly impressed at the number of trophies in all sports. (Max Wall told me that, after Dewey told him about the Limon legacy, he also made a special trip just to see the town and the school.)

Dewey was named *National Coach of the Year* in 2000, and Pricecatcher.com *Person of the Year* in 2006. He received the *Contributor* award from the Oregon Athletic Coaches Association in 2007, and more than fifty (league and state) *Coach of the Year* awards during his tenure. In 1986 he was given the *Educator of the Year* award for the Dayton School District, and in 2002 he was awarded the *Boone Alumnus of the Year* award (from the high school from which he graduated). He stated it was meaningful to receive recognition from former clasmates.

In 1996, he was named the *Pemco Northwest Coach*, and was twice given the *Kodak Coach of the Year* award. In 2002, he was one of twelve national finalists for the *Power of Influence Award* given by the American Football Coaches Association.

These are great honors, and Dewey was and would have been pleased. I have a large box with his plaques and trophies, and hope to find a suitable place where they can be displayed and shared.

When Roger Lorenzen escorted me to the platform to receive the *Oregon Hall of Fame* award he remarked, "Five times we've done this." (Roger came to the stands, and escorted me to the field for the awards ceremony after each of the State Championship games that

Dayton won while Dewey coached the Pirates. Thank you, Roger.) When Roger wrote I, I had not thought about it, but forty-two years in one small school is incredible.

At Dewey's induction ceremony into the *National Hall of Fame*, one of the representatives from the OSAA remarked, "This is not only an honor for the City of Dayton. It is also an honor for the State of Oregon." I had not thought in those terms, but it is true. And I was also humbled when representatives from both Colorado and Oklahoma were pleased to claim part of Dewey's fame.

I realize that nothing here on earth is forever, but when Dewey was enshrined in the *National High School Hall of Fame*, I celebrated his acclaim. From the halls of a small high school in Dayton, Oregon to the hallowed halls of the *National High School Hall of Fame* in Indianapolis, Indiana — one man's incredible journey to be the first coach from the State of Oregon so honored in the twenty-six years such honors have been bestowed is humbling.

CHAPTER **31**

The "Mystery" of Jake Ryan

Around eight o'clock one morning, Dewey had a call from a young man who said he was "Jake Ryan," and was moving from Texas into the Dayton School District. "Jake" said he was home-schooled, and that his parents were in Texas finalizing the move. He was to stay in Salem with his sister, "Penny," until the paperwork for the purchase of the house was signed.

After chatting for a few minutes, Dewey told "Jake" to meet him at the high school, so they could go over what needed to be done. He then called me, and said, "I don't know if I'm dreaming, but I just had a call from a young man who said he is moving into the Dayton District. He told me he is six feet two inches tall, weighs two hundred pounds, and has been playing football in Texas. I pinched myself to see if I am dreaming, and I think I'm awake. I'm going to meet him at the high school in an hour so I'd better get going. I don't want to be late. I'll see you later. Love you."

Dewey and "Jake" met at the high school, and they talked before they went to the Education Service District (ESD) in McMinnville to see what papers needed to be filed so "Jake" could play. (Dayton once had to forfeit a game because the proper paperwork for a home-schooled player had not been filed with the ESD, and Dewey did not want that consequence again.)

The young man involved in the forfeit was a resident of the

Dayton District. He had played the previous year, and had passed all his classes. His mom was told by the ESD that everything was in order, but something was evidently not done correctly.

Two weeks into the 1997 season, the Dayton Athletic Director called Dewey, and said the school had forfeited the game. Dayton won that game by the score of 44-22. Dewey's indignation at that announcement was profound.

Dewey felt that a fine should have been levied against the school, rather than taking the game from the players who had worked so hard for the victory. He never got over what he felt was the unfairness of the situation.

After meeting with "Jake," Dewey learned that he wanted to play in the Friday night football game. "Jake" said he had worked out with his team in Texas, and had played in one or more games there. Dewey told him that he would not be allowed to play until all the forms, etc. had been taken care of. Then he brought him to meet me. He was a nice-looking young man about six feet tall and maybe two hundred pounds, and he definitely looked like a football player.

After Dewey and "Jake" left McMinnville, they drove around Grand Island (part of the Dayton District), and looked for "Jake's" home. "Jake" ran out of gas, and Dwight Ediger came by and provided gas.

The Dayton Athletic Director received a phone call from a "southern college" several days later, wanting to know if "Jake Ryan" would be playing in the football game Friday night. After Dewey and "Jake" parted, Dewey did not see "Jake" again. Dewey had a phone number for "Jake's" sister, "Penny," but all he got when he called was a fax sound. (He called that number many times.)

But Dewey didn't give up, and was still optimistic. Several evenings after practice, he had his players go to the Grand Island area to see if they could determine what house the Ryans could possibly move into. The search was in vain. Dewey decided "Jake" wanted one last chance to play high school football; that he was, most likely, already out of high school.

THE "MYSTERY" OF JAKE RYAN

I thought the farce would have been a good joke for another coach to play on Dewey, but if that had been true, I am sure the coach could not have kept it to himself. He most likely would have enjoyed the joke so much he would have asked Dewey about "Jake." Dewey said, "I would just like to meet 'Jake' on the street, and ask why he did what he did." He was curious about what set the whole thing into play.

"Jake" later appeared at John F. Kennedy High School in Mount Angel with a similar story. Randy Traeger said, "One day this big kid showed up at school, and wanted to be on the football team. He was wearing jeans, a rodeo buckle, and cowboy boots, and he looked as though he was about twenty-five." "Jake" did not enroll at JFK, as he met snags similar to those he encountered at Dayton. He was later seen in Gervais, where it was reported that he played in a junior varsity game.

Randy said, "We looked across the field, and one of the coaches said, 'Isn't that the kid who wanted to play for us?'" "Jake" played in that game, and seemed satisfied with his prowess.

Dewey, himself, was not above a little joking. He once called Jay Phillips, a friend who coached at nearby St. Paul, and said, "I have one of your players – he moved into the area, and his father works in St. Paul. His dad does not want his son to play eight-man football, so he moved to Dayton and will commute, so his son can play for the Pirates." Dewey said there was a stunned silence on the other end of the line. The story was a total fabrication, but he got a chuckle out of it.

CHAPTER 32

Dante — The "Toast of Dayton"

As an eighth-grader, Dante Rosario, a four-year letterman at Dayton, a four-year starter for the University of Oregon, and now a Carolina Panther, did not turn out for the football team. (Dante preferred basketball to football.) On a Friday evening early in the season, Dewey and Dante met on the football field. They talked before the game, and Dante assured Dewey he would be out for the team on Monday. They shook hands and sealed the deal, but on Monday Dante did not appear. Dewey was disappointed, but . . . oh well! (That was not his first or his last disappointment!)

The same thing happened Dante's freshman year. Dante Rosario was not at practice the first day. The next afternoon, Dewey sent a caravan of football players out to get him. Roger Lorenzen, the high school principal, called Dewey and reported, "Coach I just saw several football players going out the Webfoot (the road on which Dante lived). I don't know what they're up to, but they might be going to have a party."

Dewey assured Roger, "No, I sent the team out to get Dante. He didn't report for practice and we need him." (Dewey didn't care that Dante preferred basketball to football – he encouraged all players to participate in multiple sports, and he wanted Dante on the team.)

Dante's freshman year was successful, but when his sophomore year arrived, the same thing happened. Dante was not at practice!

Dewey once again sent the team after him. By the end of his sophomore season, Dante began to have a love for football.

When the time for Dante's junior season rolled around, he was there. Dante said, "He was actually the one who kept me in football. Coming into high school as a freshman, I wasn't really excited about playing football. He just made sure I kept with it, and kept working at it. He was almost like a father figure to me. He kind of guided me, and showed me the way." Dante worked hard, and was a "force" on the field.

At the beginning of the summer of 2002, Dante attended the University of Oregon football camp, and was awarded a "full-ride" scholarship. Dewey and Dante were both thrilled.

We went by the high school several days later, and Dante was on the track working on his starts. I walked out to congratulate him on his scholarship, and I asked, "Are you excited about next year?" (The next year was to be his first season as a Duck.) He told me, "I'm excited about this year." He looked forward to the upcoming season -- his senior year at Dayton. I was impressed both with his work ethic and with his attitude. (And to cap Dante's very successful high school career, Dayton won the state championship in 2002.)

I told Candy, "Dante is going to have to work his way through college." She replied, "I thought he had a scholarship." I said, "That's what I mean – he's going to have to work his way through college." (And he did!)

Dante's mother, Yvonne (Bonnie) Rosario, was a student of Dewey's in the early '70s. While attending a football game at Dayton when Dante played, she remarked to Dewey, "Football is a lot like a battle – the coach is like the general as he directs his troops from the sidelines." Dewey said, " You're right, and the battle can only be won if the participants are disciplined and work hard as a team. They have to be prepared and pay attention to detail – strategy is involved, but it's a team effort."

One fall afternoon, when Dante was a sophomore at Oregon, our telephone rang. The caller said, "Hi. Is Dewey there?" I said, "No, he's at practice." He said, "Good. This is your nephew, Mark, and I plan to visit next Friday night and I want to surprise him before the football game." I said, "Oh that will be exciting! Then you'll get to go to the Duck game on Saturday." Mark said, "What's a Duck game? I said, "It's a game at the University of Oregon, and Dewey has a player there."

Mark called several times before the planned visit and always prefaced his calls with, "Is Dewey there? This is Mark." The phone rang one afternoon before Dewey left for practice and the caller said, "This is Mark. Is Dewey there?" I replied, "Yes, he's watching films, so we had better talk quietly."

There was a pause at the other end of the line while my information was assimilated. Then the caller said, "I need to talk to him about practice this afternoon." (OOPS! Wrong Mark.) It was an assistant coach. I don't know what that Mark thought, but I had to wait until the next time I saw him to tell him why I responded as I did. I was embarrassed, and I am not sure that the coach understood.

Mark Sullivan called later and we got the arrangements finalized. Dewey was surprised when Mark walked onto the football field as the team warmed up for the game, and he accompanied Dewey to the Oregon game the next day. They had a wonderful time.

A BAREFOOT BOY FROM OKLAHOMA

One of Dewey's proudest coaching moments was when Mike Bellotti, the University of Oregon coach, came to him at the conclusion of practice before Dante's first season, and said, "Both offense and defense have claimed Dante, so I made the decision. He will be on offense. Dante is ready for *PAC-10* football right now. He is fundamentally sound, and is prepared and ready to play – he will not red-shirt." (Dewey had often been asked if he thought Dante would red-shirt.) When Dewey came from that session, he "busted his buttons" with pride.

Dewey and I were blessed to be in attendance at the first University of Oregon game in which Dante was given the ball to carry. That was particularly memorable – that a player from a small high school "North of Nowhere" could play on the field with the "big boys."

And I can still feel Dewey's pride when I watch Dante on nationwide television. When Dante makes a successful play, when he completes a successful block, when he catches a pass and scores a touchdown, when I see him on the "big screen," I rejoice with Dewey at his success. (Dewey always enjoyed watching his former players when they moved to the next level, and he would be proud to see a player from the small town of Dayton make it in the NFL.)

CHAPTER 33

Footprints on the Field

Football tradition runs deep in Yamhill County, Oregon. Linfield College (in the heart of Yamhill County) has a great football legacy with a national record fifty-three consecutive winning seasons (at the conclusion of the 2008 season). Linfield College is ten miles from Amity and ten miles from Dayton.

Dewey felt blessed to know Joe Smith, current Linfield College head football coach, as well as Paul Durham, Ad Rutschman, Ed Langsdorf, and Jay Locey, all former head coaches at Linfield. At the Linfield football camp several years ago, Ad told Dewey he enjoyed watching him work with his team and his players. (Ad and Dewey once visited during a baseball game, and a fellow remarked, "Just think how many years of football knowledge is being tossed around there.")

I recently spoke with Chris Casey, the head football coach at Aloha High School. He said, "When I coached the line on defense at Linfield College, I told Dewey that he spent more time with the D-line than I did during pre-season. He was always out there and was always learning. Chris and Dewey developed a great relationship and Dewey valued the friendship. They contacted each other several times after Chris moved to Whitworth College in Spokane, Washington.

A BAREFOOT BOY FROM OKLAHOMA

Football was Dewey's passion, and he was a student of the game. He loved it. Several years ago he had a call from Bill Stautz, a coach from South Carolina, who had picked up on his offense from the Internet. They talked at length, and Dewey sent Bill a video of a Dayton football game. They discussed that game, as well as strategies, by phone and mail. After Dewey died, Bill called and wrote a letter to offer his condolences.

There are so many "Dewey stories," I cannot start to relate them all. Almost everyone who ever met Dewey, whether they played for him, coached with him, or just knew him has a story, and I am trying to gather as many of them as I can. They keep cropping up. Many of them involve physical impossibilities, but that makes the telling even better.

Jeff Hill said he was drop-kicked into the stadium (an impossible feat), and Randy Freeborn tells that he was picked up by the bar on his face mask, and firmly planted in mud for his insubordination. A play was called during practice, but Randy told the quarterback to run something else. Dewey told Randy, "Freeborn, you're not the quarterback." Randy replied (quietly, of course), "Well, you're not either," but he was heard. Randy says the next thing he knew he was firmly planted in mud (but he did not grow -- and I don't believe he made many "asides" after that incident). Randy was highly publicized that season, and he said, "I guess 'Coach' either didn't read the newspaper articles about me, or he just didn't care."

Dewey once asked a fellow who no longer coached, "Don't you miss coaching?" The reply was, "You have to be crazy to put your livelihood in the hands of teenage boys." (Dewey chuckled about that. He loved the challenge -- he loved high school football -- he loved the intrigue – and he loved high school kids.)

After the homecoming game one year, Dewey noticed that the opposing coach was covered in mud. The other coach was upset, and Dewey received a cold reception. That fellow wouldn't shake hands, but Dewey didn't comment until the other coach said, "I didn't appreciate your half-time activities." Dewey said, "Why is that?" He was told. "They put a spotlight on your team as they came onto the field and they didn't see me. They ran over me, and I was trampled in the mud." Dewey apologized, but the other coach never forgave him for the incident.

Dewey was once called to the principal's office to meet with a disgruntled parent. The parent wanted to know why his son had not received honors in football. Dewey said, "I'm sorry, but your son did receive All-League honors, and was honored at the end of the season. You should have known that."

The fellow was delighted, but was unaware of his son's awards until Dewey informed him. That father had not attended any games, and did not know what had happened on the field. (Just something to complain about? Dewey had difficulty believing a father did not know more about his son than that.)

The Pirates won their 26th straight game in 1996, and the last time they had suffered a loss was in the quarterfinals in 1994 when Weston-McEwen defeated them. The Dayton offense was described as "one-dimensional." No passes were attempted in that game, the semi-final round of the playoffs. Mike Lorenzen, quarterback for the Pirates, said, "We put everybody up to the challenge. Everybody knows we're not going to pass. We play 'heads-up.'" (The Pirates were delighted to avenge the 1994 loss suffered to those same TigerScots.)

With the win against Weston-McEwen, the Pirates of Dayton were described as a "football dynasty." Dewey was asked to explain Dayton's success, and he reported his recruiting efforts had never made much of an impact. He said, "To tell the truth, I really don't know how we've been able to be successful for so long. You would think with all the success we've had, that every kid in Dayton would want to play football. But, that's not the case. We have forty kids on our roster this year, but there's no reason we shouldn't have sixty five."

A BAREFOOT BOY FROM OKLAHOMA

But when the players were asked they always pointed to Dewey, and said he was the reason. Dewey credited his assistants with much of his success. Emory Blackwell had coached with him for eighteen years, and Jerry Sutton had been with him for seven. He said, "I also get a lot of volunteer coaches that help out." And while he did not always get the numbers of players out for his team that he would have liked, he and his staff seemed to get the most from those they had.

Before school dismissed for the summer in 2003, Dewey took a group of players to the University of Oregon Ducks spring training camp. He asked them not to let him miss the Salem exit on the way home, but they were talking and listening to music; then Dewey realized they had passed that exit about twenty miles back, so had to leave the freeway at Woodburn and go through Newberg. (Dewey enjoyed the occasion and the company, and was distracted by the music and the conversation. He liked to think he was one of the "boys.")

One story that Dewey enjoyed telling was about a team that was ahead by six points. That team had the ball on the twenty-yard line with little time left in the game. The coach instructed the players to try to get a few yards on their first possession, and then to punt the ball. The team was successful, and reeled off about fifty yards. After that great run, the players got into punt formation, and punted the ball. When the game was over, the coach walked onto the field and asked the player who punted the ball, "What in the world were you thinking?" The frustrated player replied, "That we have the dumbest coach alive." (Dewey never tired of telling that one.)

Scott Knutson was the quarterback for the Pirates on the 1995 state championship team. He wrote an essay nominating Dewey as *Coach of the Game* for a Portland Trailblazer game. He was awarded a pair of game tickets, and Dewey was one of twelve coaches selected for the honor. As Scott and Dewey sat watching the game, Cal Kearns and his sons (Cal's three sons played for the Pirates) were in attendance, and Cal remarked, "Dewey should be here." Then, he looked across the court and noted, "But . . . 'Coach' is here." They enjoyed the game, and were at floor-level. Dewey said it was amazing to be that close to all those tall basketball players.

When Dave Cooley died unexpectedly, Dewey was asked to speak at his funeral. Dave had coached at Jefferson near Salem, and his teams had opposed Dewey's several times. He was an assistant coach in Salem at the time of his death. Dave and Dewey shared the same "quirky" sense of humor, and had many fun times together.

Dave told of the time that he took his team to Hawaii to play a game. When the team checked into the hotel, he noticed a number of *Playboy* magazines behind the counter. He told one of his assistants, "You'd better go back to the lobby and get those magazines." But it was too late. The magazines were gone when he got there.

Dewey stopped by Roger's office after the funeral, and he repeated one of the eulogies expressed at the service. Reportedly one of Dave's assistants took the junior varsity team to another school to play, and his team was behind, but on the verge of scoring with no timeouts remaining. It was near the end of the game, so one of his players faked an injury so the team could have an "injury timeout." His team scored and won the game. The coach returned from that game and told Dave of his strategy. Dave's response was, "What do you suppose your team learned today?"

As Dewey left Roger's office he said, "I wonder what my kids learn from me when they leave practice. Is that what I'm teaching? Am I teaching them to be dishonest and use such tactics to win? I hope not."

Another humorous Dave Cooley story involved a first-year teacher. Dave told the teacher the superintendent wanted him to greet the buses in the morning as they discharged their passengers, and to note how many male and how many female students got off the buses.

As the students left the buses in the morning, that task was not too difficult, but after school, it was total chaos with students going in all directions. It was an impossible feat to count the students as they boarded the buses, and the teacher became frustrated. Dave told the other faculty members, so the entire faculty got a big laugh as they watched the action from the faculty lounge.

Dewey was also asked to speak when the Gervais track was

dedicated to Ordie Hoye, another of his football buddies. Ordie was a long-time coach at Willamina, but began his coaching career in track at Gervais. He was a "dyed-in-the-wool" coach and loyal to Willamina and to kids. One time we attended a basketball game at Willamina, and Ordie spotted Dewey and asked, "What's the "Father of Football" doing here?"

Ordie died before Dewey's hospitalization, but we did not attend his "Celebration of Life," as it was not held until the week after Dewey's operation. Dewey had great respect for Ordie, and would have attended had it been possible. (Marjorie Hoye reported that a volleyball game was scheduled for the Willamina gym the Saturday after Ordie's death, and he would not have wanted to interfere with any regularly scheduled sporting event, so the celebration was postponed for a week.)

Dewey adhered to the premise that a high school student has four years in which to play sports, and that he or she should take advantage of the opportunity. If a player opted to work rather than play football, he would be told, "You have the rest of your life to dedicate to work, but only four years in which to play football. If you miss this opportunity you will likely regret it for the rest of your days." He firmly believed that the game of football is a great deal like the "Game of Life."

Before Dayton played Santiam-Christian in 2004, a newspaper reported that the game would be played at "Dewey Sullivan Stadium." There is no "Dewey Sullivan Stadium."

Several years ago, the School Board asked for nominations to name the track when it was completed. One of Dewey's students wrote an essay suggesting it should be "Dewey Sullivan Track." The suggestion was made to the School Board, but the superintendent said the proposal could not be considered. He said that the track couldn't be named for a living individual.

The field was then named, "Joel Palmer Track." Dewey's name is on the football scoreboard, but that is the extent of the recognition he has received at Dayton.

For several years, a banner hung in the gym denoting the years that league championships were won, and there are two bracket boards from the state championships of 1985 and 1986. (Championships were also won in 1995, 1996, and 2002, but those years have not been acknowledged by Dayton. And the banner no longer hangs in the gym.)

Of course, I realize that there is little room in the school for such trivialities, but most schools would be honored to have such success. However, I applaud Dewey's achievements. He not only left his footprints on the football field, he left his fingerprints on my heart and my life.

CHAPTER **34**

Those "Pesky Pirates"

The game between Dayton and Umatilla in the 1991 playoffs was considered one of Dewey's greatest challenges. The Pirates were behind 7-6 with less than three minutes left in the game. *THREE MINUTES*. Those three minutes seemed like an eternity.

The Pirates got the ball on the Umatilla two-yard line, and engineered a touchdown for the 14-7 victory. Dayton appeared doomed when the drive started. The Pirates were in a fourth-down and *FOREVER* situation several times, but managed to eke out the victory in the last twenty-three seconds. (Umatilla did not allow Dewey into the "crow's nest," so he and Butch Jumalon stood across the field, and radioed plays to the coaches and team.)

As Dayton scored the winning touchdown, one Pirate fan can be seen on the game tape, jumping up and down in jubilation. (Those "Pesky Pirates" had done it again!) Dewey often showed films of that game, as well as the 1985 game between Dayton and Enterprise. Those were two of the most memorable games he coached during his career at Dayton. The perseverance shown in those games demonstrated the value of not giving up.

Dewey rode with me from the game between Dayton and Central Linn in 2005. He wanted to go by Monroe High School to learn the outcome of the game between Monroe and Santiam-Chrstian. When we arrived at Monroe, Max Wall told Dewey that

Steve Woods, the S-C coach, asked, "Are you going to share with Dewey what happened in our game?" Max told him, "I don't have to tell Dewey anything. He has been here for the entire second half of the game."

That prompted one of Dewey's favorite stories. A newspaper account reported that Dewey left the game at Central Linn at halftime, and went to Monroe to get a "first-hand" look at the upcoming opposition (the Eagles of Santiam-Christian). What a great story! It was not true, but it made interesting reading, and it certainly piqued interest in the next week's game. Dewey and Max got many chuckles from that. Max told Dewey, "Good luck if you can beat that team. They're the 'real-meal-deal!'"

The Pirates won the game the next week 29-21, and Dayton was the first team to defeat the Eagles on their new field. Joel Mason, quarterback for S-C, was quoted, "I read about him (Dewey Sullivan) in the newspaper, *USA Today*. I think it was like a year or two ago. He was on the list of the most winningest coaches."

That game was touted as a contest between Dewey Sullivan and Joel Mason. Dewey loved that story, and was quoted as saying laughingly, "I don't think I can keep up with him." (He thought it hilarious to be pitted against a teenager with "wheels.") Joel Mason and his brother made a "dynamic duo" of quarterback and receiver, and were difficult to cover.

Midway through the third quarter of the Dayton/Santiam-Christian game, the Pirates were behind 21-14. However, the Pirates controlled the ball, and behind the excellent blocking of the line, our grandson, Zack, pounded his way down the field.

Dayton took the lead with four and one-half minutes remaining, and added the final score with just over a minute to go. After the 29-21 victory, the S-C coach said, "Dayton took the ball and rammed it down our throat. We knew what they were going to do, but were unable to stop it." (The two schools had been rivals for years, but the rivalry heated up in the 2000s, when the Eagles came into their own.)

I dreaded the game between Gladstone and Dayton the entire

THOSE "PESKY PIRATES"

summer of 1973. But Dewey welcomed the challenge. (In his philosophical way, he figured the Gladiators put their pants on one leg at a time, the same as the Pirates. The Gladiators had won the state championship the previous two years, and I was in awe of them and their accomplishments.)

When I saw them at the state basketball tournament, I considered them to be a "class act." Their cheer squad was definitely "first-rate." And then when I saw the number of car dealerships and businesses on the way to the game, my fears were realized. The downtown commercial strip in Gladstone far surpassed anything in Dayton.

Gladstone was certainly "big time" compared to Dayton. Dayton had two grocery stores, a couple of taverns, a barbershop and a beauty shop, but no car dealerships. There was no commerce.

Gladstone led 6-0 at the start of the fourth quarter of the game, but Steve Lambert broke off-tackle, and romped down the sidelines for the winning score. Dayton held on for the last four minutes of the game, and won 8-6. That loss was the first for the Gladiators on their home field.

After that win, Dewey received letters and phone calls of congratulations from around the State of Oregon. One evening he told of several letters he had received, and I asked what he had done with them. He said, "I recycled them." I said, "Please bring them home so I can see them." He did, and I began collecting them. I have many letters and cards, which I have collected in scrapbooks.

When Dayton traveled to Philomath in 1991, the Pirate team was decimated by injuries and the flu. A discussion was held about canceling the game, but it was decided to proceed as planned.

The Pirates were in awe as they went onto the field. Philomath had almost as many coaches on the field as Dayton had players. The Philomath coaches were arrayed in team coaching gear, and Dayton's "rag-tag" team was definitely outclassed. But Dayton prevailed 20-7.

Dewey cried at the conclusion of that game. He was so proud. *(HEROES CRY TOO!!)* What a victory! Some "fickle" fans opted not to go to that game. One told Dewey, "I just couldn't bear the thought of watching Dayton lose."

The Pirates began the 1988 season with two losses, and Dewey said, "We could have won both those games. In each of those games, we were ahead in the fourth quarter." But in the fifth game that year, Dayton launched an offensive knockout on Santiam-Christian by defeating the Eagles 56-21. Then the Pirates went on to win the next nine games. They scored a total of one hundred and forty-four points in three games. Dewey said, "We've improved a lot from the first part of the season."

In the final league game with Gaston, Jeremy McLoud scored touchdowns on runs of twenty-one, three, seventy and fifty-eight yards in the 38-10 win, and led the Pirates to another league title. The Pirates rushed for 319 yards, and assembled a 346-yard attack.

In the last seven regular season games that year, Dayton scored 338 points for an average of 48.2 points per game (after losing the first two games). When asked if he were nervous before games, Dewey said, "I'm nervous about every game . . . every game. I'm nervous until we get down to the last three minutes, and then if we're up by twenty or more points, I can relax a little."

In the quarterfinal round of the playoffs two weeks later, Dayton defeated Grant Union 36-26. The quarterback for the Pirates, Vince Miguez, completed three of four passes for fifty-two yards. Each completed pass was on third down, and each was good for a first down. The Dayton Athletic Director said, "I was astounded by the number of people who made the trip to John Day. I thought there were an equal number of Dayton and Grant Union fans. It was nice."

But in the final minutes of that game, it became apparent that something was wrong. A defender caught Jeremy McLoud from behind. Jeremy was a speedster and a great running back, so no one (almost no one) caught up with him on the football field. Jeremy had pulled a hamstring, and the team paid dearly the following week. In a school the size of Dayton it is devastating to lose a starter.

In the semi-final round of the playoffs the next week, Dayton lost to the Crusaders of Salem Academy. The Pirates led 8-7 in the fourth quarter, but a Dayton touchdown was called back. It could have been the winning touchdown, but a clip nullified the score. Ironically, the penalty was after the fact, and was on the opposite side of the field from the action. Salem Academy then intercepted a pass that led to the final score of 14-8.

The Salem Academy coach, Frank Bain, said, "If you look at the flow of the game with Dayton, the Pirates win. I don't know how we ended up winning. I feel for Dayton. Our kids have a lot of respect for Dayton. Dayton is well coached." Dewey said, "It was there and we didn't do it." The following week, Salem Academy defeated Heppner by the score of 14-12 for the championship.

Dayton went 0-9 before dropping to 1-A in 1982. Tom Smythe, the McNary High School head football coach at the time, quipped, "That's awful. They should have fired Dewey for that one."

As Dewey went to the locker room at the half of the game between Dayton and Willamina that year, a Bulldog fan leaned over the rail, and inquired, "How does that feel, Sullivan?" He replied, "Not too good." He told me, "I think that she was shocked. I guess she thought that I would yell at her."

As we left the Central High field, I told Marvin Lorenzen, Roger's father, "We're going to win some games this year." The Pirates lost to Y-C, and were close several times, but never pulled off a victory. Dewey had faith in his system, but when the team went 0-9, I asked him, "How do the players feel?" He replied, "They know this system works. Things just didn't work out for us this year."

Dayton's record was 40-8 in the five seasons before the winless season, and the worst regular season record after that was 6-3 in 2003. Dayton's record from 1982 until 2005 was 198-17 in regular season play, and 127-9 in league play. The Pirates advanced to the playoffs every year from 1982 until 2007 – a state record of twenty-six consecutive seasons.

CHAPTER **35**

Tributes — 300th Win Celebration

There were many tributes paid to Dewey at the celebration for his 300th victory and for the *Coach of the Year Award*. These are but a few:

Coach – Thank you for teaching me as well as countless others the values that shape our lives today. You are a role model for everyone in the community. Charles Fisher '90

Remember – Our son will never play football. *YEAH RIGHT!!* Tim and Andrea Payne

Lynn Freshour – Best mentor a young coach could ever have. Thank you for all you have given to athletics. The positive influence you provided to me in those early years of my coaching career were vital as I moved on.

Larry Black – Starting out a career I could not have asked for a better role model. Thanks for everything. I'll always be a "Pirate."

Terry Calhoun – It was a great night. I always liked the love you had for your wife and kids as well as those around you. Ohio State had "Woody," Alabama had "The Bear," Dayton has "Dewey." You're a great role model for a man and coach to look up to.

Jennifer Woodward – Thank you so much for all the encouragement you have been to Jack. It's great to know he is in such good hands when he's at practice all those hours.

Bruce Bilodeau – I hope my youngest son gets the privilege to play for you also. Thank you, Coach for all you have done for all you have taught me.

Dewey and Vera – thanks for the wonderful influence you have had on our family. We're proud to call you friends and are glad we moved back to Dayton to share in the fine football tradition. God bless you!! Jan Bunn

Don Baird – Thanks, Dewey, for being more than a coach.

Rod and Nora Losier – Remembering the time Dewey and Vera came down to the coast for a visit. I especially remember Dewey asking me if I "liked" it on the Coast. I always said. "Yes." Rod really enjoyed coming over to the Sullivan house and watching films and talking Xs and Os (I just thought it was hugs and kisses). Rod is fortunate to have had the opportunity to student teach under Dewey. Dewey and Vera are two of the most influential people we have ever met. Rod has always gotten very good advice from Dewey.

Francis Dummer – Dewey – You're a legend in our time. Thanks for being you.

Mark Blanchard – Thanks for the great influence you have been on our boys. We appreciate the integrity and high values you have both lived and taught. They were proud to play for you and we're proud that they were part of your winning history. Thanks to you for everything.

Corwin Brown – Dewey – Thanks for coaching me in more than football but also life with its ups and downs.

Lonnie and Pam Burbank – You've been a wonderful role model for the Dayton community. You've earned the respect and admiration of all of us. We are all proud of you and we thank you.

Ezra Koch – Dewey – Your record is really awesome! But winning games is only the sideline of great training of a great number of young men! The impact of your devotion and training will be remembered by generations of kids, parents and friends – of which I'm proud to be one!

Terri Freeborn – Thanks for being my most favorite biology teacher – I really did learn a lot, both about biology and football!!

TRIBUTES - 300TH WIN CELEBRATION

Chuck Wert – Thanks for being a significant influence in my life. I learned more about strength, character and teamwork from you than anybody else. I'm proud to be part of your legacy!

Gene Forman, President Oregon Athletic Coaches Association – Dewey, I want to congratulate you on the tremendous honor and recognition you recently received as "National Coach of the Year." Realizing that a lot of credit goes to the players and coaches over the years, I also know that most of the credit belongs to the person who set the direction the program would take and follow. Again, congratulations for the success you've had for so many years and for the impact you've had on so many people.

Jim Albright – I've always appreciated Dewey's "no-nonsense" philosophy on life. I am glad to have learned early in life not to look for excuses but to find a solution and it all reflects back to Dewey's influence.

CHAPTER **36**

Dewey at the Shrine Game!!

Dewey enjoyed the Shrine games, and frequently went to Lewis and Clark College to watch Fred Spiegelberg, the legendary Medford coach, as he prepared his team for the *North-South Shrine* game. (The *North-South Shrine* game is now the *Les Schwab Bowl*, and is for the 4-A, 5-A, and 6-A classifications.) Dewey attended several practices, and enjoyed watching practice (his own as well as that of others).

Spiegelberg was second on the wins list for Oregon football at the time, and Dewey considered it an honor to be near a coach of such stature. He did not imagine he would reach that pinnacle in wins, or that he would get to coach a Shrine game, but he looked forward to attending the game each year.

But Dewey got to coach in three *East-West Shrine* games. (The *East-West Shrine* game is for the 1-A, 2-A, and 3-A players.) He was excited the first time he coached. Ironically, the first and the last times he would have been the Shrine coach, were not to be. Santiam Christian defeated the Pirates in both 1984 (the first year), and in 2005 (the last time he would have been eligible). Those were two of the three losses Dayton suffered to Santiam Christian while he coached the Pirates.

Before 1984, the coach selected for the game was from the team that won the State Championship the previous fall. When the rule was changed in 1984, the coach from the team that won the league championship was selected. That designation is now on a rotational basis of four years.

The Pirates had many league championships while Dewey coached, but did not win a state title until 1985. The new rule allowed Dewey the opportunity to make three appearances. (Of course, under the original system, he would have had the honor five times.)

Dewey sent more than forty players to Baker City to play. (Both Barry and Brent had the honor of playing in the game, and had wonderful experiences there.) Dewey enjoyed the games, and only missed two Shrine games while he coached at Dayton. (One of those was while he was in Africa.)

It is an honor, not only to be selected to play in that game, but to coach there. In 2003 Dewey was given a lifetime pass, and I attended the game on that pass in August of 2007. That game was dedicated to his memory, and marked the 55th anniversary of the game.

The first time that Dewey coached the Shrine Game (1989), the coaches were asked for suggestions on improving the format. Dewey suggested they increase the length of the quarters of play from twelve to fifteen minutes as in college, thus allowing more players the opportunity to play. He said, "They're no longer in high school, so they should be allowed to play college quarters." He also suggested they decrease the time spent by the team in Baker City from fourteen to ten days. That saved money on room and board as well as activities. His premise was that the players were to be in condition when they reported.

Norman suggested that the coach with the most experience should be the head coach rather than giving that distinction to the coach from the largest school, as was the practice until 2004. The Shriners adopted all three suggestions.

The second time Dewey coached the Shrine game, the coaches were impressed when the players from the West team held a meeting after practice. They thought the team was getting "fired up." After the meeting, a team spokesman came to the coaches and said, "As a team, we've agreed we're being worked too hard. The East team is not being worked nearly as hard as we are." (Mutiny on the Field?)

Dewey looked at the other coaches and suggested, "Why don't we do the *Truck and Trailer* drill? That might 'do the trick.'" That drill was initiated, and no more team meetings were held. There was no more "insurrection in the ranks."

One year I arranged a trip to Denver on Amtrak, and then remembered that Dayton had a player selected for the Shrine game. I realized we would just return to Portland, and have to prepare for the return trip to Baker City, so I arranged for us to get off in Baker City the day before the game. We spent two nights in Baker City, and then got on the train for the return to Portland the morning after the game.

On Amtrak, we sat across from a young girl named Ariel. She took a liking to Dewey, and her mission was to record a license plate from every state in the Union. She kept a log of those she saw, and to help in her endeavor, Dewey pointed out cars with different plates. He enjoyed visiting with her much as he would a grandchild. They played Parcheesi, etc.

We enjoyed the Shriners' parade in downtown Baker City the morning of the game, and then made the trek to the stadium on foot. The Dayton player had a good game, and we enjoyed it. Baker City was not a regular stop, so we had Amtrak flagged down early the next morning for the return trip to Portland. Our strategy worked great, and it was a different venue from that to which we were accustomed.

We saw foxes, antelope and other animals, as well as many beautiful birds from the Amtrak car. We appreciated wildlife, and the vantage point from the rail car was better than that from a car on the highway. (When Mike Rainy came from Kenya he told Dewey he was disappointed not to see more wildlife in its native habitat.)

The last time Dewey coached the Shrine game was in 1997. The

A BAREFOOT BOY FROM OKLAHOMA

Pirates won the state title in 1996, so two players from Dayton were on his team (Ben Bunn, III and PJ Oleman), and that was special to him. (The team that wins state is allowed two players.)

Since that was Dewey's third coaching stint, he called Ralph Patterson and told him, "I should let someone else have the honor since I've been allowed to coach there twice." Ralph told him, "You old 'fart' — you earned the right to be here, so you get over here." Dewey went, and he had a great time.

The Shriners roll out the "red carpet" for the players and the coaches. Coaches are given jackets (green for the West team and red for the East team). Dewey had two green jackets from his previous appearances, so he asked for a red one the final time.

The Shriner's Hospital for Crippled Children and Burn Victims does miraculous things for the patients with whom they work. The two teams are taken to tour the Portland facility, and to meet the patients. They are then transported to La Grande, where they are housed in the dorms at Eastern Oregon University.

The medical procedures performed at the Shriner's Hospital are done at no charge to the patients or their families. One visit to the Hospital makes you appreciate the generosity and the dedication that makes it possible.

The game held in Baker City is one of the biggest moneymakers the Shriners host. They auction a steer and raise several thousand dollars. Different Shrine clubs buy the steer, and then donate him to be re-sold. It is a tribute to mankind to see their generosity.

Cole Morgan from Yamhill-Carlton, Zach Burdon from Willamina, and our grandson, Zack, were selected to play in the 54th Shrine game in 2006. Cole's father played football for Dewey in the '70s, and Cole's grandparents flew to Portland from California to see the game. We enjoyed meeting and visiting with them before and during the game. His grandmother was the successful bidder on one of the footballs signed by the game participants, and she was proud of her grandson's prowess on the field.

CHAPTER 37

"Brother of Simba"

As a boy, Dewey became infatuated with the continent of Africa. It was his dream to go to Kenya, but he thought it beyond our financial means to do so. We were members of the New York Zoological Society, and one evening when we came from work, I found a brochure advertising a twenty-four day trip to Kenya. The participants were to stay in tents in the Mara amid the abundant wildlife. I handed the brochure to Dewey, and said, "Dewey, this is your trip – you can stay in the Mara with the animals."

He read the literature and said, "Oh, my gosh! That's the trip I've dreamed of. I've always wanted to camp out amidst the wildlife of Africa. This is my boyhood dream come true."

We called the next morning, and were assured that Dewey could have a spot if we got the deposit in immediately. We mailed it that day, and there was a lot of preparation to be done. He had to get his passport and apply for a visa. He purchased a text, a click-counter (to count wildebeest), and other paraphernalia. He had six weeks in which to assemble everything. It took the entire six weeks, but he made it.

The day before his departure, he called me at work and asked, "Can you come home and help me get things organized?" I have everything ready, but am having trouble getting it all packed." I arrived to discover chaos. It was a whirlwind of activity with no seeming objective. He had things strewn around our spare bedroom, but with a little thought and much organization, we managed to get everything assembled and packed, and he was ready.

After six weeks of anticipation and preparation the day arrived, and Dewey left on schedule. When he got off the plane in Nairobi, he was so excited that he kissed the ground. He enjoyed that trip and loved camping in the Mara. He felt he had come home and said, "It was a long and tiring trip, but I was so excited I hardly realized it. I was just so happy to be in Africa."

He became fast friends with Mike Rainy, the director of the camp. Mike, a graduate of Reed College in Portland, Oregon, is a blood brother of the Maasai, and he and his wife, Judy, have resided in Kenya for more than forty years. Mike's camp was Dewey's ideal venue, and he visited it three more times (four times total). Mike has done research on the wildlife of the Mara, and plans to write a book about his observations. I hope he lives long enough to accomplish his goal.

The group slept on cots in tents, and did their own dishes. (Dewey took a bag for dunking his dishes, but I believe he had help from some of the female participants, and didn't get his "lily-whites" wet).

Cape buffalo visited the campground at night, and Mike told the group to be careful not to startle them. Mike's recommendation was, "Get behind a tree if you encounter a buffalo." Dewey was frequently out at night, and saw the buffalo, so he also warned the other participants to use caution.

Evidently the women in the group thought Dewey and Mike were joking. (They did not believe that the buffalo grazed in the camp area.) One morning the buffalo stayed later than usual, and when the campers stirred, the buffalo stampeded through the grounds. After the excitement died down, a frightened group of ladies told Dewey, "You weren't kidding, were you?" He replied, "What did you think kept the grass mowed around here?"

Dewey's first trip was during the annual wildebeest migration. He saw those animals cross the Mara River, where several met an untimely end in the jaws of the crocodiles. He had seen the migration on television, but to see it in person thrilled him. The group sat for an hour or more just enjoying the spectacle.

"BROTHER OF SIMBA"

The group studied the Marsh lions, a pride of more than twenty lions. (When Dewey saw his first lion in its natural habitat, he was so overcome with emotion that he almost jumped from the lorry.) The last time Dewey went (the time I visited with him), the pride had been decimated. Also, the pack of wild dogs they tracked and studied had contracted distemper from the dogs of the local tribes. It broke Dewey's heart. He loved the wildlife, the people and the landscape, and he watched every documentary he could find about Kenya. He also read extensively about the country.

Before he returned to Oregon, he went shopping and purchased several handbags and other memorabilia. When he showed his treasures to Candy, she chastised him for not bringing more. She said, "Dad, I love those purses and things. Why didn't you bring more?" He said, "Darn it, Candy, I hate shopping." But on his next trip, he brought her several items, as well as a box of chocolates from Switzerland to placate her.

He brought back spears, shields and other keepsakes, as well as beautiful carvings made from wood. Some of Candy's most special mementos are bracelets made from elephant hair. She is proud of those, and she remembers her father when wearing them.

Dewey's second trip to Africa was in 1985, after the first of the five state championships won while he coached the Pirates. It was a National Science Foundation tour, and began at the beginning of Christmas break. He knew the routine, so the preparation for that trip was not as difficult.

When we arrived at the Portland Airport for his departure, we found that his flight had been cancelled due to fog, so he re-booked on another airline. That threw the timing of his connections off, and he arrived in Salt Lake City to learn that his connecting flight to New York City had been given clearance to leave the airport. (As his plane from Portland landed in Salt Lake City, the one he needed to be on to go to New York had started to pull away from the gate.)

The airport personnel radioed ahead, and Dewey's connecting flight was detained until he got to the second gate. He did an O.J. *Simpson* jump of three or more feet to get on the flight to New York. (The O.J. maneuver was a television ad campaign before O.J.'s run-in with the law.) He said, "I'm glad you weren't with me. I don't think you could have made that jump." (I am certain I could not have. Rather than landing on the aircraft, I most likely would have ended up on the tarmac below.)

Dewey's luggage was checked through on the original airline, and he did not get it until two days before his return. He borrowed clothes from other participants, and photos show him in unfamiliar clothing. On that tour, he met Larry Vereen, a professor of science from a small college in South Carolina. Dewey told Larry, "The only way to see Africa is to go to Mike Rainy's camp and stay in the Mara."

When Dewey arrived at JFK Airport in New York City, he found that it was almost time for his flight to depart. He went to the ticket counter where an agent took his ticket. The agent looked at the ticket, and told Dewey, "You're not scheduled on this flight." Dewey said, "But my wife scheduled this trip back in September." (It sounded like a good idea at the time.) The agent said, "Wait a minute while I consult with my supervisor."

As the time for departure approached, Dewey became worried. He had no ticket, and had another flight to catch after he arrived in Madrid. He saw the agent behind the ticket counter, so he waved at him, and the agent gestured he was working on it.

After a frantic few minutes (which seemed like an eternity), the agent returned and gave him his ticket. Dewey was ushered into "first-class" seating in the top of the jumbo jet where he relaxed and enjoyed the flight. He was served gourmet food, and he said, "I was served large prawns and other delicacies, nothing like I was accustomed to in coach."

When he met his tour group in Madrid, he asked, "How did you like those prawns?" They looked at him to see if he were joking (which he wasn't). He said, "The only way to travel by plane is in 'first-class.' I had more legroom and the food was delicious. It was great!" He had fun, but missed his family at Christmas, and said, "I enjoyed the trip, but I missed Christmas at home. I won't travel at that time of year again."

That group stayed in the *Treetops*, and in other lodges in Kenya. Dewey said, "It was good to see how others view Africa, but I enjoyed camping out in the Mara (Mike Rainy's camp) far more. I wanted to stay out all day on game drives, but I was the only one who wanted to." (The group came in at five p.m. for cocktails, but Dewey did not drink cocktails. He preferred the game viewing drives and seeing the country instead.) Armed guards greeted them at one airport, and Dewey said, "That was scary. I was glad to get out of there."

When he returned to Mike's camp in 1986, Dewey was the only guest. He enjoyed the one-on-one exposure. They had many game drives to see the wildlife, and at Dewey's insistence, stayed out in the Mara too late one night. (You are to be in camp, not out in the Mara after sundown, but Dewey liked to stay as long as possible.)

They drove some distance in a deep gorge, before they realized they were being spotlighted from the escarpment above. Mike said, "Oh, oh! We're being spotlighted from above. We're not supposed to be in the Reserve after dark. I'm going to turn off the lights so they can't see our vehicle." Dewey said, "I didn't know we weren't supposed to be here this late. You'd better not hit the brakes because they can locate us by that."

Mike said, "Thanks for reminding me. We don't want them to know where we are. We had better get out of here." (While they traveled without lights, they almost ran into a herd of elephants.)

When they returned safely to camp, Dewey asked Mike, "What would have happened if we had been apprehended?" Mike put out his hands, and told him, "The rangers would have asked for money first, and if they didn't get that, they would have taken us to jail." (I am sure you do not want to go to jail in Kenya.) Dewey breathed a sigh of relief, and said, "Whew! I'm sure glad that didn't happen."

In one village, a native woman asked Dewey to extract her tooth. *(DR. DEWEY!!* He might have been a good dentist had he been trained, but he had no training.) Mike told him he probably resembled a dentist who had previously visited her village.

Dewey traveled light, so he did not take a camera with him on that trip. However, he took one with him on his other safaris. I am glad he took as many photos as he did. We framed several of his photos (a lion, a cheetah, and an elephant), and he was proud of those pictures.

He visited Lake Victoria and was amazed when he saw hundreds of pink flamingos. He said that sight was incredible. (Actually I believe flamingos are white, but the water in Lake Victoria is so rife

"BROTHER OF SIMBA"

with red algae that the red overcast on the white feathers results in pink, thus pink flamingos.) They also traveled near Mt. Kenya and Mt. Kilimanjaro, and he was awed.

The first three times Dewey visited Mike's camp, two of the *Samburu* tribesmen were *LaRolle* (sp) and *Lokatari* (sp), but only *LaRolle* was there when I went in 1995. He considered them good friends. *LaRolle* got enjoyment from asking, "Dewey, where's *campi*?" Dewey pointed in the direction he believed the camp to be, but was incorrect each time until his final day. Dewey said that there was rollicking amusement when he pointed in the right direction.

Dewey was enthralled with the big cats, and his nickname among the helpers was *Brother of Simba*. *LaRolle* asked him how many wives he had, and he said, "I only have one wife. One is more than enough to keep me busy providing her with clothes, etc." *LaRolle* told him he also had only one wife, but was building his herd of cattle so he could acquire a second one. I guess wives are a "status symbol" in Kenya (a symbol of wealth or just another "headache?").

Larry Vereen visited Mike's camp a year or two later, on Dewey's recommendation. Then, in 1989 Larry, Bill Tomasini and Dewey agreed to meet there. When Bill was a student at Linfield College, he student taught with Dewey, and they became good friends. They attended many football games and wrestling matches together.

In the early spring of 1989, Bill called and told Dewey he would accompany him to Africa if they could go to Europe for ten days first. Dewey agreed and the arrangements were made. Bill and Dewey stayed in bed and breakfasts, and traveled by Eurail around Switzerland, Spain, Italy, and France. They visited the Netherlands, and they went to a post office in Italy to purchase stamps. They had difficulty communicating with the personnel there. One fellow demonstrated air travel by waving his arms and simulating flight. Bill and Dewey found that particularly amusing.

Bill was a reserve on the Gresham Police Department, so they visited several police departments. In one town in Italy, Bill purchased a full police uniform. The policemen in the department were delighted to learn his name. "Tomasini, Tomasini," they exclaimed.

Dewey enjoyed touring the countryside and the villages, and seeing much that Europe has to offer, but was anxious to get to the Mara. In his mind the only destination in the world was Kenya (the cradle of civilization), and he had a wonderful experience each time he visited.

Bill purchased a camcorder before that trip, and he and Larry Vereen recorded their experiences on tape. I have videos of their travel through Europe, and of Dewey dancing with the Samburu, and at the hippo pool. It is amusing to see their exploits.

Mike had purchased an infrared light and camera before they arrived in the Mara, so they often went out at night and watched the activities. That was a favorite time for Dewey. He loved seeing the creatures under the cloak of darkness.

I am thankful we have those videos. Bill edited one tape, and titled it, *Sleeping Through Europe on Thirty Dollars a Day*. Dewey is seen sleeping on a boat, on the train and on the tram. (He borrowed a canteen from Brent, and one night a hyena came to the door of the tent and confiscated it. The hyena dropped the canteen when he

"BROTHER OF SIMBA"

heard the clank it made. Brent still has that canteen, complete with tooth marks.)

Dewey traveled to Mike's camp four times, and I accompanied him on his fourth trip (his fifth trip to Africa, but his fourth to Mike's camp). He retired from teaching in 1993, and I went with him during February and March of 1995. We had a wonderful time. He wanted to show me what he had experienced.

It is a tiresome trip when you fly practically non-stop from the United States to Kenya, and we were exhausted when we arrived. We stopped in Amsterdam for a couple of hours, but other than that, and for changing planes, our trip was without a break. Upon our arrival, we spent two nights at Mike's headquarters near Kajiado. That alleviated our jet lag, and prepared us for the trip to the Mara. We took several daylong jaunts while we were there, and we were able to see many creatures in their natural habitat.

After the two days spent recuperating, we were ready for the daylong trip to the *Maasai Mara*. The Mara is in the *Great Rift Valley*

of East Africa, and on the way we encountered zebra, giraffe, hyenas, etc. We passed several structures built far out over the Valley, but did not go out on any of them.

There is a fee to view the Valley from those vantage points, but they looked as though they were not well constructed. I could imagine falling several thousand feet to the floor of the *Valley*. Some (or likely most) of the construction in Kenya is of poor quality, and those viewpoints looked shaky to me.

A zebra was in trouble our first night in camp. Mike and Dewey said, "Get into the lorry so we can see what is happening." I said, "I'll just stay here and wait for you. You go ahead and see the action." They laughed and said, "You can't stay here by yourself. Get in the lorry and let's go." I did, but was relieved to find we were too late for the kill. However, I was teased about my desire to avoid death.

We visited the site the next day, and could see no evidence of predation. I told Dewey, "I really don't want to see death on a "first-hand" basis. It's hard enough to watch on television. Why can't the predators and their prey co-exist peacefully?" He said, "The predators have to eat also. That is part of the 'chain of life.'" (I wanted the animals to get along together and not eat each other. That was the one aspect I disliked about Africa.)

I could accept the outdoor "privy," and the black rubber shower bag with the slatted floor for the water to drain away, but I did not want to witness a kill. However, I nearly saw one on one of our drives. A topi was in trouble with a hyena, so I read a book while Dewey and Mike's son, Gaby, watched the kill. I did not want to see such encounters, and I avoided them as best I could.

We visited during the rainy season, and the second night in camp I got up and found I was standing in water an inch deep. I woke Dewey and said, "Oh, my gosh, Dewey. There's water all over the floor." We promptly stowed our luggage on chairs, and the tent had to be moved the next morning.

We visited a native village, and that proved interesting. Mike Rainy had known the villagers for years. There are commercial villages that charge a fee for admission, but the one we visited was an actual village where people lived. At night the cattle and goats are brought into the enclosures to keep them safe. Those enclosures are made from reeds and branches with thorns on them to discourage the predators (lions, hyenas, etc.).

To make the huts waterproof, mud and dung is combined and plastered over the thatch. The villages are moved periodically because the ground gets churned up, and becomes soft from the urine and feces deposited by the animals. As we entered the enclosure, my shoes dipped into the mud and manure. Oops! When we got back to Mike's camp, I had a difficult time cleaning them.

We were invited into one of the huts, and there were calves and baby goats just inside the entrance. A fire was in the center of the hut, and the places where the family slept were clustered around the perimeter. It was truly communal living. An opening in the center of the roof allowed smoke to escape, but it was smoky and dark inside. We sat around the fire on stools, and a gourd with clabbered milk was passed around. Dewey tried it, but I declined. (Dewey didn't

◂ A BAREFOOT BOY FROM OKLAHOMA

grimace as he tasted it, but I am not adventurous. I am not a good tourist due to my reluctance to try new things.)

A small boy of about two took a liking to me, and held onto my hand. He was cute and wore only a shirt (when he turned around you could see his little buns). Mike and the tribesmen had a good visit, and Dewey and I were excited to be in an actual village, and to see how the tribesmen lived.

One morning we found several dead hyenas, and it was learned that the local tribesmen from another village had poisoned them. Mike went to the authorities, and brought two armed gentlemen back with us in the Toyota. There was a heated conversation with the tribesmen, but they agreed to stop poisoning the carnivores. I think. They repeatedly said what sounded like, "Un doggie, doggie," or something like that. It was *Greek* to me.

The storks and other birds fed on the hyena carcasses, so the poison was going through the food chain. The poisoning was instigated because the hyenas preyed on the cattle of the tribe. Mike explained that Dewey and I came to see the wildlife, and that Dewey was on his fifth trip to Kenya. That seemed to have some influence on their decision (but, who knows?).

Every night a couple of bush babies (nocturnal African marsupials) visited our tent, and we wakened to hear them chattering. They got on top of the tent, leaned down, and peered over the edge to see what was happening. We saw those little faces peeking in. One night I woke Dewey and said, "Come watch." We watched them play with the bar of soap at the wash table. The soap slipped through their hands (paws) as they looked around as if to say, "Why? What is this stuff?" It was comical and they were cute. They have huge eyes and are cuddly-appearing.

Bush babies are dear creatures, but Mike told us they are not pet material. He told of one couple that adopted several of them, and kept them in their house as pets. The little rascals urinate on their hands to get friction when they climb up and down a pole, or on other things inside the house (or outdoors), so it reeked of urine. Phew!!

As the sun was setting one evening, we saw a herd of impala, and it made the most amazing picture. To see the bright rays reflected off the tawny hides of the impala was incredible. We took several photos, but no picture could capture the beauty of that scene. The wildlife we saw was beyond anything I had ever imagined, and was more beautiful than any picture could portray.

The hippos were amusing as they grunted and snuffled at the "hippo pool." We watched them in their antics, and we listened to the noises made as they surfaced. (Hippos kill more tourists than any other animal in Africa.) They did not look dangerous because they were comical appearing and seemed docile, but we gave them a wide berth as we viewed them from a small ridge above where they "bathed." Crocodiles were also seen in the "hippo pool." (The crocs feed on the hippo calves when they are given the opportunity.)

A BAREFOOT BOY FROM OKLAHOMA

Dewey saw several leopards on his African adventures, but the only evidence of a leopard's habitation I saw was a gazelle in a tree. Leopards kill their prey, and carry it into the tree for "fine dining." That makes their food less accessible to lions, hyenas and other scavengers.

On one drive, we encountered a herd of elephants. The matriarch charged our vehicle, and attempted to use her tusks as a "can opener." She was fast and agile, but Mike avoided her by swerving as he drove. He told us that her herd had likely been invaded by poachers, and that prompted her aggressive behavior. We left the area after several minutes of dodging her.

Another time we sat for almost an hour in the midst of a different herd of elephants. That herd was not as aggressive as the first. Mike dubbed one baby elephant, *Babar*, as he was mischievous and cavorted among the adult elephants much as an impish child would do in a group of adults. *Babar* did the most hilarious things. He pranced around and irritated the adults. He was into everything, and we chuckled at his antics. We also saw herds of giraffe, and it was amusing to watch them "prune" the tops of the trees from their great height.

"BROTHER OF SIMBA"

Dewey also saw several rhinos on his trips, but I was not as fortunate. Rhinos are rare and not often seen, so it is a source of interest to encounter one or more. We saw several herds of cape buffalo, and one morning we came upon a pride of lions asleep in a grove of trees. Our vehicle was about four feet from them, and we sat and observed them for fifteen or twenty minutes. There was a kill in their midst, and they were sprawled in contentment, their bellies distended by the food they had consumed.

The mongooses were amusing – it was hilarious to come upon a group, and see the sentinel signal the family that danger approached. We also enjoyed the wild pigs. The young ones were funny as they scuffled with each other and snuffled in the dirt.

And one afternoon we encountered several hyenas. (We had seen many on the plains, but that time we were "up close and personal.") One was a young cub, and he stood on his hind legs and sniffed at our vehicle. He looked like a puppy and appeared cuddly. Of course he was not cuddly, but was a wild animal. You are not to touch or interfere with the animals, so we sat quietly and watched the action.

Another time we saw two lionesses with seven or eight small cubs. Those babies were so cute. On Dewey's first trip to Africa, he told me that they encountered a lion. Mike's son, Gaby, was quite young, and he told Mike, "Dad, that lion is looking at me. What should I do?" Mike said, "Move back from the edge of the lorry and stay there." (I guess you hope the lion won't leap into the lorry?) I know I would stay back if there were a lion nearby!

One morning, we came upon a newborn Thompson's gazelle. It was the smallest animal – no larger than a kitten. I did not want to see such a dear little thing get eaten, but we proceeded from there and did not see any carnage that day. We just enjoyed the beauty of the herd. And another morning we sat for half an hour watching a group of young topi as they raced across the plains.

The sounds of the ibis and the African eagles, the calls of the egrets and the herons were awe-inspiring. The birds of Africa are incredible – the variety of birdlife is truly astounding. The crowned cranes were spectacular. They were so beautiful in their plumage, and the secretary birds looked as though they had quill pens stuck in their elaborate hair-dos. We marveled at the colors as well as the diversity of bird life, and we watched the weaver-birds weave their nests.

There is a constant humming and buzzing throughout the day, and the night sounds are eerie and to be remembered. Dewey said he was reminded of Africa when he heard the doves cooing at our home in Oregon in the mornings. He loved the sounds of the birds and of lions roaring.

One adventure Dewey did not realize was to camp near Wildlife Safari in Winston, Oregon. He wanted to hear the roar of the lions at night. He suggested that as an alternative to another trip to Africa.

We saw some of the smallest animals as well as some of the largest ones. I wish I had kept a diary of what we saw (from Mike's descriptions and names), and what we did. We had a wonderful trip, and I understood why Dewey was enthralled with Africa. (Actually, that is one of the reasons he was attracted to me. When we were classmates in Boone I stated I wanted to visit Africa, and I believe Dewey thought we were kindred spirits.)

"BROTHER OF SIMBA"

I wanted to go to Africa, but I did not have the all-consuming passion for it that Dewey had. After his family and football, Africa was his top interest here on earth. In his mind, nothing could compare with what Africa has to offer. Seeing wildebeest on their annual trek – seeing lions and hyenas in their natural habitat -- sitting in the midst of a herd of elephants – all overwhelmed Dewey. He enjoyed his experiences immensely, and could have enjoyed those times all day.

Before we returned to Oregon, we visited the *Nairobi Museum*. We sat in the rail car from which the lions took the Indian workers while the *Tsavo Bridge* was under construction. During nine months in 1898, two large male lions killed and ate nearly one hundred and forty railway workers. (The book, Man-Eaters of Tsavo, is based on that occurrence, and the film, Ghost and the Darkness, is predicated on it. Dewey enjoyed *Man-Eaters*, and read it several times.)

One maneless male lion is on display in the *Nairobi Museum*, but I believe the actual culprits are displayed in the *Field Museum of Natural History* in Chicago. (Dewey thought a better venue for displaying those lions would have been to capture and show them alive.)

And before we knew it -- it was time to return to Oregon. As we prepared to return, Dewey turned to me and asked, "Well, are you ready to move to Africa?" He astounded me. I had not contemplated such a move, and was at a loss with the possibility. I was stunned and said, "I've never thought about it." (He would have loved to live in Kenya from December until August, coming back to Oregon to coach football.) Of course, we did not do it. All I could think of was the paperwork, etc. necessitated by such a move.

On our return flight, monitors in the cabin showed where the aircraft was, and how far we had traveled. Each time I looked at the monitor, I vowed I would not do so for at least another twenty minutes, but I inevitably checked it about every five minutes. That flight got so monotonous. After his first African safari Dewey told of the exhaustion he experienced, and I encountered it "first-hand" when I went with him. It was a long time before I wanted to fly again.

When we arrived at the Minneapolis/St. Paul Airport, Dewey asked, "Do you want to rent a car and drive home?" I said, "No, that be more tiring than the rest of the plane ride." (We would have been much more fatigued, had we driven the remainder of the way.)

(I worked with Dr. Thomas Yonker, a professor at Linfield College, for many years and he told me to select a photo from which he would paint a picture for us. I typed a book for him, and he painted that picture in return. I told Dewey to pick something, so he chose one with a lioness on a fallen tree, and a male lion on the ground below. Dewey was pleased with the finished painting, and it hangs proudly in our family room.)

Dewey hunted as a young man, but later looked at hunting, and decided it was not a sport (his philosophy was that the animals were not willing participants in a hunt). He felt that for it to be a sport, both participants must participate willingly. He did not hunt again, and became adamantly opposed to hunting. (He had a love for all God's creatures.) Jerry Sutton says I jinx him in the arena of hunting.

Any time I know he is prepared to go hunting, I tell him not to get anything.

Several years ago I told Dewey, "I would like for you to go to Africa one last time." His reply was, "I don't think I want to return. I have seen Africa five times, and the wildlife was still fairly plentiful each time I visited. I don't think I want to go again."

(He also did not want to see what had transpired there. He did not want to see the lack of so many lion prides, or the decimation of the packs of wild dogs.) He liked to see animals in their natural habitat, and he enjoyed going where he could see them. The abundance of wildlife was the reason he loved Africa so much. He loved what God created.

CHAPTER **38**

Aloha!!

We had seen Hawaii on television . . . the sunshine . . . the white sand beaches. All that beckoned us. After Africa, our top choice for a vacation was Hawaii, but we could not afford the tickets. So when the 1980 football team gave us the airfare, we were elated. We went during spring break of 1981, and stayed in Larry Groth's condominium (Larry was a player for Dewey in 1965-67, and his brother, John, played for Dayton from 1977 until 1980).

We drove Larry's Volkswagen around Oahu, and had a wonderful time. We toured the Polynesian Cultural Center and the Bishop Museum. Dewey snorkeled in Hanauma Bay (the water of the Bay was so clear he could see far below). I sat beneath an umbrella while he snorkeled. He reported that the fish were spectacular, and he was enthralled with the diversity and colors. We were grateful to that team for their kindness, and we were indebted to Larry for providing our transportation and lodging.

We enjoyed Hawaii so much that we went again fifteen years later. We went in February of 1996, and watched the Pro Bowl on a Sunday afternoon in the sunshine. What a beautiful, warm day! We saw John Elway, Jerry Rice, Drew Bledsoe and Jerome Bettis. We left Portland in freezing weather, and returned to warm rain and flooding.

◄ A BAREFOOT BOY FROM OKLAHOMA

It rained steadily for two weeks after we returned. Dewey was scheduled to go to Tacoma to receive the *PEMCO Northwest Award* on that Saturday, but a mudslide on the I-5 corridor between Portland and Tacoma closed the highway. I tried to schedule a flight from Portland to Sea-Tac (the Seattle-Tacoma airport) on Saturday morning, but the airlines were booked. Dewey did not make it for the presentation, but PEMCO understood, and his award was mailed to him. It is a beautiful plaque, and he was proud of it.

The last time we went to Hawaii was in 1999. Dayton defeated Regis 24-0 in the quarterfinal round of the playoffs. Before I left for the semifinal game the next week, Dwight Ediger called, and asked if we would like to join him and his wife on the Island of Hawaii when football season was over. I didn't pause. I happily told him, "Yes!" I made reservations, and I thought it would be a wonderful surprise for Dewey. I told Dwight not to tell him until after the title game.

The Pirates played Sherman County in the semifinals, and won the game 42-36, but five team members were injured. (Nine starting positions on both offense and defense were lost to those injuries.)

Dewey was devastated by the injuries to so many, so when I went to the field after the game, I informed him we were going to Hawaii. I told him a week earlier than I had planned, because I felt he needed a "pick-me-up." (Dayton lost the title game to Amity the following week. The trip to Hawaii did not make up for the loss, but it helped.)

We had a marvelous time and Hawaii in December was great. We visited the volcano and Dewey snorkeled with the sea turtles. We sat in the sun. We had dinner at *Bubba Gump's Shrimp Factory*, and we unwound from the football season. We saw many things of interest and appreciated the opportunity to relax. Hawaii is always a "fun" destination.

CHAPTER 39

Travels — Florida

Florida, the "Sunshine State," was another exotic destination for us, and we visited three times. Each time we were there, Dewey insisted we go to the serpentarium in Kissimmee. On our first visit he asked the snake handler, "Do you ever see any rattlesnakes outside?" The reply was, "One morning a large rattler was found on the front step, and I promptly captured him and brought him in."

We toured the facility, and Dewey enjoyed watching the handler "milk" the venom from several snakes. He walked among the displays, and was curious about the creatures there.

After we left the serpentarium, we headed to Cape Kennedy, and found a small rattlesnake on the highway. Dewey put the car into reverse and backed up. He found a stick to use in getting the snake off the road, so it wouldn't be run over and killed.

Dewey asked me to take a photo of him with that snake, but I would not get anywhere near that thing. I stood about twenty feet away, and Dewey told me, "You've got to get closer than that to get a good picture. Come on. You're okay. That snake won't get you."

He was disappointed in my lack of appreciation for his skill in snake handling, and for his "bravery" – his foolishness? When he saw the resulting photo he asked, "What were you doing? You can hardly see 'my' snake." (I stood so far from the action that the picture was long-distance, and the snake looked like a worm.)

A BAREFOOT BOY FROM OKLAHOMA

When we visited Circus World, the largest tiger imaginable was on display in a glass case. Dewey was amazed at the size of that beast. He had a love for the big cats, and enjoyed the tour.

Dewey's cousin resided in Fort Myers, so we drove down and stayed a couple of nights with him and his family. We visited Sanibel Island, and reveled in the beautiful, white sand beaches. We saw pelicans and other birds and were enthralled. The emerald-jeweled waters were spectacular, and the sunsets were awe-inspiring. The shades of mauve and lavender stretched like strips of ribbon across the sky. It was a veritable palette of color. The balmy climate and the pristine beaches were mesmerizing.

We stopped at several stands where we purchased fresh-squeezed orange juice. Tree-ripened fruit far surpasses any that is picked green and then allowed to ripen during transport, and it was so refreshing.

As we headed to the airport to return home, we took an airboat ride, and Dewey served as the pilot. The airboats were fun to ride, and we zipped around the lake for a few minutes, but needless to say, he got the boat hung up in the reeds, and I feared we would miss our flight. We didn't. He had a second sense about such things, and he worked on a different schedule than I did.

Sharon accompanied us on our third trip. She told her assistants at the Stayton Library, "My brother thinks he's going to get me to the serpentarium, but he isn't. There's no way I'm going to visit rattlesnakes." But when we arrived at the sepentarium, she elected to go inside, rather than sit in the hot car.

She said, "I really don't want to do this, but it will be better than staying in the car in the parking lot." She became absorbed in watching the handler "milk" the venom from a poisonous snake. She might not have appreciated the visit as much as Dewey did, but she learned something that day.

An article in Reader's Digest later that year, told of the snake handler being bitten by one of the snakes, and about his struggle for survival. Sharon enjoyed reading about where she had been and someone she met.

Each of the three times we visited, we enjoyed *Disney World* and *Epcot Center*. We visited Italy on our last trip, and opera songs were being sung. Dewey asked one of the gentlemen, "Where's *Figaro*?" He was told, "He'll be here this afternoon." He loved *Figaro*, and wanted to hear their rendition. He was amused at the reply — even though he did not get to hear the song.

The night before we returned to Oregon, Dewey went on an alligator "hunt." Sharon and I stayed at the condo, and he went alone. The hunt was conducted in airboats, and the alligators were spotlighted. They were not touched or harmed in any way. They were just spotlighted. He said it was fantastic to see those big eyes gleaming red in the spotlight. He had a wonderful time. It was something he had seen on television, but did not think he would have the opportunity to do.

On his return trip to the condo, he pulled to the side of the road, rolled down the car windows, and listened to the night sounds. He thought of the Native Americans and told us, "I imagined I was a Native American in the 1880s. With all the noise from the insects and the frogs (the chirping and the singing), you couldn't hear someone sneaking up on you." He had a memorable experience, and said it was incredible to hear the cacophony of the sounds of the Everglades at night

CHAPTER **40**

North to Alaska

Barry was a butterfly collector, and traveled to Alaska many times. He invited Dewey to accompany him when he went in 1987. Dewey was excited because he wanted to see grizzly bears in their natural habitat. They had several humorous experiences on their trip.

At the campsite the first night, Dewey jumped from the pickup, rubbed his hands together, and declared, "I'm hungry! What's for supper?" Barry whipped out several tins of *Campbell's* soup, and said, "We're having soup for supper." Dewey looked at him askance. "Is that all you have? I don't like soup. What else is there?"

Barry said, "Well, Dad, welcome to my world. That's what's on the menu for the next two weeks. That's what I eat when I'm on the road." Dewey's disappointment was palpable (I'm sure he was ready for a big juicy steak). He survived, but he insisted they stop for burgers, etc., every chance they got.

At one cafe they ordered hamburgers, and Barry noticed blood coming from Dewey's mouth. He said, "Stop, Dad! There's blood on your mouth. Your burger is awfully rare – we'd better send it back to be cooked again." When they examined the burger, they discovered a toothpick in it. Dewey had stabbed himself! Barry laughed about that and kidded Dewey unmercifully.

They slept in the back of Barry's pickup, and one night Dewey got up frequently. Every time he got back into the pickup, he rolled over to kill the mosquitoes clustered on him. The sheet used for lining his sleeping bag was bloodstained. He got up so often that he tired of opening and closing the canopy, so he finally left it open. That disturbed Barry, because he did not want a mosquito invasion. (They must have made a "dynamic duo." They were probably like an old married couple arguing with each other.)

Another evening they crawled into the back of the pickup, but did not latch the canopy well. They had looked for bears that day, and saw none. But when they crawled into their sleeping bags, they heard a noise. First there was a rustle. Then there was a scratching, and it got closer and closer. Dewey whispered to Barry, "Do you suppose it's a bear?" Though they had looked for bears, they were not excited by the possibility of one visiting them at night.

Dewey quietly got out of his bag, and crept to the rear of the pickup. He tentatively leaned out of the canopy to see. The tailgate fell with a BANG. They both jumped about six feet in the air. No grizzly was under the pickup, but rather they found a vole (a small rodent). But the excitement far eclipsed anything they had seen during that day. They lay in their sleeping bags and rolled in amusement. *DEWEY'S BIG ADVENTURE!!*

Marmots often visited the pickup at night, and crawled up on the axle to get to the salt accumulated there. They made a great deal of noise with their skirmishes. Many brown bears were seen, but Dewey was disappointed they did not see grizzly bears, as that was one of the reasons he had looked forward to the trip.

In the early morning hours, three days before their planned return to Oregon, Dewey nudged Barry and said, "Let's get going – I miss your mom. We've been gone ten days, and I'm ready to go home." Against his better judgment, Barry grudgingly got out of his sleeping bag, fixed something to eat (more soup?), and loaded the pickup.

They drove throughout that day and the next, and pulled into our yard about ten o'clock in the evening. I heard a commotion, so I went out and found that the travelers had returned. I was happy to see them, and amazingly, they were still speaking to each other. (Ten days together in the wilderness . . .)

After they returned, Dewey showed slides of their trip to his classes. During one presentation, a student looked at a picture of Barry, and asked, "Who's that old man with you?" (Barry had not shaved for several days, and was rather "grody" looking. Dewey thought that was hilarious. Barry was thirty-two at the time.)

CHAPTER **41**

Other Travels

We visited Jonell in Denver in March of 1982. It was the beginning of spring break, and when we arrived at the airport, we found that our flight was jammed. I said, "This flight looks overbooked. We might be able to get "comp" tickets if we volunteer our seats." After we were seated, the flight attendant came down the aisle (as if I had programmed the scenario), and asked for two seats. We stood up to volunteer our seats, but then were told that only one seat was needed.

When we sat down, I looked at Dewey and said, "We don't have to travel together." The words were no more out of my mouth when the attendant came back and said, "We still need another seat." Dewey did not look back. With "single-minded" determination, he was out of his seat like a shot from a cannon. He was gone. (Once I said, "We don't have to travel together," his decision was made. And with Dewey, if he made a decision, he acted on it.)

I did not think too much about that, until I realized that, under our seat, we had a box of canned fruit from his mother to be delivered to his sister. A box of twelve jars of canned fruit is a heavy load. And as if that were not enough, he also left his huge, heavy coat with me (and it was a big one.) He was determined to get a free ticket, and he volunteered his seat in the blink of an eye, before I could even say goodbye or think of the implications.

A BAREFOOT BOY FROM OKLAHOMA

The plane did not pull up to the airport in Denver, so I maneuvered my load down the steps to the field, and then back up to the concourse. I waited about ten minutes for Jonell to come to the waiting area, but she did not arrive. I went to the desk, and asked for change so I could call her. Change was not available, so I considered stowing the fruit and the coat in one of the lockers, but didn't. (That was fortunate since I could not have gotten back to that area to retrieve those items).

When I finally decided I had waited long enough, I trekked up the concourse to the gate. I was not appropriately attired for my adventure (I was wearing a dress and high heels -- oh, my aching feet). As I "huffed and puffed" toward my destination, I stopped frequently to rest my load on whatever was available (most often an ashtray along the wall, as smoking was allowed in airports at that time).

I struggled up that long, winding road. It was a battle all the way, but I finally got the fruit to the street level of the airport. When I arrived at the gate, I found that people were not allowed down the concourse to meet incoming passengers. (In 1982, it was common to greet your guests as they disembarked, but it is not allowed at all today.) That was why Jonell had not greeted me. There had been no announcement, so I had no inkling why Jonell was not there to meet me.

I stowed the fruit on a seat at the shoeshine stand, and sat down for a "breather," and to "recoup."

After I caught my breath, I left the fruit and went down a level to retrieve my luggage. When I got to the baggage claim area, I found Jonell. She stood there, and was prepared to go home to wait for me to call. We retrieved my luggage, and returned to the shoeshine stand to get the fruit.

Dewey's mother later asked, "Why didn't you just leave that box in the airport? You shouldn't have worked so hard. It wasn't worth all that trouble." In retrospect, I should have, but with my determination ("pig-headedness" has been suggested), I got everything to Denver safely. Mission accomplished! (Of course, in today's world, had

OTHER TRAVELS

I abandoned my load, a bomb squad would likely have been summoned.)

When we returned to the airport to meet the next Portland flight, Dewey was not on it. I looked at Jonell, and said, "I'll bet he volunteered his seat a second time." We went to her house, and waited until time for the next scheduled flight to arrive. We returned to the airport, and he was on that flight! He said, "I almost received a third ticket, but a seat on my last flight was not needed. It looked as though it was, but they worked it out."

Dewey was "comped" two round-trip tickets for his "sacrifices," and was pleased with his efforts. (One of those tickets got him to New York City for his first trip to Africa. We saved a lot of money with his adventure, and were glad he volunteered his seat.)

We were fortunate to be able to accompany Frank and Julie Kline to Mazatlan four times, and had wonderful experiences each time. (The Klines are veteran Mexico travelers, so they paved the way for us.) Those trips were fairly snag-free. We took our grandson, Zack, with us the last two times we went, and he loved it. He said, "It's awesome."

We went to St. Maarten in August of 1992, and had a fabulous time. We stayed on the Dutch side of the Island, and toured it, as well as the French side. I am not supposed to tell Dewey's story, but since he's not here to defend himself, I feel I can. When we arrived on the Island, one of the "attractions" we heard about was a nude beach. We were not looking for it (at least I was not), but the next day, as we drove around, we saw several cars parked nearby. We got out and walked down to the beach. (We had found the nude beach!)

Dewey enjoyed himself until he saw a man's bare buns. (He was a much more "visual" person than I am.) He turned to me and said, "Let's get out of here." I thought that was a funny story, but he didn't find it amusing, and did not want it told. (I'm sorry, Dewey.)

As we prepared to leave for an extended trip in 1966, I heard an announcement on the radio, "Vera Sullivan has won the *Pepsi-Cola* shopping spree contest, and will be shopping at Edwards Market in Dayton." I was excited and could hardly wait for Dewey and our children to arrive from school so I could tell them. I received official notification a couple of days later, and the time and date were established. It was a five-minute spree conducted without the use of a shopping cart – just what I could carry.

The first thing the kids requested was television dinners. To them the epitome of fine dining was "tv" dinners. We had never had a "tv" dinner, and I admit, "tv" dinners were not high on my list. Candy said, "Mom, what we want most is "tv" dinners. We've never had any, and our friends get them." Jack Edwards owned the small local grocery where my "spree" was to be conducted, and he asked me what cuts of meat we wanted, and what other items we preferred.

The big day came, and it was simple to cover the necessary territory. But five minutes running back and forth with your arms loaded is a lot of time. (Not that I complained. I was happy for the opportunity.) I selected $625.25 in groceries, and the man who conducted my shopping spree finished it with a couple of cartons of Pepsi. To us a windfall of that amount was astronomical. We felt fortunate (I would feel that way today should I be so lucky), and were grateful. In today's world, that does not sound like a lot of money, but Dewey's annual salary was less than $7,000 at the time.

When we left for our trip a couple of days later, we were still "flying high" from our good fortune. We had purchased a small tent at the Montgomery-Ward surplus store, so we packed it and our camping gear and supplies into a box Dewey constructed before school dismissed. (At last we had an "honest-to-goodness" tent – no more canvas over ropes for us.) We loaded it into the trailer, piled the kids into the station wagon, and took off to see the United States.

We had lived in Dayton for one year, and had been away from Colorado for two years. We had not seen some of our relatives during that time, so we spent six weeks on the road leisurely traveling and visiting. We meandered through eastern Oregon, Idaho and Wyoming before going to Colorado.

When we arrived in Colorado, we stayed several days with Sharon and her family in Steamboat Springs. We enjoyed the beauty of that area. In the summer everything is beautiful (probably in the winter also if you ski, or are a winter sports enthusiast). We did a lot of sightseeing, and we fished in the small stream that ran by their home. When we left Steamboat we stopped by Meeker to renew acquaintances.

In Canon City, we visited my mother and stepfather. The big attraction there is the mile-high bridge over the *Royal Gorge*, so we took the kids across it, and we also took them for a train ride through the *Gorge*. The kids were excited when we finally arrived in Fowler where Dewey's parents lived.

We spent a week in Fowler, and then drove to Hays, Kansas and visited Windle and my brother, Elmer, who lived there. My nephew, Brad, told me recently that, when we visited them in Hays, Dewey and our sons went downstairs with him and his dad.

Elmer had weights there, and Barry and Brent struggled lifting those weights. After several exhibitions, Dewey said, "You guys get out of the way, and let the *BIG GUY* lift. (Brad was probably six, Brent nine and Barry eleven at the time.) They turned it over to Brad, who lifted the weights with no problem. (Brad later learned that Dewey had instructed Barry and Brent to get on both sides of the bar behind him, and to give him added "heft," by lifting on the bar.)

A BAREFOOT BOY FROM OKLAHOMA

When we left Kansas, we spent two more weeks in Fowler before we left for California. On the way to California, we camped in Mesa Verde, the Grand Canyon and Lake Mead (near Las Vegas). We stayed with my stepsister in Anaheim, and went to Disneyland, Sea World and Knott's Berry Farm. We also visited my cousin in San Diego. We attended the Shrine football game at the Rose Bowl (the L.A. Coliseum), and we crossed the border into Mexico, so the kids could say they had been in a different country.

When we went to the Shrine game, Dewey stated he wanted to attend a high school game in every state in the Union. (Unfortunately, that is one aspiration he did not realize. His buddy, Garnet Wright, told him he would go with him, but it did not happen. Dewey could not coach and attend football games elsewhere. But he attended high school games in Colorado, Washington, Oregon, Arizona and California.)

Dewey was assigned as the photographer (or archivist) for our trip, so he only saw the activities through the viewfinder of the movie camera. We took the scenic route back to Oregon, and drove through San Francisco. We camped in the Redwoods and had a wonderful time. When we returned to Dayton, it was nice to see what had happened while we were gone.

CHAPTER **42**

NSF Fellowships — Southeast Missouri State

Dewey was awarded three National Science Foundation (NSF) fellowships. The first was during the summer of 1963. Then he had another in the summer of 1964, and one in 1968. The experiences afforded our family during those summers were priceless.

We lived in Meeker when Dewey accepted his first fellowship. That summer, we spent eight weeks on the campus of Southeast Missouri State College at Cape Girardeau. The college is located on the banks of the Mississippi River, and many of the escapades mentioned in the works of Samuel Clemens *(Mark Twain)* occurred in that area. We visited many of those sites, as well as other historic locations. Living on the banks of the Mississippi gave us a wonderful opportunity.

As we prepared to leave Meeker for Missouri, we loaded our small trailer, and were off to see the world (not to see the "wizard"). We visited Dewey's parents in Fowler, before we drove to Lamar, Colorado to spend the night with Sharon and her family. We knew it was going to be extremely hot and humid on our trip, and as our car was not air-conditioned, we elected to start early, and get most of the travel completed before the hottest part of the day.

When we left Lamar, we got up about one o'clock in the morning. Dewey went into the bathroom to shave, and Sharon's daughter, Kathy, heard us stirring. She got up to see what was happening.

A BAREFOOT BOY FROM OKLAHOMA

Dewey's shaving procedure amused her, so she perched on a stool and watched. She said, "Uncle Dewey, what are you doing?" (I guess she had not seen anyone shave and it fascinated her.)

Before we left we awoke Sharon, to ensure that Kathy did not try to "escape" with us. (Dewey once told Kathy something, and her reply was, "Uncle Dewey, you have your brain in backwards." She was precocious, did hilarious things, and had many amusing retorts.)

When we drove through Kansas, small turtles were on the highway, and were being smashed by the traffic. Our children were intrigued, so Dewey stopped and put a couple of them in the car. That did not last long. They urinated on the floorboard, so we stopped and released them. For shelter, we tied a rope between two trees and flopped a heavy canvas over it. That served as our "tent" for the time it took us to get to Cape Girardeau.

Our second night in Missouri, we were deluged by a torrential rainstorm, and our makeshift "tent" became soggy. It was already heavy, but with the added moisture, it took days to dry. The humidity was oppressive.

It was more than a week later that we finally considered the "tent" dry enough to fold up. (Things did not dry readily in that climate, and when we took showers in the dorms we could never seem to get dry. We felt damp no matter how much toweling we did.)

Dewey studied herpetology and botany at Southeast Missouri State College, and he was the first student in the herpetology class to capture a timber rattlesnake. The instructor lectured from atop a fallen tree. When he moved, Dewey checked underneath the tree, and found the six-foot long snake.

The capture was publicized in the local newspaper. (I still have that article.) Dewey later took Barry and Brent to the classroom to see "his" snake, and they were fascinated by its size. The botany professor used poison ivy as one of the specimens to be identified on a test, and one student got a horrible case of poison ivy.

We visited local sites of interest, and our children caught fireflies at night. Dewey went to St. Louis to watch the Olympic trials. He attended a St. Louis Cardinals game and saw Stan Musial play. On Sunday evenings we, along with several other participants and their families, crossed the long bridge that spanned the Mississippi River into Illinois for a seafood buffet dinner. Those times are recalled with fondness, and were highlights of a memorable summer.

One night the herpetology class hung the snake bags (in which the captives were placed), in a closet in the dorm. A snake escaped, and an alarm went through the dorm the next morning. We (mostly wives of the participants) tiptoed around gingerly while going about our daily activities. I had done laundry earlier, and had carefully picked up each item before putting it into the washer. (I didn't want to be the one to find the snake.) About ten o'clock a scream was heard, and we knew the "escapee" had been located.

We rushed to the second floor, and found that the snake had taken up residence there. It had wrapped itself around the leg of a desk. (I do not know why we met there, as none of us had any intention of dealing with it. I guess we were curious!) It was a harmless water snake about six feet in length, but when we saw its length, we gasped in surprise (harmless or not). That was one long snake.

A visiting professor (not a herpetologist) was staying in the dorm, and he took the snake catcher and attempted to get the snake into a snake bag. Marty, the resident of the room where the snake decided to hide, screamed when she saw the length of that snake, and rapidly evacuated the scene. All we saw were long, brown legs running down the hall. The professor eventually captured the "escapee," and things returned to normal (Normal? With a snake on the loose in a dorm with a bunch of women, what is "normal?")

Dewey and another participant went fishing at the Lake of the Ozarks one evening, but did not catch any fish. The other fellow apologized, but Dewey said the experience was incredible, just to be out on the lake at night. He had a fantastic time. We established lasting friendships with other participants in that and other institutes, and at the time of Dewey's death, received letters from many of them at Christmas.

During the summer spent in Cape Girardeau Dewey encountered bigotry, true prejudice and racism. His eyes were opened when he saw that the African-American participants were refused service at the small cafes where they stopped on their field trips. (As a child he recalled that the swimming pool in the small town of Fowler, Colorado did not let the Hispanic youngsters swim with the whites. Since he and his brothers played with those children on a daily basis, he was baffled.)

(In May 2006, Dewey and I accompanied John Patterson to California to visit Yosemite and other places of interest, and were fortunate to visit *Calaveros County* – the place immortalized by Bret Hart as well as Mark Twain, i.e. *The Celebrated Jumping Frog of Calaveros County*.

We stayed in Angel's Camp, and toured the area of the *Jumping Frog Contest*, which was held the weekend after we left. That was our last trip together, and is "priceless" in my memory -- the tie-in between *Angel's Camp* and *Cape Girardeau* was of special interest to us.)

CHAPTER 43

NSF Fellowships — Montana State University

Dewey's second National Science Foundation fellowship was to Montana
State University in Bozeman, Montana in 1964. On weekends, we hiked and fished -- we camped in Yellowstone -- we had a super summer. Dewey studied microbiology, and the kids and I played.

I accompanied Dewey to a lecture by Werner von Braun, and I took swimming lessons with our children. They thought it hilarious as they watched me try to learn the things they already knew.

Candy recalled that one of their favorite outings was when we visited one hamburger stand that sold fifteen hamburgers for a dollar. We indulged the kids on those burgers, and the boys stoked up because it was a treat to eat anywhere other than at home. (Our kids enjoyed eating out, and didn't care that the patties were small.) Dewey encouraged the boys to eat to promote their growth. He wanted them to be big, strong football players.

Dewey stayed in the dorm that summer, and the children and I stayed in a basement apartment. I cannot remember why we had separate residences (I'm certain it had something to do with finances), but he visited us during the week and on weekends.

After the children were in bed one night, there was a knock at the door. I was frightened and roused them. We prepared to exit through the rear door, but whoever was there went away. We did not learn who our night visitor was (possibly someone who lived there previously, or who wanted to visit a former resident). Anyway, it was frightening, as I was alone with the kids.

The weekend we camped in Yellowstone, a buffalo (bison) wandered near as we were setting up camp. Candy yelled, "There's a cow . . . a moose . . . a buffalo." Dewey told our kids, "Get up on the picnic table and stay quiet." We saw many bears, moose, etc., and enjoyed watching them.

As we prepared to leave Bozeman in August, it snowed. We had seen photos of Yellowstone in winter, and to get snow that early in the season gave evidence of things to come. We were happy to leave before winter settled in.

Dewey read extensively about the Native American peoples and their culture, and empathized with them about the treatment they received from the white man. On our return trip to Chehalis, we visited Browning, Montana and other sites of interest (battlefields and museums), and had hopes of returning at a later date. (But, we did not get to do so.)

CHAPTER **44**

NSF Fellowships — "Johnny U."

Dewey was selected for his third NSF fellowship in 1968, after we had moved to Dayton. That fellowship was to Western Maryland College in Westminster, Maryland.

Mrs. Robinson was *Number One* on the pop charts, and Johnny Cash performed at Folsom Prison. Dr. Martin Luther King and Senator Robert Kennedy were assassinated. It was a time of revolution, and it forever changed the nation and the world.

1968 was the year of *Burn, Baby Burn*, and social unrest was rampant. It was a tumultuous time. We passed some of the larger cities on the way to Maryland, and we saw the smoke from the riots. The Civil Rights Movement was in full swing, and it defined who we were as a nation – who we became. The Beatles gained prominence. Young people rebelled against authority. Anti-war demonstrations were rampant. The country was in turmoil, and issues over race became primary in the minds of Americans.

We were excited as we prepared to leave for Maryland. It was to be the most extensive trip our kids had been on, and we anticipated showing them the Washington, D.C. area. Dewey and I had been there in 1956, but Candy was only two at the time, and Barry not yet one, so we wanted them to experience the nation's capital when they could better appreciate what they were seeing.

The summer in Maryland was one of the highlights of Dewey's

coaching career. The Baltimore Colts summer training camp was held in Westminster, and for Dewey to be able to be on the field with Johnny Unitas and Ray Lewis was awe-inspiring.

We rented a house next door to the home of a doctor with eight children. There was no lack of excitement for our kids that summer. At night they used flashlights to signal the neighbor children from the second floor bedrooms. They took swimming lessons. We attended the Colts practices. And weekends were spent sightseeing and touring various spots of interest.

We visited Gettysburg, the White House, the Smithsonian, Madison Square Garden, the Washington Zoo, the Statue of Liberty, and other attractions. One weekend was spent in New York City, and we camped overlooking the city. We could see the lights of the city below. (I doubt we would want to do that today.) We went to Indianapolis, and we walked on the Indy 500 track. It was a treasure trove not only of science and football, but of culture and history as well. We had an incredible experience.

(After trekking around the Smithsonian on my recent trip to Washington D.C. for Dewey's induction into the *National Federation of High Schools Hall of Fame*, I marveled at how we kept up with four kids milling around the many exhibits. I am amazed that I wasn't accused of child neglect, due to my inability to keep up with them, particularly Barry who was more adventurous than most.)

I cannot think of a better venue. Dewey appreciated the opportunities provided by the Colts training camp, and he was in coach's heaven. Imagine the excitement and the exhilaration experienced by a small town football coach from Oregon, who got to watch Johnny U. in action, and to be near Bubba Smith and Coach Don Shula.

Armed guards didn't escort players and coaches on and off the field in 1968, and Dewey was delighted that Coach Shula invited him to spend time with the team. He was on the field as much as he had time for. Our entire family became fans of the Baltimore Colts.

The memories of that summer remained special in our minds. I took several photos of our two sons with Johnny U., and I had one made into a poster (after Johnny U. signed it). The boys also had Johnny U. sign a football, and then proceeded to play football with it (the $1,000 football??). At the conclusion of practice most days, Johnny U. spent time throwing passes to our sons. He showed them passing routes, and was a gentleman. We had many wonderful experiences.

(A couple of years prior to our time in Westminster, Gino Marchetti played for the Colts, and years later, Dewey felt privileged to become acquainted with his niece, Jennafer Marchetti, who became one of his surrogate daughters.)

While we were in Maryland, the new Dayton football stadium was built, but we missed the construction. A scrap metal drive and an auction by the Booster Club served as fund-raisers that spring. Erle Parker and other club members went to the bank to get a loan for the remainder of the money needed for the project.

Dewey accepted the invitation to go to Westminster before the stadium became a reality. He did not get to help with (oversee?) the actual construction, but Bill Stoller kept him up-to-date on what happened. Bill was quarterback for the Pirates, and he frequently wrote to Dewey to keep him apprised of the progress.

When we first moved to Dayton, the games were played on a field at the end of the high school, where the middle school is now situated. An old scoreboard was used for scorekeeping, and the scores were changed manually from the back of that board. Our boys were pleased that they were allowed to change the scores on that scoreboard.

When it became evident that the new stadium would be built, Dewey and several Booster Club members visited other stadiums around the Willamette Valley to get ideas. The actual construction began before school dismissed for the summer, and Dewey spent every spare minute at the construction site. He stepped on a nail, and had to get a tetanus shot.

He was allowed to drive one of the bulldozers used in leveling the ground, and was thrilled. It made him feel important and he appreciated watching and helping with the construction. (He hated missing the building of the stadium, but couldn't be in two places at once.) He spent a great deal of time "supervising" the project until we left for Westminster.

The stadium was completed in time for football season, and forty years later, it is still in good condition. There are pockmarks from spikes during track season, as well as other evidence of "wear and tear." But it is one of the nicest stadiums in the Willamette Valley, and is something to be proud of.

A construction worker walked into the principal's office the next fall, and asked, "Where do you want this D-8 Cat?" The principal was astounded. He said, "A D-8 Cat? Who ordered a D-8 Cat?" The worker said, "I had a call for one to clear out under the new stadium." (The worker was sent on his way – a D-8 Cat would have demolished the new structure.)

When Dewey attended the National Science Foundation summer schools, we saved his stipend (most participants spent theirs). It was not hard for us to forego the restaurant meals, doughnuts, etc., that the other participants enjoyed (and considered necessities). We still had fantastic times at each of the locations where he studied.

The stipend was not much ($400 - $800 depending on the length of the summer session), and was to help with living costs (including gasoline -- at that time much less than one dollar per gallon – which in today's world is unbelievable). But when you traveled several thousand miles to your destination, it was expensive. We were happy for Dewey to have the opportunities afforded by the NSF experiences. His horizons were expanded through them, and we as a family were blessed.

CHAPTER 45

I Love Shopping for Cars!

One thing Dewey didn't mind shopping for was a car. He loved cars, and he helped many people in their search for the "right car." He was an avid reader of *Consumer Reports*, and did thorough research before shopping. He was usually available if someone indicated an interest in buying a car. We spent many Saturdays assisting in a purchase. He loved looking at cars, and he also enjoyed spending the money of others more than his own.

In the late '80s we went car shopping with Sharon, and she outlined to the salesman how much she could spend. They could not reach an agreement, so we left. (That was not the way Dewey recommended she handle the situation. He told her to keep her financial situation to herself, but Sharon did not listen to him.)

After our day of shopping, we had dinner at Dewey's parents' home. While we were eating, the phone rang. It was the salesman. He said, "I've worked the figures, and I can meet the terms you laid out." Sharon refused, saying, "Since you couldn't agree when I was there, I'm not coming back to Hillsboro. No deal." When she got off the phone, Dewey was mystified and said, "What's wrong with you? Why didn't you agree to his terms? After all, you're not going to marry the fellow."

Another time Dewey sold one of Sharon's cars at a garage sale. She had a Datsun "Honey Bee" for sale, and he talked one of her customers into buying it. I thought he should have offered to help Randy Freeborn at his car lot, but he did not pursue that venture. (Randy played for Dewey in the '70s, and now has his own lot.)

In 1992, Norman was looking for a Toyota Camry in a burgundy color, and Dewey was delighted to help. He had visited a car lot in Albany the week before, and told Norman, "I know where that car is. I was in Albany last week, and they had it in the exact color you want." They drove to Albany and Norman bought it. Sorry, Randy, but that was before you had your own lot.

When Lexus came to Portland, we visited so Dewey could take a test drive. After we walked around the car lot for several minutes, it became evident we were not considered "viable" customers. (I guess we didn't have the "aura" of a Lexus buyer.) Dewey was disappointed, but "Oh, well!!

Before that event Dewey and Dave Cook visited a lot in McMinnville. Dave drew the salesman aside and said, "Don't pay any attention to that guy. He's just looking. Take care of your other customers." Dave later told Dewey what he had done, and they had a chuckle about it. (Windle sold cars for a while and he told Dewey, "Car dealers would classify you as a WORM.)

Dewey liked cars, old and new (or just cars in general). He particularly loved "old cars," and often went to classic and antique car shows and cruises. He thought it beyond our means to own a classic car, but after we took a look at our finances, we decided he could swing a deal. He was "off and running." (It was good for him to have a project. I wanted him to find a project car to restore, but did not think he would spend the money necessary to complete the job, so I encouraged him to get one that was ready to drive.)

It took several months of looking, but Dewey finally found a '53 Ford coupe in what he considered his "price range." One Saturday morning, he read an ad in the *Salem Statesman-Journal* and said, "Get ready. There's a car in Salem that I would like to look at." We changed clothes, and drove to Salem to see it, but the seller was not home.

Dewey was determined to see that car, so we had lunch and drove around for a while. We returned to that fellow's house several

I LOVE SHOPPING FOR CARS!

times that day. Dewey persisted, and finally located the owner. After driving the car, Dewey decided he did not want to pay the asking price, so we left.

About a month later he again had the paper, and came into the kitchen where I was. He said, "Get ready – we're going to Salem." I asked, "Why? What are we doing?" He said, "The price on 'my' car has been reduced, and I'm going to buy it." Again it took a while for the seller to appear, but Dewey was tenacious.

We made several trips to that fellow's house that day, and Dewey finally caught him and made the deal. The car likely would have sold earlier if the seller had remained at home to show it. (Dewey said he derived more pleasure from the "search" than from the actual "purchase." When he looked for something he had a mission, and he loved the quest.)

Dewey had a great time with his car. He often came to my place of employment, and took me to lunch in it. He took it to the *Amity Pancake Breakfast*. He drove it on cruises and to car shows. He drove it in parades. He even did a "time trial" with it. It was not a super car, but he was satisfied with it. He said, "We were married in 1953, so it's our anniversary car." (He was ever a romantic at heart.)

CHAPTER 46

"Keep Me Out of the Kithchen"

Dewey did not like to cook, but he loved to eat. He loved desserts, especially pie. He appreciated the finer things in life (pie, jam, etc.). He was just a good ol' country boy. Several years ago we joined a group of friends, and had potlucks while we watched boxing matches. (Boxing was one of Dewey's passions. He loved boxing.)

At one of those potlucks was heard, "Round One, Round Two, Round Three," etc. until the count got to "Round Seven." We later learned that Dewey's portions of dessert were being counted. His "fans" had fun watching him enjoy his "goodies." He said, "I hope I am never diagnosed with diabetes. I love desserts so much, it would be difficult for me to give them up."

SANDY BAKER – THE PIE MAKER!! Sandy Baker makes great pies, and one August evening she called and said, "I baked a pie for Dewey, and am setting it out on the front porch for him to pick up after practice. But as Dewey was later than normal (or maybe late as usual), Sandy called again to say she had taken the pie inside, so the coyotes or raccoons would not get it. When Dewey came from practice I said, "Sandy baked a pie for you and left it on the front porch, but when it got so late, she called to say she took it into the house."

With the hope that the pie might still be outside, Dewey and Barry drove to Sandy's house to find that the pie, indeed, was no longer there. But the outdoor motion lights came on startling them, and they felt as though they were being spotlighted.

The next morning they got an early start, and went back to Sandy's house. (They must have "dreamed" about pie.) The pie was enjoyed then (not more than it would have been the previous evening, but at least as much). (Pie for breakfast. Dewey loved it. It was a *DEWEY THING!!*)

Another time Sandy called to inform me she had baked a pie for Dewey. A league meeting was scheduled at Amity, so he got the pie, and went to the meeting. When he arrived at the meeting, he started eating it. One of the other coaches asked, "What do you have there?" He said, "I have this mom who bakes pies, and she thinks she can really bake pies, but they're awful. I just eat them to make her feel good." (Yeah, right! It was a real sacrifice!)

That was a great story to keep from having to share his favorite pie. (Sorry Sandy! Honestly, Dewey loved your pies.) He willingly shared almost anything other than pie! (He shared the love, but not the pie.)

Barry accompanied us to scout a football game one evening, and we stopped at the "Pie Barn" to pick up pies. (Charlene Hill baked great pies and they could be purchased from the "Pie Barn.") Dewey knew the locations where the best pies were to be found. We did not have plates and utensils, so when we got to the game, Dewey and Barry asked the concession stand for such, and they enjoyed pie before the game.

In the late '80s and the early '90s, the Upward Bound Program at Linfield College (my place of employment) held a competition, *The Continental Cookoff*. The students selected the menu and did the cooking, and judges rated the food items. Prizes were awarded. One year Dewey was invited to be a judge, and he accepted the invitation. "Sandwich party loaves," (sandwiches made to look like cake and iced with cheese spread) were popular at the time. Dewey took a slice of one loaf (he thought it was a cake), and saved it for dessert. After his meal, Dewey took a bite and said, "Oh, yuck. Someone put fish in this cake." (I don't think that loaf won any prizes.)

"KEEP ME OUT OF THE KITCHEN"

Before Candy and her husband, Jeff Bornac, were married, they came to our house for a celebration (Thanksgiving or Christmas), and they were amused when I asked Dewey, "What kind of pie do you want? Do you want pumpkin, apple or cherry?" His response was, "Yes!" (He wanted a slice of each.)

Candy also laughs about the time we ate with them at a restaurant, and the dessert tray was displayed for selection. Dewey said, "I want that one," and tried to take it. He thought the plastic samples were the real "McCoy." I found that hilarious, and we all had a good laugh about it.

When Dormie Groth made jam for her family each summer, she prepared a special stash for Dewey. Before she died, she instructed her family to be certain he got his jam. Dormie was a staunch Dayton fan and her sons, Larry and John, played for the Pirates and her daughter, Sue, was a cheerleader.

Denise Wall also made jam for Dewey, and one time when she and Max brought him his "allotment," Max came into the kitchen and asked, "Which is Dewey's favorite jam? Is it strawberry or raspberry?" I told him, BOTH. Max laughed, and went into the living room and told Denise, "Vera said Dewey's favorite is strawberry AND raspberry."

Dewey appreciated homemade jam. When he ate at *Shari's Restaurant*, he asked for a "to-go" box, so he could take his biscuit home to enjoy with Denise's jam. He was a jam purist (none of those little cartons of jam from the restaurant for him). He was spoiled, but he loved it. He was plied with pies, cakes, etc. at church socials or other events. He appreciated the finer things in life, particularly food.

Dewey was not a cook, and did not function well in the kitchen, but he loved to eat. He told me that, when we were first married he tried making cookies, but they were such a "flop," he did not try again. He said, "We didn't have one of the ingredients I needed, so I substituted something." (I don't know what we lacked, but he did not like his finished product.) I do not recall that specific incident, so maybe he pawned those off on one or more of his unsuspecting buddies (like he did his bologna).

A BAREFOOT BOY FROM OKLAHOMA

When a microwave appeared in the teachers' lounge the last part of Dewey's teaching career, he started taking left-overs or something else to be heated for lunch. His frequent question, "How long should I heat this?" was usually responded to with, "Two minutes, Dewey."

After Dewey retired from teaching, the "cabbage soup" diet was popular. I often fixed a batch for him to heat for his lunch, but he tired of having to heat it, so he started eating it right from the refrigerator. Yuck!

Dewey was always appreciative when I served a meal, probably because he realized that he might be given kitchen patrol if he wasn't. When our kids left home, he told me that I didn't have to cook again if I didn't want to. But he constituted such an appreciative audience, that he made it pleasurable. Actually, I enjoy cooking, but don't do much since he left.

One time I had the flu, and stayed in bed for a couple of days. I asked Dewey to fix me a cup of tea, but gave up when I could not explain where the tea was stored. It was not worth the effort. I think God knew what he was doing when He took Dewey to be with Him before me. I do not know how he would have coped with meals, laundry, etc. He was good at football, but not at household chores.

Of course, I am not good at football, or at outside tasks (or much inside either), so maybe it's a "toss-up." I also do not know how Dewey would have handled giving up football. It would have saddened him not to be able to coach. He would have been heart-broken to have to give it up.

CHAPTER 47

After Hours

One night Dewey went to Hillsboro with a group of enthusiasts to watch boxing on television. They returned late, and he was the only one in the group who did not drink, so he was the "designated driver." He kept the van window rolled down so he would not go to sleep. But he got his group home safely. (That was before the times when we had potlucks for boxing matches.)

Several times Dewey accompanied Earl McKinney and/or Wil Wilson on deep-sea fishing excursions. He suffered from seasickness, so after several such trips, he declared, "Why should I go for a fun day doing something that makes me sick?" He did not go again.

In 2003 Crystal Cruises had super deals on their cruises. It was the year of the *SARS Epidemic*, but it was also the year of our 50th wedding anniversary. Crystal re-routed their cruises that had been scheduled for China to more local destinations. Kathy Lambert got us a fantastic deal, and we had a wonderful time.

We booked our cruise to the Mexican Riviera, and one night we had lobster. Our waiter told us that we could have as many lobsters as we wanted the next night. (We each had two lobsters and that satisfied our cravings for several weeks.)

Dewey's biggest concern on the cruise was seasickness, but he was not troubled by it. I guess that was because the ship is larger than the ones used for deep-sea fishing. (Before we boarded the ship, someone gave him a patch to wear, but he later did fine without one.)

Mandated by a teacher's salary, we made use of coupons for our daily living. In the early 1980s, a restaurant in Salem, *Truffles*, advertised a Friday night seafood buffet. *Two-for-One* deals for *Truffles* often appeared in the Friday edition of the *Salem Statesman-Journal*." Norman lived with us for a time, and one Friday afternoon, Dewey came by my office after work, and said, "How would you like to go to *Truffles* for dinner?" I said, "Yum! That sounds good! I won't have to cook and I'm hungry."

We drove to our house to get the coupon, but when we got there we found that the part of the paper with the coupon in it was missing. I said, "Oh, boy! Tonight I'll bet we're going to meet Norman's latest." (Norman was quite secretive about his relationships, but we were certain that he had a "lady friend.")

We drove to the restaurant, and were ushered inside. We were escorted to our seats, and we passed right by Norman and his friend. He covered his embarrassment well, and introduced us, but we chuckled all evening about his discomfiture.

We used those and other *Two-for-One* offers for dining out, and I have utilized grocery coupons religiously for years. I have been called, "The Coupon Queen," but I'm not nearly as good about saving with coupons as some are.

For several years, Shawn Sutton was an appraiser for estate sales, etc., and she told us when a particularly interesting sale came up. We invited Norman, Sharon, and Dewey's mother and aunt to go with us to Portland to the sale. Lefty met us there, so he could see the "goodies" also. We spent the day looking at the various items. When the time came, I was the successful bidder on a box of baskets and picture frames. WHOOPEE!!

One of the items in my box was a framed Christmas card. When I got into Norman's van to return home, my purchase was being discussed. I examined the frame to see what the "big deal" was, and I discovered a fifty-dollar bill on the back!! I had paid three dollars for the box, so it really was a "big deal." I had heard of such things happening, but had never experienced such "luck" first-hand. (And the frame was not even the reason I had bid on the box.)

What a deal! I was excited and showed everyone in the van. Then I looked at Norman, and THE LIGHT DAWNED!! I said, "You put that there didn't you?" He said, "Yes, and I was beginning to wonder how I could get it back." I told him, "Well, I'm awfully slow, but had it come to me sooner, I would have asked you to pull into a *Goodwill Donor Station* so I could donate that frame. I could imagine you squirming on that."

Lefty was with us when I discovered my "good fortune," but he left before I discovered Norman's "ruse." He stopped and told Barry and Brent about my "find." I later had to tell everyone that I was the victim of a "cruel hoax." I vowed to get even with Norman, but was never successful.

The first time Dewey met Jerry Sutton, he said, "You wouldn't happen to be related to Joe Sutton by any chance?" Jerry replied, "Uh, oh! Yes, he's my brother. Why?" Dewey said, "My daughter bought a Dodge Colt from Joe when she was a student at Linfield College. She and Joe brought the car to our house, and I took a 'test drive' in it. When we finished that drive, I advised Candy to forget that car, and to look elsewhere." (It was Dewey's assumption that the car had been through the teenage "mill" of driving.)

A few days later, Candy appeared at our home, driving the "infamous" Dodge Colt. She had purchased it!! Her father was disappointed, but I guess we are all entitled to our mistakes (and that car was a mistake). It spent more time in the repair shop than it did on the road. OUCH!! She had new upholstery, etc. installed, and it looked beautiful, but was never serviceable.

She was employed on a part-time basis at the Outdoor Store in McMinnville, and she frequently had to beg rides to and from work, as the car often would not start. She carried a case of oil in the trunk, and routinely asked the service station attendants to put oil in it for her. One attendant asked, "Do you take your own steak into a restaurant, and ask them to cook it for you?" (After several such fiascos, she learned to put the oil in herself, but she soon traded the car.)

Dewey was protective of his daughters, and when the time for the "dating game" arrived, he was reluctant. Of course, he had to let go and allow them to grow up. When Candy went on her first date it was with a Dayton football player (who else would it be?).

Dewey could not abide knowing that his precious daughter – his "first-born," was going on a date with one of the young men he worked with on the football field. He loved his football players, but "family is family." (Dewey wanted to keep his daughters out of the arena of the dating game.)

That evening he stayed upstairs when the fellow came to get Candy. He refused to come down to greet the "date." When the young man arrived, he asked, "Where's 'Coach'?" I said, "He had an appointment elsewhere." (LIAR!! LIAR!!)

And Dewey was devastated when Jeff Bornac asked him for Candy's hand in marriage. He realized that he would no longer be the MAIN MAN in her life, and that he would be on the sidelines. He recalled her life as a baby, and then as a teenager. He remembered her first steps, and the way she grasped his hand as she toddled along. He remembered soothing her at night when she awakened from a bad dream. He remembered drying her tears.

And now she would be holding the hand of another. She would confide in Jeff rather than her father, and he was overwhelmed. It's so hard to let go. It seemed to him that it was only yesterday that she was a baby. Children grow up way too soon!

When Dewey heard the song, *I Was Born Under a Wandering Star*, he was convinced it was from a movie, but did not know which one. Candy came home from a date one night, and wakened him to tell him, "Dad, I just saw *Paint Your Wagon*, and your song, *I Was Born Under a Wandering Star* is in it." (The next night we went to that movie, and we also bought a sound track.)

Dewey enjoyed telling ghost stories, and he liked to sneak around to the girls' bedroom to scare them. He scratched on their window, or thumped on the wall to hear their squeals and giggles.

AFTER HOURS

They pleaded with him, "Daddy, please scare us." They loved the thrill of anticipation.

Even as long as I knew Dewey, it was many years before I realized that his first story was most often not the truth. (In fact, I bit on his stories until the very end.) He liked to get me with his humor. One time he told me something, and I repeated it to several friends before I mentioned it to him again. He was aghast. He said, "You didn't tell that did you?" I admitted I had, so I had to go back and retract my story.

But eventually I got retribution. In 1978, Dewey visited his parents in Muskogee, Oklahoma. While he was gone my friend, Margaret Macaulay, purchased a new lawnmower, and gave me her old one. I took it home, and when he returned and saw it, he asked, "Where did you get that lawnmower?" I said, "I bought it from Margaret. She bought a new one and I bought it for $100." He said, "You did WHAT??" I said, "Well, it sounded like a really good deal, so I bought it for $100. I thought you would be pleased." He said, "You didn't really do that did you?" (He was hoping I was not that stupid!) I finally had to tell him the truth before he blew a gasket. I loved it. I had gotten one over on him.

Dewey enjoyed Native American powwows, and we attended many. When our grandson, Zack, was eight we took him to a powwow at Rickreall, and he was enthralled with the drums, the eagle feathers and the dancing. We also attended many at Grand Ronde. One time we took two ladies from China (both Linfield College students) to a powwow in Canby. They enjoyed the evening, and remarked, "Their babies look like our babies."

Toward the end of our first year in Dayton, I joined a knitting group. One night a week we drove to Enid McManimie's house. (Enid was Dante Rosario's grandmother. Dewey taught with Enid at Dayton, and he also taught two of her daughters and several of her grandchildren.) As a carry-over from his college days, we were again driving around on "bald" tires. I did not work the first two years we were in Dayton, so I often drove without him. I said, " I want to change the tire the next time we have a flat." (Yeah, right??)

A BAREFOOT BOY FROM OKLAHOMA

When I prepared to go to class one evening, I found that we had a flat, so I asked him to supervise me. He instructed me in the procedure, and stood watching as several cars went by. We lived across from the high school, and the next day someone asked him, "Why did you make Vera change the tire?" He really chuckled about that. He did not mind being the object of a joke.

When Brenda graduated from Linfield College in January of 1978, she secured a position as substitute for a teacher who was on maternity leave. She moved home with us for a short period of time, and she and Dewey carpooled. She drove our car to work, and left Dewey at Dayton each morning before going to her place of employment.

Some evenings she visited friends at Linfield, and when she brought the car home, the gas gauge registered *EMPTY*. Dewey asked, "Brenda, do you see any gas stations in the hills near our home?" She told him, "No, Dad, I don't." He said, "Well, if we run out of gas on the way to school some morning, you are going to push."

Sure enough, one morning the car sputtered to a stop, so Dewey got behind the wheel, and Brenda (in her high heels and skirt) started pushing. She was laughing when a car with three men pulled up behind them. Two of them got out to help her push. She and Dewey imagined the men wondered why that "big lug" was letting a young lady push the car. It was less than a quarter of a mile to the nearest service station, so they made it okay, but they found the incident hilarious.

The youth group from the Baptist Church in Dayton planned to scale Mt. Hood one year, and Dewey agreed to accompany them. Tents were set up when they arrived at the mountain, and Dewey crawled into a sleeping bag. It was raining, and the temperature was near freezing. The next morning the mountain was closed to climbing (the snow was wet, and was as slick as ice). When the climb was cancelled, Dewey crawled back into his "nest," and went to sleep. He said, "Thank the Lord we didn't have to climb that mountain."

It was fortunate, as Dewey was not in the best physical condition he had ever been in, and he had never tried to climb a mountain before. He did not know why he agreed to accompany the group, but was happy not to have to attempt mountain climbing. He questioned his sanity. Upon his return, he said, "What was I thinking? I must have lost my mind. I have no idea how to climb a mountain."

When Brent was a youngster, one of his childish pranks was to hide under a blanket in the back of our station wagon, and have us ask, "Where's Brent?" (It was something like "peek-a-boo" with a baby.) On our way to Portland one Saturday, we stopped for gas at a service station.

When we left the station, Dewey and I chatted back and forth for several blocks. I asked where Brent was, and then several more times I said, "Where is Brent? We haven't heard anything from him for a while." When I looked over the back seat, I panicked. I said, "Oh, my gosh! He really isn't here. We've got to go back to that station."

Dewey said, "Are you serious?" I said, "Yes, I'm serious! He really isn't here!" (We had not realized he had gotten out for a bathroom break.) We immediately returned to the service station to be greeted by a very frightened and sad little boy, with tears streaming down his face. We were fortunate not to be charged with child abandonment. Most likely, Brent would have pressed charges had he known how.

Dewey's good friend, Garnet Wright, used to smoke, and one day found his son emulating him. He decided to put a quick end to that, so he got a box of cigars and took him to the basement and closed the door. When Garnet's wife, Norma, opened the basement door she asked, "What's going on down there?" Garnet said, "We're having a smoking party. It's for boys only. You just go on and we'll be up soon." His son turned white, but Garnet told him, "Just keep it up. Inhale! You're doing fine." His son got deathly ill, and to this day he does not smoke. (A good lesson.)

One Thursday evening I met Dewey at the *Pirate's Den* (the hangout across from the high school which is no longer in use), for the team meal before the Friday game. He was crushed He had received a letter from an Amity fan who was offended by a statement he made to the media. He was quoted, "Amity is a good little team." The writer berated him, stating that Amity did not have a "little" team.

Dewey's intent had been to brag on the opposition. He had not meant to be derogatory. He vowed not to speak to the newspaper again. The reason was not that he had been misquoted, but that what he said was misconstrued. He could withstand criticism, but when he felt he had offended someone, it gave him cause for concern. He did not have the opportunity to apologize to the writer of that letter, but he regretted his statement.

We went to Phoenix in 1999 (one of the years the Denver Broncos won the Super Bowl), and as we were exiting Sky Harbor Airport, were hailed by two of our former Boone classmates, Betty and Ann Chandler. Betty lived in Phoenix, and we exchanged greetings, phone numbers, etc., and proceeded on our way.

At the conclusion of the Super Bowl game, Dewey called Betty and told her, "They need to replace that John Elway. He did a lousy job today!" (Of course, he was joking. Elway had a *SUPER GAME!!*) Betty didn't recognize Dewey's voice, and responded (as any loyal Broncos fan would), "WHO IS THIS??" She was indignant that someone could disparage "her" Broncos, but Dewey thought it hilarious and he chuckled about her response.

Dewey once piloted a World War II Navy trainer plane, and I have a video of him. Sharon, Norman and I, as well as Sandy and Verlyn Baker were on that excursion. Verlyn also piloted one of the trainers, and he and Dewey got a thrill from their "Warbird Flights." Norman asked me, "Would you want to fly that plane?" I said, "No, but Dewey does many things I don't want to."

A trainer flew over football practice several years later, and Dewey stopped practice. He looked up and told the team, " I flew one of those once." They scoffed, so at Sunday night films, he started with the video of his flight. At the conclusion of that season, the team gave him a leather helmet and a miniature plane.

He also took a ride in a helicopter at the Hillsboro Airport. When Norman was taken by life-flight to Portland for surgery, he said, "Dewey, I got to do something you haven't. I got to ride in a helicopter." (I did not disillusion him by telling him that Dewey had previously done that.)

One of Dewey's favorite movies was The Gods Must Be Crazy. When Dewey saw an ad for the movie, Where The Green Ants Dream, he wanted to see it. It was to be shown at Salem Cinema, a theater where "artsy" movies are shown. Dewey did not want to go to Salem, so we visited every video rental store in McMinnville to see if we could rent it.

Of course, I was elected to check at each place (Dewey was good at appointing me for such tasks). When I asked for, Where The Green Ants Dream, they looked at me as if I were the crazy one. Needless to say, we went to Salem to watch the movie (which was about the aborigines of Australia or New Zealand).

He also liked Dr. Zhivago, but I had to twist his arm to get him to take me to see it. Zhivago became one of his all-time favorites. One of Dewey's students saw that movie, and told Dewey, "This old boy gallops on his horse to one woman, and then gallops back to the other one, with a little fighting in between." Dewey came from school that night, and with his devilish grin, told me about it. (He did not care for action movies, car chases, etc., and was puzzled when someone recommended one of such caliber to him, but he loved *Dr. Zhivago*.)

He also enjoyed John Candy in *Planes, Trains, and Automobiles*. One time, when Dewey visited Jonell, her kids insisted he watch that movie. He was hooked! He watched it very time we went to Denver. Another favorite was *A Christmas Story*. As a child, he wanted a *Red Ryder BB gun* (one of several things along with a rubber tractor he coveted, but never acquired). He enjoyed that movie, as he could relate to the events in it.

As a high school student, Dewey concocted his own weights by filling bags with sand and putting them on a bar. Those bags were his early attempt at weightlifting, and he and Lefty became avid weightlifters.

He brought the first weight training equipment into the school at Dayton, and showed kids how to properly lift weights. He was a strong proponent of weight lifting, and he struggled to get his players to train diligently. It was a work of endurance as well as a challenge to get his players to lift weights.

When he arrived at Dayton, he was definitely ahead of the curve in strength training. His shoulders were broad and his forearms huge. He looked like *Mr. Clean*. He trained with the students, and was "buff." When he retired, he donated four sets of Olympic weights to Dayton High School.

In 1967, Dewey and Dick Jones, the superintendent of schools, went to Portland and purchased a *Universal Gym* (a weight machine) for the school. We lived across from the high school, and Dewey anxiously waited for it to arrive. Brent told me that the young guys could also hardly wait for it to come.

Richie England (whom Dewey nicknamed, "Hess," as he reminded him of a former player) told me recently that Dewey pushed them hard in their efforts. "Hess" said, "We bench pressed

225 pounds several times, and then 'Sully' took over, and pressed it ONE HUNDRED MILLION TIMES. He made it look easy."

I remember how Dewey looked when we first went to Dayton. He was tall with a regal bearing. His blue eyes twinkled with humor, and they showed his emotion. He had an air of authority that was seldom challenged. He had a love for life and every day was an experience.

Tom Smythe, the Lakeridge High School head football coach, said, "I can remember Dewey in a white, short-sleeved dress shirt, red and black tie . . . boy he looked good. You looked at him, and thought oh, God, I hope their players aren't as studly as the coach. Dewey was a stud then and he's still a stud." (For a high school football coach he was definitely a "hunk.")

We went to Geary, Oklahoma four times to visit his roots. We visited several of his cousins, aunts and other relatives. There was a "Sullivan Cousin Reunion" in 1999, and we have a video of Dewey singing in the Geary Christian Church choir. He was not an adept singer, but he loved to sing.

A BAREFOOT BOY FROM OKLAHOMA

Dewey often entertained (entertained??) his football teams by singing on road trips. I do not think they truly appreciated his abilities, however. One of his favorite songs for such trips was, *On Top of Old Smokey*. He loved that song, possibly because it was popular while we were in high school. Another favorite was *The Yellow Rose of Texas*.

We visited the Air Force Academy when Shawn Finnicum graduated from there. As we prepared to leave Portland, we learned we could take an earlier flight, but to do so, we would have to take our camera and film from the checked luggage and carry it on. We unpacked, and Dewey took the camera from the suitcase, and placed it around his neck.

We prepared to go to the ceremony and did not have the camera. We thought back, and remembered that Dewey had taken it from the luggage. When he was seated on the plane, he removed it and placed it under the seat.

In retrospect he said he thought a lady's purse was under the seat, but did not report it. (I do not know why he did not mention it.) It was the camera. We encountered a thunder and lightning storm over Denver, and had to circle the airport for more than an hour, so our "earlier" flight arrived at approximately the time we were scheduled to arrive.

The fly-over during Shawn's graduation was incredible. Garnet Wright took photos for us, and one of my favorites is of Dewey wearing Shawn's Air Force cap. It is a great representation of Air Force "brass."

Garnet and Jonell accompanied us to the graduation, and we visited the Arkansas Valley after the ceremony. Garnet stayed with his mother in Pueblo, and Dewey, Jonell and I rented a motel room. The next day, we visited Al Tilton in La Junta, and had a good visit. When we returned to Denver, we were fortunate to retrieve the camera from *Lost and Found*.

We attended many weddings, funerals, graduations and birthday parties during Dewey's forty-two years at Dayton. (Dwight Ediger recently told me that Dewey and I were *Funeral Crashers*. When Wade Fergus graduated from Dayton, I let Dewey talk me into not attending the ceremony. Dewey gave his promise that we would go to the receptions afterward, so I thought we could get away with it.

The football team had an award for Dewey (they should have warned me and we would have attended). He was not in attendance when the team called for him to come forward. Wade said, "But Coach is always here." (There's nothing like announcing to the general public that you are absent. Roger Lorenzen often said, "If there is food, Dewey will be here.") I did not let Dewey miss another graduation.

While our children were growing up, we did not attend as many celebrations of life as we did in later years. When the kids moved out, we had more time for rituals and ceremonies. Due to his coaching commitments, Dewey missed some of our sons' athletic competitions and our daughters' activities, but he made an effort to attend as many as possible.

When Dewey realized how many of his former players were struggling with the problems of alcohol and/or drug abuse, he attended *Alcoholics Anonymous* meetings with Randy Freeborn. He felt the consternation experienced by those who had become mired in the morass of addiction. As a family, we had also struggled with the problems associated with such abuse.

Dewey related to the pain, and he made it his mission to learn what motivated their insecurities. He took it on his shoulders, and tried to learn as much as he could about the problems involved. He felt he might have been able to help in some way.

Several years ago Dewey heard KaiLee Arnold sing, and was impressed. He told her, "I want to be your manager." KaiLee has done several compact disc recordings, and is a talented young lady.

Of course, Dewey has moved on. He is now in heaven, and no longer struggles with earthly things, while KaiLee is on her way to stardom here on earth. She has performed extensively for various local events, and she performed at the *Third Annual Dewey Sullivan Golf Scramble* (now the *Dewey Sullivan Classic*) in August of 2008. I like to think Dewey is overseeing her success from a better vantage point than any of us here below.

CHAPTER **48**

Call Me "Grandpa"

God blessed us with four beautiful (my thoughts) children, and five wonderful grandchildren. Dewey loved children and welcomed his grandchildren. He said, "If I had known how much fun grandchildren would be, I would have skipped parenthood and gone directly to being a grandfather."

Our granddaughter, Lauren, was born October 9, 1984, and we were thrilled. We went Christmas shopping that year, and Dewey selected a cute, little red dress for her. That is amazing considering how he hated shopping, but he was proud of his selection and enjoyed seeing her in it. (That dress was one of his few "selections," and he asked Brenda about it several years ago. I believe that Brenda still has it.)

One grandchild proved not to be enough for us. Brent got into the action and married Debbie on Christmas Eve, 1985. Debbie had two daughters, Jami and Nicole, so we were suddenly blessed with two new granddaughters. (I had scheduled Dewey's second trip to Kenya, before the wedding announcement was made, so he missed the event.)

We enjoyed our grandchildren immensely and soon welcomed two more. Zack was born January 24, 1987 and Leah on February 4, 1987. Ironically our twins, Brent and Brenda, were born ten minutes apart, and their children were born ten days apart. When

Dewey's father met Zack for the first time, he made the statement that Zack could replace him as he was on his way out. (Zack's great-grandfather died in November that year.)

We often entertained our five grandchildren with slumber parties, and had some great times. Brenda and Jay had a "date" one evening, and left Lauren and Leah with us. We took Dewey's mother to dinner, and after taking her home, planned to attend a basketball game. We asked the girls if they would like to go to the game. Lauren, was six at the time, and said she would go, but Leah said she did not want to, so I left Dewey and Lauren in Dayton with the understanding that we would go back for them when the game ended.

When Leah and I arrived at our house Leah told me, "I can see in the dark, so you don't have to turn on the lights." She promptly walked into a door, and things progressed from bad to worse. She said, "I don't know why my parents left me with you." I said, "Your mom and dad have a date, so you're to stay with us tonight." She replied, "Well, they could have gotten a babysitter." (BELIEVE ME – ABOUT THAT TIME I WAS WISHING THEY HAD!!) Someone brought Dewey and Lauren home after the game, and the next day Leah's attitude had a definite adjustment. I guess she was just tired (I hope!)

Another time we prepared for a slumber party with the grandchildren. Barry and I took four of them to select rental movies for the evening, and Leah stayed with Dewey at Barry's house. She curled up in a sleeping bag, and read a book about the frontier. When she came to the part about chicken pot pie, she looked up at Dewey and asked, "Grandpa, have you ever had chicken pot pie?" He said, "Yes, I have, and it's delicious." She said, "Yuck! It doesn't sound very good." (We later took them to *Kentucky Fried Chicken*, where she tried it and liked it.)

Candy and Brenda accompanied Dewey and our five grandchildren to *Disneyland* in June of 1995. What a crew! Dewey felt the necessity of having one or more females escort their entourage to Disneyland, as he had previously had experience with a mixed group. One summer afternoon when our grandchildren were young, he took three of them and two other grandchildren, Tony and Karina Lorenzen, to a children's fair in Wilsonville.

Things went well until the girls needed a "potty" break, and Dewey wondered how he was going to chaperone the two groups (boys and girls). He asked one of the ladies at the face-painting booth to keep an eye on the boys, while he accompanied the girls to the bathroom.

When he returned, he told the boys it was their turn. They replied, "We've already gone." He asked, "Where did you go?" They pointed to the bushes, and Dewey said, "Oh, my gosh! Let's get out of here before we get into trouble. They might kick us out or have us arrested."

When they went to Disneyland, Dewey enjoyed going on the rides with his grandkids. He had a lot of fun as he watched them savor the good times. (Zack was given twenty dollars to spend, and it was gone by the end of the first day.)

Dewey said he followed our two youngest (then eight-years-old) into the gift shop. The clerk there told him they were her favorite customers. (I imagine it was a daily experience for them.) While in the gift shop, Zack and Leah purchased six-foot rubber snakes, and had fun startling people with them. When they boarded the plane for their return flight, the stewardesses made them check their snakes at the front, much to their chagrin. The stewardesses did not want them to frighten the other passengers.

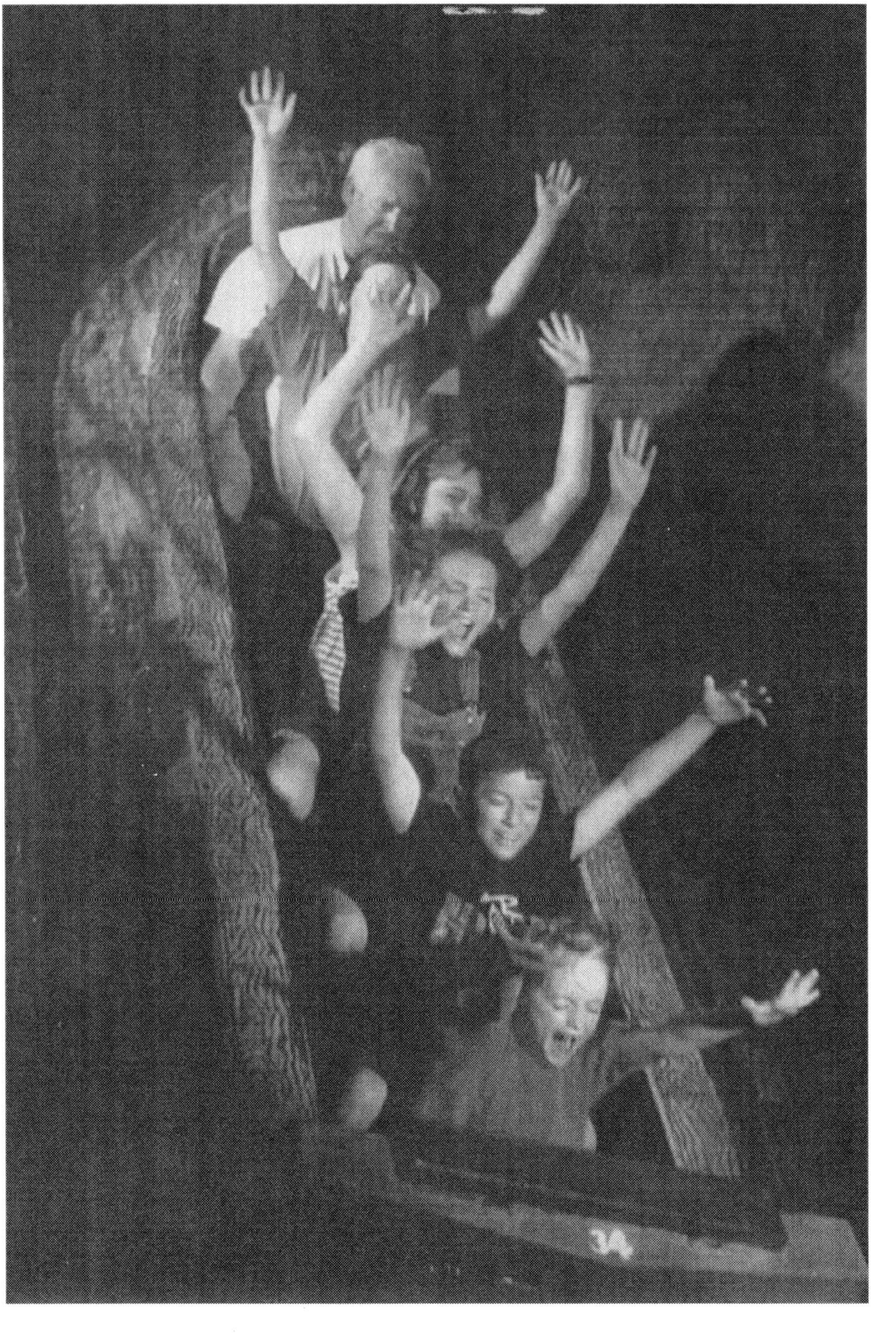

CALL ME "GRANDPA"

When Lauren was three, she loved to play school. We stopped by Megan Blackwell's home one afternoon, and the Blackwells gave us a desk with a blackboard for Lauren. We took it home and put it on our deck. When Brenda and Jay came by several days later, I told Lauren that she could have the desk the next time her parents brought her back to visit, and had the station wagon to carry it in.

I came from work about a week later, and the desk was gone. I asked Dewey, "Where's that desk that was on the deck?" He said, "I took it to *Goodwill*." I said, "What?? Oh, my goodness! I promised that to Lauren. She'll be so upset." He said, "She won't remember." I said, "Yes, she will!"

When Brenda and Jay returned, Lauren came into the house, and asked, "Grandma, where's my desk?" I said, "Grandpa took it to *Goodwill* for a needy child." She started to cry. Brenda said, "Lauren, honey, you know that we give your old toys away so other kids can play with them." She said. "But I don't like grown-ups to lie to me." (I felt terrible. Thanks a lot, Dewey.)

We often took our grandchildren to the *Oregon Zoo*, and Dewey enjoyed watching the grizzlies. He told Zack to notice the log that a large grizzly had shredded with his claws. In response Zack told him, "You're not more stronger than a grizzly." Dewey found that hilarious. Zack loved to bug his grandfather.

One day Zack was riding in our pickup with Dewey, and he put his hand on the gearshift. Dewey told him, "It's not smart to put your hand on the gearshift when someone is driving." A few days later they went somewhere, and Zack again put his hand on the gearshift. He looked up at Dewey, and inquired, "Grandpa, am I bugging you?"

Clouds of steam were escaping when we drove by the *Oregon Steel Mill* one day.. Zack matter-of-factly told us "I used to think that's where clouds come from." (Kids say the darnedest things, and have such interesting perceptions.)

One night Zack stayed with us without his sisters. When bedtime came, we bedded him in a sleeping bag in the family room, and went to bed in our bedroom. About two o'clock in the morning, he pattered down the hall to our room. Dewey got up and got him a drink, and then put him to bed on the floor at his side of the bed. Zack then raised up on one elbow, and inquired, "What are we going to do now, Grandpa?" Dewey chuckled and said, "We're going to go back to sleep, Zack!"

Another time, Barry and Zack spent the night at our house, and early in the morning, a loud cry came from the bedroom where Zack slept. Barry got up to see what the trouble was, and took Zack to the kitchen for a drink. Dewey also got up, and went to see what the commotion was.

Barry was holding Zack who held a small truck. He tugged on the wired remote, and Dewey said, "What in the world is going on out here?" Barry said, "There's something wrong with his truck. He's unhappy about it." After several minutes, Barry decided that Zack wanted the wire removed from his truck so he cut it off. That seemed to satisfy him. *(After all, big trucks don't have wires attached to them.)*

In 2001 Zack traveled with us to Colorado. We had a great time showing him the area. We visited Meeker (where Dewey once coached), and Dewey told him there were often deer on the football field. As if on cue, there were deer on the field. We met with several football players who played for Dewey in 1962 and 1963, and had a nice time catching up on what had happened in their lives.

Zack went to Mazatlan with us in 2005 and 2006. Dewey enjoyed watching Zack's enthusiasm for what he saw and did. (I guess he lived vicariously through his grandson.) The first time Zack went with us, we drove through a seedy part of town, and Dewey envisioned Zack thinking that was where we were going to stay. He enjoyed Zack's reaction, and asked, "What do you think of Mazatlan?"

When Zack was in the eighth grade, Norman and I drove to Sherwood to see him play in an afternoon football game. After going to every school in Sherwood, we learned the game would be played at seven o'clock that evening under the lights at the high school.

I told Norman to go back to Dayton so we could get Dewey to go to the game with us. Norman said, "He won't go." I said,

CALL ME "GRANDPA"

"Yes, he will." When we got to Dayton, I went on the practice field, and Dewey asked, "What's wrong?" I told him, "Zack's football game is going to be played tonight under the lights at Sherwood High School." Dewey turned to the other coaches, and said, "Carry on. I'm going to Zack's game." To this day I believe Norman was amazed that Dewey would leave practice, even for Zack's game.

At the end of Zack's eighth grade year of school, the question arose as to where he would attend high school. Dewey decided that, if Zack were to go to school in McMinnville, he would retire from football for four years, so he could watch his games. Zack had attended nine years of school in the McMinnville School District, and was firmly entrenched there. It was a difficult decision for Zack to make. But I am so glad that Zack agreed (however reluctantly) to go to Dayton.

I think Dewey and Zack had a truly special relationship, and their friendship was not in jeopardy. Candy feared their grandfather/grandson love might be harmed, but they worked it out okay. At practice, Dewey often asked Zack if the team had worked hard enough, and Zack replied, "Yes, they've worked their little hearts out," or some other such thing.

As a little boy, Zack had stated, "Grandpa is my best friend," and that relationship was what Candy worried about. Dewey picked Zack up from kindergarten, and took him to lunch on a daily basis, and they became quite close. After his last high school football game, Zack's Uncle Jeff asked him how it was to play for Dewey and Zack replied, "It was awesome." I think that surprised Jeff, but I believe the statement was heartfelt.

When Megan Blackwell was five, we stopped by her home one afternoon. On the way, Dewey had gotten sleepy, and had crawled into the back seat. When we arrived, Megan came to the car and looked in. She giggled, and asked, "How'd you get him in there?" (I guess she thought I had physically placed him there!)

Dewey doted on his grandchildren (and he had many of them — most not biological). He was called "Papa Dewey," "Grandpa Dewey," "Grandpa," etc. Spencer Payne was a baby when Dewey

303

met him. When Spencer's parents, Tim and Andrea Payne, flew to Florida to adopt him as a newborn, they could not get him released to go to Oregon, so they stayed and toured the city. At one restaurant Tim, who was forty, was told by an older gentleman, "It's really nice of you to care for your grandson." (I still enjoy reminding Tim of that.)

When Dewey met Spencer, he held him and declared, "This guy is going to be a football player." Spencer's parents, Tim and Andrea, replied, "Oh, no, Dewey, Spencer will never play football."

However, Dewey was correct, and Spencer is a multi-sport athlete, excelling at everything he tries, much to the delight of his parents, who blame Dewey for his prediction. (Dewey and the McMinnville football coach, Greg McNally, often

joked about who would get Spencer. Greg had Andrea sign a contract that stated that Spencer would go to McMinnville.)

Spencer is but one of the many young people Dewey thought of as grandchildren. Through the years Dewey attended Spencer's activities and reveled in the fact that he could be part of Spencer's life. After Spencer scored a touchdown a couple of years ago, he came to his dad and asked, "Do you think Dewey would like that?"

In January of 2008, I received a note from Spencer who was in the 7th grade at the time, and a delight, "Dear Vera, thank you for coming to a lot of our football games and always being so nice and still having time to go support Dayton. That must be hard. This year it would be cool if you could come to one of our basketball games. It was fun when you and the Mondeauxs came to dinner. We should do that again. Tell Barry and Brent I said hi. I think I am a little taller than you, too. My dad has known you for a long time. You're like a big part in our family and that's pretty cool to me. Have a Happy New Year. Love, Spencer"

Dewey's love of sports was intertwined with his love of kids, and he enjoyed working with them, and seeing them enjoy their activities. When we visited Mexico (or Africa), he could not resist the charms of the children. He gave candy to the African children who held out their hands and said, "Sweets," and he bought gum from the Mexican children we met on the streets. When we walked somewhere, he could be counted on to be the last in line, because he had to stop to see the kids.

After our five grandchildren, we were blessed with two great-grandsons. Evan was born in 2003, and Ryan in 2004. Dewey was proud of them, and loved getting on the floor to play with them. His legacy lives on through his grandchildren and great-grandchildren. (I told Zack he is an extension of his grandfather.)

Dewey often said he would like a second chance at parenthood. He felt he could learn from his mistakes. I was not so certain, and did not want to expend the energy going through a second time what we had already experienced. I feared we might repeat our initial mistakes. However, there are no "do-overs" in life. Dewey was a better parent than me in that he missed our kids, and he mourned when they left home for college. I welcomed my newfound freedom. It was nice to see them when they came to visit, but he would have kept them with us forever

To know Dewey Sullivan was to be a member of his family – a family that spanned generations, and included thousands. But unlike most of us who have our children grow up and leave home, Dewey had an unending pool from which to draw. His children (his players and students) grew up and left the nest, but were replaced by a new group the following year. Each group was welcomed into his "family." He loved each one, and was always delighted to learn how they progressed after going into the outside world – the world beyond Dayton.

CHAPTER 49

Quips and Quotes

Lyn Lumley coached football at Willamina High School for several years, and he and Dewey had a relationship that revolved around kidding each other. One afternoon at a junior varsity game, Lyn disagreed with a call made by the referee. He yelled across the field, "Hey, Dewey, I didn't know your brother was going to referee tonight." Dewey responded, "That's not my brother – that's my uncle." They enjoyed giving each other a hard time.

In our early days at Dayton, I sat near the top of the stadium for football games. I later moved to a lower vantage point to avoid hearing all the coaching that was espoused. One mother with two sons who played for Dayton was rather outspoken. The older of the two was a running back, and when the team was on offense she yelled, "Run the ball, Sullivan. Run the ball." A couple of years later, the youngest son played as a receiver, and she yelled, "Throw the ball, Sullivan. Throw the ball." I reported her statements to Dewey, and we laughed about that.

Dewey often asked Regis fans, "When am I going to get a Lulay?" (The Lulays, the Keudels, the Fesslers etc. are part of the great Regis tradition, and he wanted to coach one of them. He said about Travis Lulay, one Regis quarterback, " I think he even drove the bus, and sold tickets at their home games."

And he often asked the same about the Hawley brothers. The four Hawleys played for Amity, rather than for Dayton. He asked, "When am I going to get a Hawley?" Philip, the youngest, once told Dewey, "I will play for you if I can wear a Panther *(Central Panthers)*, a Pirate *(Dayton Pirates)*, and a Warrior *(Amity Warriors)* on my jersey." Dewey said, "We can do that." But it did not happen.

The Hawley brothers graduated from Amity, and had illustrious football careers. (Dewey had known the family from the time the boys were small, and he derived a great deal of amusement from the skirmishes that occurred in the van when Sharon Hawley came to pick up or deliver game tapes. Dewey enjoyed childhood scuffles, and he frequently instigated them.)

Several years ago, Dewey called Justin Sutton, and asked him to be ball boy for the Pirates. Justin was not at home, so Dewey left a message, and when Justin retrieved the message, he was excited. He called his grandmother and told her, "Coach called and asked me to be ball boy." She asked, "Well, what did you say?" Justin replied, "Grandma, I accept!"

As one of his memories Justin said, "I have many memories with 'Coach,' but the one I will remember the most is when my Grandma Sutton and I went to see 'Coach' in the hospital. We saw Vera, Brent and some other family members. Brent and I went to see 'Coach' in his room, and the doctor said that when 'Coach' squeezes your hand that means 'yes.' I asked him, 'Am I the best ball boy you've ever had? He squeezed my hand, and that made me feel special.

"I also remember another moment. When I visited 'Coach' in the hospital, Barry said, 'My dad will always be an angel on your shoulder when you're playing football.' That was the most emotional moment of my thirteen-year-old life. I will always love 'Coach.'" Justin S. (a.k.a. Sutt) 07/06/07

One fan of Dayton football bet Dewey he could not make a certain young man into a football player. She said, "I'll bet you five dollars you can't make 'so-and-so' into a football player." Dewey responded, "You're on! I think he can be a player, and that he will be successful." The gauntlet was thrown and the contest was on.

That fan kept tabs on the young man's progress, and she attended a Friday night football game a couple of years later. She wanted to see if the young man was still out for football. He was, although he had quit earlier that season. (One afternoon Dewey was late to practice, and was greeted by that player who was not in uniform. Dewey asked, "What's wrong?" Why aren't you suited down for practice?" He was told, "I quit." Dewey told him, "You can't quit – we need you." He told one of the assistant coaches to get him back into uniform, so the coach took him to the locker room and suited him up.)

Dewey had the media interview that player after one of the games his senior year. The next day he called that fan and said, "You'd better read Saturday's paper. That interview means I win our bet. You owe me five dollars." The next time she saw Dewey, she handed him a wadded-up five-dollar bill. With that, I told her, "Dewey wouldn't accept defeat. He quit the team, but Dewey made him get suited back up. He wouldn't let him quit." She said, "That's not fair. You wouldn't let him quit. I want my money back."

Joe Kelly assisted Dewey for several years, and he and Mike Misely drove nearly one hundred miles daily on a round-trip basis. Joe told me, "I considered it an honor to just stand on the sidelines with Dewey. A new state record was set every time Dayton won a game. I was there when a reporter interviewed him after a game, and when she finished, Dewey asked her, 'Can you get me into the movies?'" Dewey was teasing, but it sounded good. *DEWEY IN THE MOVIES??*

Dewey was once asked, "If a movie were made on your life, who do you think should play you?" He said, "I think Jack Palance would be ideal." (Palance, the quintessential tough guy, died about the same time Dewey did.) However, I think that Jimmy Stewart, as in *It's A Wonderful Life*, or Alan Alda, would be more appropriate.

One year at a league meeting, Dewey listened to an opposing coach extol the merits of his team, but he did not comment. After several minutes of regaling his listeners, the other coach looked at

Dewey and said, "You old fox — you're loaded aren't you?" Dewey was amused because his teams were most often not "loaded," but he utilized each player to his maximum potential. He played the hand he was dealt, and he played it well.

Corey Sutton remarked, "It's amazing. We play with twelve people (with Dewey on the sidelines), and everyone else plays with eleven. (It was stated, "When a team plays against Dayton, they're not just playing Dayton, they're playing Dewey.")

He had great relationships with players from neighboring schools, and when the coach from a local school moved to another position, several players told Dewey if he would coach them they would work hard for him. One of those young men sat with us at a basketball game, and talked "football" all evening. He even gave Dewey his undivided attention when the dance team performed at halftime. His focus was on football, rather than on the dancers. I told Dewey that young man was really "into" football.

However, one of his own players, Caleb Kearns, who quarterbacked the Pirates for four years, told me, "Vera, you have to realize we have dreamed of playing for Dewey Sullivan since we were little." I told Dewey, "You can't desert the little town of Dayton. I won't go to any of your football games if you do."

One afternoon, Caleb announced to the team, "We'll be off the field tonight by five o'clock." Someone asked, "How do you know that?" Caleb replied, "Because I set the sprinklers to come on at five o'clock." Sure enough, the sprinklers came on as Caleb said, and Dewey conceded that practice was finished.

Dewey's offense was the *Full-House T*. A news reporter or someone else, often said it was a boring offense. When Dewey heard that, he grinned (his slow, lazy, "devil-may-care" grin), and his response was always, "What's boring about winning?" His teams were successful running his offense, and he added plays and strategies to it through the years, but he stayed faithful to what worked. He said, "If it's not broke, don't fix it."

Dewey, ever a student of football, was fascinated by the *Bandon* offense instituted at Bandon by Coach Don Markham. In the early

'90s Bandon consistently defeated the opposition by scores of 50-0 or more. Dewey visited Bandon twice, and attended practices and interacted with the team. We stayed in a motel, and he spent a lot of time on the field. (His assistants took his practices for those times.) He adapted the offense, and combined it with his own strategy. He dubbed it "The Bandit."

Frank Buckiewicz, the former football coach at Pacific University, assisted Gaston when Dewey first experimented with the *Bandon* offense, and when Frank came down from the crow's nest at halftime of the Dayton-Gaston game, one of his players asked, "What is Dayton running?" Buckiewicz replied, "How the heck should I know?" Dewey chuckled when he learned about that.

Dewey was also fascinated by the single-wing offense. He regretted that, when he first went to Dayton, he did not listen more carefully to Earl McKinney, the Dayton basketball coach, who was knowledgeable about the single-wing. (He said he was just a "punk kid," and felt he knew more than the "old-timer." He was sorry later.) Coach Max Wall uses the single-wing, and came to Dayton in 2001 to work with the Pirates. That team did not accept the offense, but Coach Wall is successful with it.

CHAPTER **50**

Letters

I have reprinted several of the letters Dewey received over the years, but I apologize to those who have written letters that are not included. If a sequel to this book is printed, I will add more. My apologies. (I do have enough letters to make several more books.)

"Dear Coach – You've taught me more than just football. You've taught me about life and about caring, discipline and responsibility. Most of all, you've been a good friend. When I was in the hospital, you visited me often. That showed me how much you cared. You treated me with respect on and off the field. Sincerely, Oscar Garcia #32"

"Dear Coach -- When I started as your manager, I didn't realize the effect you would have on my life. You helped turn a little boy into a man. I learned responsibility from you and that brought on maturity. But, most importantly, I learned to believe in myself. Love, Jason Herring"

"Dear Coach, I have been with you for three years and have never had anybody teach me as much as you did. I thank you for that. I wish I had another year of football left. You're the greatest. I just wish we could have won the state title for you. Love, Josh Sutton #21"

"Dear Coach, You've taught me more than just football. I learned about self-discipline and what it takes to win in life. You have helped me overcome my fears and build self-confidence. Thank you. Sincerely, Donny Smith #52"

I also have several letters from parents of players from opposing teams. Dayton won the state championship in 1996, and an especially poignant letter is from Paul and Merlyn Skeen: "Dear Coach Sullivan: Congratulations on your state football championship! You have a great team and you do a wonderful job coaching. We just wanted to write you a letter to thank you for what you did for our son, Cameron Skeen, after the football game you played here in Nyssa. As parents, to watch your child hurt as much as he was after our loss to you, was almost too painful to bear. As quarterback he shoulders much of the responsibility for the team and the blame when they lose, as he was doing that day.

"When you came up and spoke so highly of his performance in the game and were so complimentary, we saw his whole demeanor start to pick up. You made him believe in himself again and for that we can never thank you enough. As parents we try to help our kids through their tough times, but it means a little bit more when it comes from someone else. You helped him deal with a tough loss a little bit easier and time will make that day a little less painful. We can't thank you enough for taking time to speak to him and caring about a kid that was a complete stranger. You'll always be someone very special in our book. Good luck in the future and keep up the good work."

From a former player: "Dear Coach: Congratulations on a great season and a great winning streak. Now that it is over you really have something that you can look back on for the rest of your life and cherish. You have built up a truly outstanding program at Dayton of which the whole community and alumni is proud. Winning and winning streaks are nice, but the really important part of your program is what individuals, like myself, gain from working with you. You have a strong and positive impact on your students and players. The lessons I have learned from you as a former student and player still influence decisions I make in my professional and personal life today. You are one of the few people in my life who has had such a strong influence and I am all the better because of it. Congratulations again, Coach, and thanks for coaching me. Very truly yours, Frank E. Stoller"

From Rich McCullough, the Superintendent of the La Grande School District in 1985: "Dear Dewey: As you may have noticed, I am not prone to routinely sending congratulatory letters. However, Saturday's game with Neah-Kah-Nie gives me pause to comment on your years as head football coach at Dayton High School.

"While the State Championship is a small part of your success at Dayton High School, such a benchmark is an opportunity to take stock. You have built a program that reflects the best things about high school athletics. Parents and students who have worked with you over the last twenty-one years compliment you with their respect, affection, and loyalty.

"Dayton is very fortunate to have you. I consider it an honor to have worked with you in the interest of youngsters. Please give my best wishes and congratulations to Vera, who has played such a key role in your success."

After the 1996 season he received several letters of congratulations. One particularly inspiring one was from Mrs. Helen Fare whom he had never met and did not get to meet: "Coach Sullivan and Squad: Congratulations! I have read every newspaper report this season (and last) on the progress of your boys and their great efforts. I have enjoyed reading about 'your history' as a coach and mentor... I love football, baseball and basketball in that order... I only wanted to tell all of you how happy I was with your win yesterday and with your past record. Good luck Pirates for the future."

A note from Marv Heater, Executive Director of the Oregon Coaches Association, December 4, 1996: "Congratulations on another great season and another State Championship. What a great job you have done at Dayton. I'm looking forward to next year and your setting the state record for most career wins."

From the Dayton School Superintendent: "Dear Coach Sullivan, on behalf of the Board of Directors of the Dayton School

District, I want to congratulate you on a truly outstanding football season. A second consecutive state championship is a tremendous accomplishment, particularly in view of the many talented players you lost through graduation. This second championship is a credit to your remarkable coaching ability, as well as the high quality of your program.

"The success of any organization or team starts with the attitude, commitment and ability of its leader. Your dedication to the team members, your commitment to excellence and your coaching ability are indicative of your leadership. The mutual respect between you and your players is evident in everything the team does and has a significant impact on the success of the program. The Dayton community is indeed fortunate to have you here, giving of yourself in the many ways you do. Thank you and congratulations on a job well done. Sincerely, Gary Peterson"

And he received one from Al Ashcroft, head coach of the Sheridan Spartans, "Dewey -- Congratulations on another great season. You, your coaches, your players, and your fans set standards that we others can strive for. It's tough sometimes always looking up at you guys, but I know the work you put in and appreciate the dedication you make. Congratulations!"

He received a congratulatory note from Shawn Stanley, now the head coach of the West Salem Titans, "Coach Sullivan, Congratulations on your 300th win and your much deserved national award. You have truly honored the game of football with all of your hard work over the years. I would love to sit down and talk football with you sometime."

After the 2002 State Championship, "Congratulations on an outstanding season and winning the 2002 2-A State Championship. Coach Sullivan, you and your staff can be very proud of the fine student athletes who represented you, Dayton High School, and the entire Dayton Community, playing with tremendous sportsmanship and class at Saturday's State Championship game.

"The Dayton Team showed up prepared, focused and they executed a well thought out game plan. High school athletics teach

LETTERS

our young people so many valuable lessons and Saturday was no exception. Reg McShane, Superintendent, Amity School District"

And from David Wu, Member of Congress, "Dear Coach Sullivan: I would like to commend the hard work and good sportsmanship of your Varsity football team. I followed the season with great interest and cheered for both 2A finalists, both from the First District, knowing both teams could not be champions. Congratulations on your victory! Again, congratulations on a terrific year and best wishes for continuing academic and athletic accomplishment."

"Dewey and Vera, Congratulations! A just end for countless hours of dedication for the benefit of the young men on your team. You two continue to be an inspiration for my wife and me. What do people mean when they say we don't have heroes to look upon today? Enjoy the glow! Randy & Lynnette Traeger Family -- 'He rises by lifting others.' — Robert Ingersoll (1833 – 1899)"

In 1996, Vince Baker wrote an essay for one of his classes at Western Oregon University, "Dayton High School just won another 2-A state championship! They have one of the best records in Oregon and are well known for winning football games. The winning has not come by itself. It has taken 32 years for Dayton's football coach to take his program where it is today. His teams won state championships in: 1985, 1986, 1995, and 1996. He is the second all-time winningest coach for high school football in Oregon.

"His name is Dewey Sullivan, but I call him Coach. He is the best thing that ever walked into my life. He is not just known as a coach to me, he is a mentor. He has shown me that hard work will pay off, encouragement keeps one to task, life is not always fair and equal, and that each person is important. He did not yell at the top of his lungs but took you through a task until you understood it. He explained it from all points of view, so you could understand it better.

"One day he made me go through a certain task until I got it right. I kept doing the same thing over and over. However, it made me a better person because he taught me that after keeping with a task it would pay off in the end . . . I remember a playoff game against Weston-McEwen. My team was ranked number one and Weston-McEwen was not ranked . . . My team came to this game thinking we were going to win by 40 points, but we lost by two points . . . Things equaled themselves out the next year because we won the state title . . . The teams Coach worked with were not the biggest, quickest, smartest, or most athletic. He took kids that were not any of these things and turned them into some of the best players . . . He saw each individual as important and realized the value in him or her.

"One of the kids on my team was always in trouble. He had the hardest time in school, getting Saturday detention and not showing up for school. All those things followed him to the football field. He made sure that kid went to Saturday detention. Coach saw value in him. I did not see why he was doing that but he cared about every football player on and off the field. He saw value in everyone. He taught me this and I try to do the same to everyone I meet.

"When thinking of a mentor, I knew right away who my mentor is. He has shown me the way to live life, not by words, but by example. He showed me that in life you should have fun. He was wise and knew what life was all about. He is the person I look up to and is my mentor. His name is Dewey Sullivan."

After the first game of the 2006 season, with Regis (which Dayton won 22-21) Dewey received a note from John Kuppenbender (the former head football coach at J.F.K. High School in Mount Angel): "Coach Sullivan – just a note to congratulate you on your opening game victory over the Rams. It is no small accomplishment to have your team ready every game, every season, for so many years. I am proud to know you." (The 2006 season was Dewey's last.)

CHAPTER **51**

Things I Have Learned

"It's not the years in your life – rather it's the life in your years that matters."

-- Abraham Lincoln

Dewey was my favorite teacher, and I learned many life lessons from him – I learned that life is what you make it, not what you have been given. I learned you should not give up, that by giving your best effort each day you get the most from what you have. I learned you should give more than you get, that by sharing you get more from life than you could imagine. I learned you should give to those less fortunate than you, and you should give back to those who have done so much for you. The only real happiness comes from giving not from receiving.

Dewey taught me – always squeeze the toothpaste from the bottom of the tube (not the center or the top) – always put the toilet tissue roll so the tissue feeds from over the top (not from beneath the roll) – always tell someone how you feel (that you love them) – you never know how much time you have left or if you will get another chance – don't use money to measure wealth.

We change – the world changes – tomorrow will be different than today. We can never go back to what once was – we can only greet each new day with anticipation.

Go as far as you can go. You're the one who sets the standard for how high you can fly. Don't let someone else do it for you.

Dewey's nephew, Rueben, said he taught Dewey things also. After Dewey died he wrote, "To my Uncle Dewey, It has been a great blessing being your nephew these 30 years. My mind is full of memories of the times we shared and my heart holds forever on to the person you were. I love you, Dewey Sullivan. If knowing you momentarily is a blessing, then being your nephew is like having a gift hand-wrapped by God.

"For as much as I know I will miss your presence, I know I will greatly revel in the joy of your humor, in awe of your passion to learn, and an admiration of your beautiful life with Aunt Vera...there are many things that make you a hero more than an uncle, and for that reason, you will live forever. Therefore, it does not sadden me to know that you may not hear these thoughts, for they are purely the product of celebrations.

"I will mourn your loss for a while, but when I am strong again, I will forever brag to the world that my uncle was Dewey Sullivan...I am grateful to God because you made me laugh, helped me learn, and were someone I'd like to be more like. I'm glad I was able to teach you a thing or two also...like when I was a young boy and I showed you how good those 'nilla wafers are when dipped in milk. When I remember you I automatically smile, Uncle Dewey.

"I write this not to say goodbye but to say 'peace be with you'... for peace will be ours together some glorious day and my heart will know you. Thanks, Uncle Dewey. And give Uncle Norman a giant hug when you see him. With love and milk-soaked 'nilla wafers. Rueben"

Charity Baker Kuiper wrote: "The day of Dewey's service many of the speakers mentioned several of the wonderful traits displayed by Dewey. Personally, I think they all missed a very important one – fidelity. Dewey was a faithful man. He was faithful to God and his relationship with Him. He was faithful to you, Vera.

"Because of his commitment to his marriage I always felt safe to be around him. He was a gentleman and he treated his female students like ladies. He was faithful to his family — I know not perfect and not always a "sweetheart," but he was faithful to his job — both as a teacher and as a coach.

"I am sure, with his record and knowledge of the game of football he could have gone other places to coach and teach. However, he gave 42 years of his life to a small town called Dayton. A town that will never be the same without him, but a town full of lives touched by him. I know — I was one of the many who was changed because of him taking the time to care."

CHAPTER 52

The Glory Years

With Dewey there were no "outsiders." He treated the members of his football team with respect, and they became part of his family. He encouraged brotherly love. No one was looked down upon, and all were treated as equals. It mattered not to him whether you were the child of a school board member, or the son of the "town drunk." He tried to help his students and players look up to their parents. He did not bring demeaning incidents to the attention of others.

The star football player was treated the same as the manager or the water boy. He had no stars, and discontinued the practice of naming the *MVP* (Most Valuable Player), etc. when he arrived in Dayton. He was often asked to name his best team or the best player he ever coached, but he refused to make such distinctions. He loved them all.

Three weeks after Dewey's team celebrated his 300th victory, he received a letter notifying him of his selection as *National Coach of the Year*. He was humbled and excited. The Booster Club proposed a dinner in celebration of the honor, but he was embarrassed. He said, "I don't know if that would be a good idea. What if no one comes? It will be embarrassing to have a celebration if no one attends."

But they came. Dewey was "roasted," and he thanked those who attended. He remarked, "Most people don't get to attend their own funerals and hear what people have to say about them, but I did. I got to hear what others think. It is humbling to hear these tributes."

Dewey was amused at many of the tales told. He said, "I love these stories. They are great." He did not consider himself a speaker, but I have a note he wrote for his speech, "If I could talk like some of those guys we would be at 400 wins by now."

He was asked to sit on the stage at the celebration, but by doing that, it became evident that he missed talking to those who meant so much to him through the years. So he stationed himself at the entrance to greet each one. He became the "official greeter," and was delighted to see many he had not seen for years. He had not wanted to be feted, but was happy to renew old acquaintances.

Dewey had tickets to the USC-OSU football game in 1967 when Oregon State won 3-0. USC was ranked Number One in the nation in college football, and the win was decided by a thirty-yard field goal in the second quarter. Barry went with him, and I listened to the game on the radio. When OSU scored the field goal, I thought it would not stand, but it did. O.J. Simpson was the USC running back and almost broke for a run and possible score, but the Beavers contained him. Barry was delighted to be able to go to that game. It was a memorable game for both of them.

Dewey attended all the football practices and games he had time for. He went to Linfield College practices, Western Oregon practices, Oregon State University practices, University of Oregon practices, McMinnville High School practices, as well as football camps and spring training at Western Oregon University, Willamette University and Linfield College.

Dewey was often asked to speak, but he usually refused. He preferred to listen and learn. He did not consider himself a public speaker, and did not like to be the center of attention. When his Pirates were not playing or practicing, he watched college, high school, junior high or *Little Guy* games. He was a frequent visitor to coaches' clinics, and was well known in coaching circles, particularly in Oregon.

Dewey did speak several times at George Fox College (now

THE GLORY YEARS

George Fox University) in the early '70s while they still had a football program. He met John Hackworth through one of those presentations. John came to Dayton and helped with football while our sons were in high school. He later coached at Sherwood, and when Sherwood played Bandon for the state championship in 1999, Dewey attended a practice.

When someone had a question, he was ready to help with strategies and plays "one-on-one." He often received calls from coaches around the Willamette Valley asking for advice. (And most often, those coaches won by taking his advice. One of those coaches was Randy Nyquist, of the West Albany Bulldogs. The Bulldogs won state championships in 2007 and 2008.)

Devising plays and helping on offense and defense were what Dewey enjoyed most. Several years ago I ordered a book on trick plays (I thought he might be bored after so many years of coaching), but after reading it, he said he had seen everything it covered.

However that book stirred his creative juices, and he devised his own *Finnicum Series* for the championship game in 1996. His plan was for the team to score a touchdown on the second possession.

The biggest problem with the *Finnicum Series*, (if it could be considered a problem), was that the team almost scored on the first possession rather than the second. Several former players were at practice that week, and Dewey told them, "Watch for this new play – it's a sure touchdown." The Pirates scored on the second possession as planned.

It became his mission to be certain all players had food after a game. If a player called his mother to ask for a ride from practice or after a game and Dewey heard him, he insisted the call end with, "I love you, Mom." If that player had not told her he loved her, Dewey had him call her back to tell her. He taught respect for the opposing teams and for facilities. Barb Cruickshank recently told me she still gets misty when her sons end their calls with, "I love you, Mom."

Dewey was a master strategist, and he could assess the assets of his players. He used them to their best advantage. He assigned them to the positions he felt they were most suited. If a player was pulled from the game because he made a mistake, Dewey explained what the mistake was, and he tried to correct it before sending that player back onto the field.

He loved to get insights from others and compare notes. He mentored many, but was always ready to be mentored. I have never met anyone who was as inquisitive about everything as Dewey Sullivan. He had an analytical mind and left no stone unturned in his quest for knowledge.

After a Little Guy game one mother reported that Dewey said, "Way to go, Ranger. Keep up the good work." The little man told his mom that Dewey knew who he was. (He was not thinking that his name was on the back of his jersey).

It meant a great deal to the young players when Dewey went to one of their games. He knew that, and he attended as many as possible, but his priority was to scout games that had an impact on his own schedule. When he finished scouting those games, he attended college and *Little Guy* games, and other high school games with no bearing on his season's outcome. If there were no games to scout with implications on his season, he went to a game for the fun of it (for the joy of football).

Dewey enjoyed high school football, and was convinced that teenage boys play for the joy of the game, not for money or other rewards. He attended college games, especially when one or more of his former players were playing, and he watched pro football (I am certain he would have watched Carolina Panthers football now that Dante Rosario, a 2003 graduate of Dayton, is playing for them). But he was a firm believer in high school football.

Dewey was a humble man, but of course, he wanted to win. He said, "Who plays a game to lose? No one puts that much effort into losing." The purpose of playing is to win, but with winning there is pressure. When the Pirates won thirty-six consecutive games, it was devastating to the team and the coaches to lose. In three short years the agony of defeat had been forgotten.

On the Saturday morning before Dayton played John Day of Grant Union in 1987, Dewey's father told him, "Son, it's only a football game." (Dayton lost that game by the score of 15-6, which broke the thirty-six-game win streak.) His father died the following Thursday (on Thanksgiving evening), and Dewey was in much turmoil during that time.

Dewey respected his players, and commanded the same respect from them. He also had the respect of players from opposing teams. Many of those players (from opposing teams) were in attendance at his celebration of life. Dewey said he wanted to be a coach, but he became so much more. He became a student, a teacher, and a coach.

Dewey coached in the '50s, the '60s, the '70s, the '80s, the '90s and the 2000s. He mellowed through the years. His former players often remarked how "soft" the old coach had become, but Dewey still related to his players in much the same manner in 2006 as when he started coaching in 1959. He just changed with the times. As the years passed, he became a kinder, gentler coach – he loved kids and football and put the two together well. Attitudes and expectations may have changed, but kids are much the same today.

He said, "I don't know how I ended up in a career where I'm often in the limelight. For someone who hates publicity as much as I do it is ironic.

Dewey had the God-given talent of making you feel loved. Love played an integral role in his life. He loved God, he loved his family, he loved life, and he loved football. He was thinking football when God called the last play and took him home. He reached heights most of us as mortals only strive to attain. Each day was an adventure, and he looked forward to it with anticipation.

To be as successful as Dewey was, in a small public high school, year after year, is a remarkable accomplishment. Without the luxury of recruiting, or of having a large pool of players from which to choose, it is almost impossible. It is even more amazing when you consider how well Dayton did during Dewey's tenure.

CHAPTER **53**

Forever a Pirate — AARGHH!

"What is brought out from the memory is not the events themselves but words conceived from the images of those events which have left their footprints stamped upon the mind."

-- St. Augustine

"Yesterday is but a dream and Tomorrow is only a vision. But Today well lived makes every Yesterday a dream of happiness and every Tomorrow a vision of hope."

--Sanskrit

The first team that Dewey coached was with the *Silt Pirates*, and the last team he coached was the *Dayton Pirates*. He may have strayed along the way, but he remained a *Pirate* throughout his coaching career.

Dewey started college to become a physical education teacher, but added biology and science to his studies, and he became the biology teacher at each of the schools where he taught. He loved science -- he loved kids — he loved football. He often went to the locker room of the opposing team after a game, and told the players what a good job they had done, whether they had won or lost the game.

At the conclusion of the 1992 season, Corwin Brown presented

Dewey with a black and white photo of his team in their stances. Dewey remarked, "I don't know how it was captured on film, but you have each man in perfect position."

John Imlah and Randy Rohde accepted the basketball coaching position at Amity High School several years ago. Dewey went to them before the Amity/Dayton game and asked, "Do you guys know what you have let yourselves in for?" John told me they both agreed, "No, we don't know." After Amity defeated Dayton, Dewey said, "I guess you do know what you're doing. You did a good job. Congratulations!"

Dewey once remarked, "I have never won a football game, but I can take credit for some of the losses." He prepared for every game, and took each one seriously. He tried to leave no strategy unexplored, but sometimes the execution fell short of expectations. Randy Traeger, head coach at JFK High School in Mount Angel, runs much of Dewey's offense, and he told me recently, "It's a great offense and a tribute to a great man."

A loss on the scoreboard was not as hard for Dewey to bear as it was for him to lose a player. He said, "You hate to lose the kid. He might not help the team that much, but the benefits he could get from the team experience is better than anything to be derived from other activities. This would certainly help him, but it does happen. You try your best to get him back, and keep him out. Kids learn life lessons on the football field. You don't know what they go through at home. Sometimes it's their fault -- sometimes it's a family situation. There are no bad kids, but there are kids who make bad choices. Sometimes they are victims of circumstances, but our job is to help them overcome their situations."

Dewey had a library of scout tapes, and knew where they were. He could recall what school had run what play, go to his library and select the correct film. He and Max Wall often talked football for hours on the phone, and they diagrammed plays using a dry erase board. Dewey enjoyed those sessions. He loved to "talk" football – even by phone.

Several years ago, Dewey appeared on the sidelines of a junior varsity game at a neighboring school. One of the coaches from that school said, "What are you doing here?" Dewey replied, "Well, Dayton was ahead when I left home, and I came to see what was going on over here."

When Jeremy McLoud was a sophomore, he did not have a letterman's jacket. Dewey asked, "Why don't you have a letterman's jacket?" Jeremy told him, "My mom is a custodian, and we don't have much money." The next day he had a jacket with the letters, etc. (Jeremy's father died shortly after Dewey's father did, and Dewey said, "I'll be his father now.")

We attended a practice and scrimmage as Taylor Barton from Beaverton prepared for his freshman year at the University of Colorado. We also attended one of the Denver Broncos training camp sessions. Dewey loved attending football practices, and he never tired of them. He said he enjoyed the practices more than the actual games. I believe it was the strategy involved, as well as the contact with the players.

One year a friend of Dewey's, who was also a coach, told him that he was going to run his offense. Dewey told Max about that, and Max laughed and replied, "The only similarity between what he runs, and Dayton's offense is that they both use a football. Dewey loved that analogy, and got a chuckle out of it.

He had fans from other areas, as well as from Dayton. One of those was Charlie Anderson from Nestucca. Charlie and his wife drove all over the State of Oregon to attend Dayton football games. Charlie's daughter was a student at Nestucca High School, and she asked him why he was willing to drive so far to see Dayton play. After seeing the game between Dayton and Nestucca, she told her dad she understood. Dewey appreciated Charlie's support, as well as that of Truman Arnold.

Truman lived in McMinnville, but started going to Dayton games in 1983 when he had a grandson who played for the Pirates. Truman drove to most Dayton games including playoff games, and once got an eighty-dollar speeding ticket. He usually stayed until halftime, and then he left with the comment, "This game is history."

A BAREFOOT BOY FROM OKLAHOMA

When we went to Nyssa in '96, one of Truman's grandsons was in the stands. At the half, we looked up and saw Truman approaching. The grandson said, "Oops! I see Grandpa coming, and I didn't drive more than three hundred miles just to go home at halftime." (He disappeared until after the game.)

Another fan was Rich Ward. Rich's son had not played for Dewey, but Rich became an ardent fan, and attended most of the Pirate games. He went to football practices, and his wife, Gail, was also a fan of Pirate football (when she wasn't having her nails done). Barry fondly dubbed Gail, *Miss America*.

One year, when the lineup for the varsity traveling team was announced, Juan Morales, a freshman was designated. Juan immediately broke into tears. Dewey asked, "What's the matter?' Juan replied, "I don't deserve to go with the team." Juan's attitude impressed Dewey. Juan worked extremely hard, and had a successful football career at Dayton. He was a "force" on the '85 championship team, and played in the East-West Shrine game in Baker City.

Pontus Inerup was an exchange student from Sweden in 1988, and fell in love with the game of football. Before he returned to Sweden, he purchased a video recorder, and had copies made of all his game tapes. (I believe he played college football in Europe, and is now a surgeon.)

Fabian Garcia played opposite Larry Ramirez in 1990, when Dayton met Vale in the semi-final round of the playoffs. Fabian was five feet nine inches tall and weighed one hundred fifty pounds, and Ramirez was six foot six inches tall and weighed more than two hundred fifty pounds.

Larry later played for Oregon State University, and he and Fabian became friends. Fabian told the OSU coach, Jerry Pettibone, that he had played against Ramirez in the semi-final game between Vale and Dayton. Coach Pettibone looked at the disparity in the size of the two, and scoffed. Fabian said, "Ask him." When Coach Pettibone asked, "Did you play against that little guy?" Larry said, "Yes, I did."

FOREVER A PIRATE - AARGHH!

Fabian said, "Coach told my parents to feed me doughnuts in order to get some meat on my body. He taught me to never give up. He motivated me and gave me the courage to play the game of football." Fabian flew from New York for Dewey's celebration of life, and he planned to attend the induction ceremony in Washington, D.C., but was unable to make the trip.

When Nate Lindell was a senior at Dayton High School, he came into Dewey's classroom and told him, "Coach, I really feel sorry for you next year." Dewey asked, "Why is that?" Nate stood for a few minutes, and then said, "No, it's like a puzzle. You'll put the pieces in their proper places." And Dewey did. (Oftentimes he shifted the players from the positions they played in junior high or at some other school, and somehow made the pieces fit.) Dayton won league the next fall, and advanced to the quarterfinal round of the state playoffs.

Football was Dewey's passion. I remember watching a junior varsity football game one night in Portland between two opponents we knew nothing about, simply because it was football. Dewey was intrigued with football lights. If we were somewhere at night and he saw lights, he tried to find the game.

Dewey appreciated his former players when they came to our house to watch films. Bo Jacks came with his dad, Matt, several times, and was football savvy. After one play Bo said, "That is what we run." About three years ago Ben Bunn, III (who was a volunteer coach for the Pirates), came to watch films with Dewey, so I went into the bedroom to read. When the house was quiet for several minutes, I thought I had better check to see what was happening. Dewey was asleep, and Ben was too polite to wake him.

Ben said Dewey backed the film up, and then played it forward repeatedly at a specific time, just as if he were awake and watching. He had watched that film so many times it was committed to memory. Dewey enjoyed watching a game film with anyone who was willing to help him "break it down."

Lonnie Turner student taught at Dayton, before going to Culver

A BAREFOOT BOY FROM OKLAHOMA

in 1975 and 1976 to teach and to coach football. Culver won the state title both years Lonnie was there. He told Dewey, "Dewey, I have a better record than you do. My teams were undefeated while I coached at Culver, and they won two state championships." (Imagine, going to a school, coaching for two years, and winning back-to-back state championships before retiring from coaching. A 100% win record!)

Tom Johnson who played for Dewey in the late '70s, and his sons, Barry and T.J., played in the 2000s, said, "The thing about Dewey is that everybody respects him, and he's loved every kid who has played at Dayton." (Dayton teams made playoff appearances for thirty years, and had fifteen semi-final and six title appearances during the time he coached at Dayton. But it was about more than winning – it was about kids.)

Dewey had many plays in his playbook (which was in his head), and many of those plays were used in practice, but were rarely seen in a game. When Dayton was successfully in the lead in one of the championship games, Dewey told Roger Lorenzen to call any of the plays he wanted to run. (Dayton plays were run in a specific sequence, but in that game they were run for no particular reason.)

Dewey mellowed over the course of his coaching career. He said, "All it takes these days is a glare to tell players they need to improve. I'm a lot softer than I used to be. I think you probably have to be today. Also, as you get older you sort of mellow out." (Having grandkids possibly helped too.)

When a new player moved to Dayton several years ago, Dewey had members of the team meet the family, and help unload their belongings. He knew it was difficult to leave friends, and to move to a new locale, particularly as a junior in high school. He empathized, as he had experienced first-hand the sadness and the homesickness involved with leaving your friends.

One of the most "memorable" events in Dewey's coaching career in Dayton was in 2005, when Thomas Bunn took a flying leap off the infamous Dayton Bridge. Thomas and a group of guys (and maybe girls) had been "tin-canning" cars. (The cans are tied on a fishing line, and strung between the two sides of a bridge. When a car gets over the cans, the line is raised and is hooked by the car. A terrible racket ensues, and frightens the driver of the car.)

There is a walkway on one side of the Bridge, but not the other. Thomas was on the side without the walkway, but in the excitement of the moment, he forgot that, and when the next car approached, he raised the line and took a leap. Only then did he realize his mistake.

Thomas tucked as he fell approximately fifty feet. He landed in the blackberries and thorns. Had he landed a little further on either side, he would have dropped into the small creek (most likely knocking himself out and drowning), or onto the rocks also possibly (or probably) resulting in death. He fractured his wrist, punctured a lung, cracked a vertebrae, and had several broken ribs from his "leap of faith." The place he landed is now dubbed "Bunn's Landing."

Thomas told his father, "Coach used to play that prank when he was a young man." (But Thomas, I hate to blow your cover. "Coach" had to ask what "tin-canning" meant, so he learned something new that day.) Thomas played football for the Pirates that fall, and has served his country in the U.S. Marine Corps in Iraq and Afghanistan. His mom said, "When Thomas walks out the door, I turn him over to his guardian angel."

Max Wall and Bill Crowson came to see Dewey at Dayton later that spring. When they left, they went toward Salem rather than Amity. Dewey started after them, but then realized they were going to assess "Bunn's Landing." Max had previously visited the site, so he knew the story and shared it with Bill.

I received a phone call from Claire DePietro one night while Dewey was at football practice. She told me her family had purchased a home on Grand Island in the Dayton School District, but could not take possession until school started. There was a problem in that the family was staying with relatives in Albany. Her son would be a freshman at Dayton that fall, and could not get to practice until they moved.

Charley had played junior high football in Virginia the previous year, and loved it. Dewey was tired when he came from practice that evening, but he returned her call. "Hello, this is Dewey Sullivan. I understand you have one of my players over in Albany. What can we do to solve the problem?" After some discussion, he arranged for Charley to stay at our home until the family could move. Poor Charley was homesick during the two weeks he spent with us.

Claire brought Dewey a fabulous fruit tart when the family picked Charley up at the end of the first week. With treats like that, Charley could have lived with us on a permanent basis. I am surprised he "escaped," as Dewey loved pastries so much. I do not believe Claire ever attended a Dayton game, but when she came to take Charley home after each game, she asked in her accent, "Did 'Sharley' make a touchdown?" She was proud of him and of his accomplishments.

Charley adapted to the Dayton scene, and excelled in school and in sports. He loved football, was a great football player, and was an asset to the Pirates. After graduation he played for the Wolves of Western Oregon College (now Western Oregon University), and he had a successful football career there.

Sheridan football coach, Brice Ingram said, "At Dewey's last Linfield football camp, we were trying to perfect a play. Dewey walked up and asked, 'What are you guys doing?' I told him, and he stepped into the center of our group, and proceeded to show how it should be done. It worked as slick as a whistle. I called him The Silver Fox."

Dewey often said, "As a coach, if you haven't been fired, you haven't been there." He consoled coaches who had been fired. He told them it was a blessing in disguise. As an example, he frequently mentioned one of the winningest coaches in the State of Oregon who was fired but went on to be successful. He was told, "But you would never get fired." Dewey replied, "They would love to fire me. After all, they fired Tom Landry didn't they, and he was a much higher profile coach than I am. All they would have to say is that I can no longer relate to today's youth."

That is the truth, but he had a remarkable talent for working with young people. He could walk into almost any group of football players, and get down to "brass tacks" with them. He truly loved young people and the game of football.

The ironic thing is that Dewey actually got fired from coaching football. When he was the coach of the Meeker Cowboys in Meeker, Colorado, he was the head football, assistant basketball and head baseball coach. The football team had a dismal two years while he coached there, but his baseball teams made it into the playoffs both years. (He had not played baseball or coached it, but was successful at Meeker.)

The School Board removed Dewey from his position as football coach, but wanted him to remain as biology teacher and baseball coach. (The School Board did us a favor – we just didn't realize it at the time. That failure made Dewey all the more determined, and he proved himself worthy of the title of "Football Coach.")

The Meeker Cowboys were a young football team, and Dewey felt they would be good the following year. He told the School Board, "If you don't want me to coach football I'm out of here."

Dewey showed his resilience by not accepting defeat. (Failure is the opportunity to begin again – this time more intelligently.) It would have been easy for Dewey to lose his way, but he was persistent and became successful. It was our belief that God led us to the small community of Dayton to fulfill His will. Once Dewey was asked by an interviewer, "Why are you so confident?" his reply was, "Because I know I can do the job."

Norman was also fired from two positions as basketball coach. At one school, he did not start the son or sons of a school board member, and the superintendent called him into the office and asked him to start a certain player. Norman said, "Well, he's not as good a player as this other young man. He gets playing time, but he's not a starter."

A BAREFOOT BOY FROM OKLAHOMA

The superintendent looked at Norman and said, "If I tell you my job is on the line, would that make a difference?" Norman replied, "In that case we'll change the rotation (the player in question was a senior, and the starter was a sophomore.) I've been trying to get the younger players experience for next year."

Norman changed the rotation of the players' time on the court, but at the end of the school year, he and the superintendent were both dismissed. (Six weeks before his dismissal Norman shared with us his glowing reviews that told how well he related to the students. The reason for his dismissal was totally counter to what his initial review stated. In six short weeks, the assessment had changed.)

Norman ran the summer basketball program at the second school before he left for an extended tour of the United States. The school board knew of his plans, and a letter dismissing him from his position was posted the day he left for his journey. That letter awaited him when he returned.

(There's nothing like confronting your demons.) At that school, two sons of a school board member were on his basketball team. One was a good player and saw quite a bit of playing time. The older of the two was a great kid, but was not as talented as his younger brother, so he saw less time on the floor. (Politics and the School Board!!!)

About three years ago, several coaches were asked if they thought Dewey's record could be broken. Kent Wigle, Marshfield head football coach and second on the list of winningest coaches in Oregon was quoted, "I don't think that you are going to see that kind of longevity." (Kent won his 300th game in 2007, and retired from coaching in 2009 with 307 wins.)

When Dayton played at South Umpqua in 1977, Kent was the coach. Dayton lost 20-14, and Kent and Dewey agreed Dayton should have won that game and that South Umpqua should have won the contest when the 1979 game was played at Dayton and the Pirates won 20-13.

Tom Smythe, the head football coach at McNary at that time said, "That's not going to happen. Coaches don't stay in the game because they work too hard and get burned out after five or ten years."

Corey Sutton said, "I think records are made to be broken. I think the record will be broken someday, but I think it will take an amazing person . . . I think it will be a long time."

CHAPTER 54

Coaching Staffs

Roger Lorenzen assisted Dewey in football for ten years. Roger was the varsity quarterback for two of the four years he played football for Dayton. He knew the offense and what Dewey wanted, so he was invaluable to the program. He had a "feel" for what play would likely work. In August of 1988, Dewey was disappointed when Roger called to discuss his impending move to Amity as Athletic Director.

Dewey appreciated Roger's loyalty and assistance, but knew that a move was inevitable. After the discussion, Dewey wished Roger the best, but realized the Pirate dynasty would take a direct hit.

There is an affinity between a coach and quarterback, and Dewey and Roger shared a common knowledge of football. They had been through "fire and brimstone" together. They had worked together for so long that they were tuned to the same wavelength.

After Roger left the Pirate program, Dewey went to the crow's nest, and enjoyed the better vantage point, but he missed the contact with the players on the sidelines. He stated several times that he would like to be in both places at the same time. After Roger's departure, Dayton lost the first two games, but still won league and advanced to the semi-final game of the playoffs.

Dave Cook came to the program in 1972, and he helped immensely. Dave had played football at Willamette University, and he and Dewey spent countless hours going over tapes and plays.

A BAREFOOT BOY FROM OKLAHOMA

Jerry Sutton began coaching with Dewey at Dayton in 1990, and Dewey appreciated his help. He valued Jerry's input. Jerry is one of the most "kid-oriented" assistants Dewey had, and each season, the team members asked if Jerry were going to coach. Jerry worked well with young men, and appreciated the game of football. He had the respect of the players, and he was loyal and dedicated.

Dewey and Jerry spent hours scouting games, and going over films. They broke each tape down "play-by-play," and studied what each Dayton player had done in a game. They also assessed what the opposing players had done. Dewey appreciated any coach who was willing to watch tapes with him. He loved having someone help him analyze films. I was no help because I liked to watch a game as it had been played (not to have plays run back and forth multiple times as they liked to do). I could not sit through one of their screenings.

Mark Hawley assisted Dewey one year, and they also spent hours going over game films. When Mark assisted, a breakdown of the game was in Dewey's hands the morning after a game. Mark and Jerry gave hours of their time to the Pirate football program on a volunteer basis.

Jim Massey played pro ball for the New England Patriots, and came to Dayton several times to help with practice. The players were impressed with having a former pro player help, and Dewey valued his input. Jim later became the head football coach at Yamhill-Carlton, and then was an assistant at McMinnville High School. When Jim's season was finished, he willingly shared his knowledge.

During Dewey's last ten years of coaching, several former Pirate players served as volunteer coaches. He was thankful for their assistance, and he appreciated their knowledge and loyalty. He valued those who had played under his system -- those who were loyal to him and to Dayton football.

But not everything went without problems. Several years ago, Dewey was informed by one of his former players that, at a junior high practice, he watched in frustration, as the team was instructed to run a certain play. The play was demonstrated incorrectly and the team struggled. He finally stepped in and showed the team how to run it correctly.

At the conclusion of practice, the coach called the young man aside and told him he did not appreciate being shown up in front of his team. Dewey said, "Well, he's right, but he's also wrong. He could have come out to our practices any or every night of the week to see how we execute a play. He didn't do it. You probably shouldn't have shown him up in front of his team, but he was wrong in not learning how to do things correctly. After all, don't the kids deserve our best effort and dedication?"

The last two years of Dewey's tenure, he designated Matt Jacks as the offensive coordinator. Matt played for Dewey in the '80s, and was an astute student of Dewey's offense. The two of them thought along the same lines and they often went over films together.

One coach who had teams that opposed Dewey's, moved to a larger school, and Dewey talked with him about his move. The fellow said, "Dewey, if I had it to do over I would not have taken this job unless I had been given oversight of the entire program – junior high through varsity. After the fact, it is too late to go back and make that request, but before I took the new position, I could have asked for that responsibility."

Dewey had the luxury of junior high loyalty when Larry Black and Lynn Freshour coached with him. They attended the high school practices so they could learn what the varsity ran. There was continuity during that time, and when the players got to high school, they were familiar with the program. Dewey always welcomed the junior high coaches to practices.

He provided the opportunity for anyone interested to step in both to help and to learn. He welcomed questions from the junior high coaches as well as from the high school assistants. He tried to make the learning process as seamless as possible, and appreciated anyone who wanted to break down a game tape.

For years Dewey had the benefit of loyal and interested

coaching staffs. But a few times he was bedeviled with those who did not do as he requested. He carried the weight of the team on his shoulders.

It was only in the last few years that his directives were not followed. When it became evident that several assistants turned off the headphones, and didn't listen to Dewey's instructions and questions, he was deeply disappointed. Such disrespect is unconscionable. The hardest thing for him to understand was why someone would do something like that.

He always thought the best of others, and did not believe that such traits could actually be exhibited. He loved people, and didn't think anyone could intentionally sabotage another. (His naivete was one of his most endearing traits.) But when he had to face reality, it was a bitter pill for him to swallow.

After Dewey had struggled with the situation for a time, I told him, "Why don't you fire those assistants who are disloyal?" He said, "Vera, I can't do that. I have never fired anyone in my life, and I don't intend to do so now." (He would not have been allowed to fire them anyway. He was only directly involved in hiring one or two of them in his forty-two seasons at Dayton.) But Dewey was willing to overlook such disloyalty.

Every organization functions better if all work together for the good of the program. During Dewey's last years of coaching, he was frustrated when one or more of his assistants went "behind his back" and did their own thing. Loyalty and respect are essential in any organization, and football is no different.

I remarked recently that I wondered what Dewey could have accomplished with more dedication from his staff. After I considered my statement, I realized that he was most likely a better coach because he did not rely heavily on others. Possibly he became as successful as he was, because he knew whom he could trust.

Dewey knew he was forgiven and he forgave. He was better about forgiveness than I am. I have difficulty forgiving those who I feel wrong my husband's memory. He often told me I need to be more forgiving, but I still struggle with that.

His motto was, "Never pay back evil for evil to anyone. Respect what is right in the sight of all men." -- Romans 12:17

"For if you forgive men when they sin against you, your heavenly Father will also forgive you." -- Matthew 6:14

CHAPTER **55**

A Tale of Three Horses

One of Dewey's ventures in the early 1970s was to purchase a horse. He loved horses, and as a young boy in Colorado often "borrowed" one from their landlord. He said, "I could have been locked up for horse rustling."

When friends learned that Dewey wanted a horse, they told him he could keep one on their property on the Willamette River. With that offer, Dewey set out to find a horse, and in the search, he visited several students with horses.

Candy and one of her friends "test-drove" one particularly round horse, and they both slipped beneath her. It must have been comical watching the "slow-motion" slide. Dewey and Candy got a chuckle out of that.

Dewey spent several weeks "horse-shopping," and our kids were delighted when he finally settled on a specific horse. We purchased Stardust in May, and moved her to the property on the River. (One of his life-long dreams was realized with that purchase.) After Dewey purchased Stardust, he decided we needed a second horse.

We went to an auction in June, and found what, we thought, would be the perfect kid's horse. That horse let his owner get beneath his belly, and he stood placidly while anything was done to him. Little did we know, that he had likely been drugged. After a few days in our possession, he became very rambunctious. Since he was white, we named him, Silver. He was a fun horse for Brent, but he was a handful for him and for everyone else. Dewey and our kids had a great "horsey" summer and visited the horses often.

But wait. You've only met two horses. Let me tell you of the third horse. One crisp fall morning, when the leaves had turned from green to yellow, and the autumn air had a bite to it, we went to the River to check on the horses. The kids ran down the path, but immediately came back up the hill shouting, "Stardust had a baby – Stardust had a baby." They were so excited. We hurried to see, and sure enough, Stardust had a beautiful colt by her side. He was brown with a large white "J" emblazoned on his forehead. Naturally we named him Jay.

He was not of show stock, but we didn't care. We had a "baby horse," and he was a darling. Well, he was almost a darling. (He kicked and bucked, but with work, he became docile and was fun to work with.)

We spent more time checking on the horses after that experience. But we never stopped teasing Dewey about being a biology teacher, and not realizing that the horse he had chosen was with foal. Our kids loved having a colt to rear, and he had a good life with them.

Several summers later, Dewey and Brent brought Silver to our home in Dayton, to stay in our backyard. A neighbor boy stopped by and asked to get on him. When he "saddled up," he gave him a prod with his heel. You did not do that to Silver. He was out of the "chute," and off to the races.

As I came from work, a white horse complete with rider, galloped in front of my car. Dewey and Brent were in the pickup in hot pursuit. They captured the "runaway" down by the Yamhill River, and Brent rode him to the area where the horses were kept. Dewey said, "No more rodeos." We were fortunate that no one was injured in that escapade.

Another time Brenda rode Silver, and he took off up the hill. Dewey yelled at her, "Hold on tight and stay on. Don't fall off!" But when they neared the top of the hill, she "bailed," and landed in a blackberry thicket. She was scratched and shaken, but otherwise unharmed. She didn't do much riding after that. She preferred to groom rather than ride the horses.

The second winter we had horses, Dewey and I were on our way to Corvallis to watch the state championship football game, when we learned that the water in the Willamette River was rising rapidly. We were in a hurry, but we changed direction and went to the River to rescue them.

When we got to the River, Dewey got Jay and I got Stardust. I had trouble with Star, so he told me to let her go. When I released her, she turned and went back to the River, and Silver followed. Stardust was the dominant horse, so had Dewey been leading her, the others would have followed, but I released her. We succeeded in getting Jay safely to dry ground, but Dewey spent the next week going to the River to try to get the last two horses to safety.

Each morning he called the Corps of Engineers to see how much water was released into the Willamette River. He knew when he absolutely had to bring the horses to dry ground. When it became evident that the time had come, and there was to be no more delay, he and Dennis Withnell went to the River and crossed. Dewey was in waist-deep water, but he succeeded. When he got Stardust across, Silver followed obediently like a puppy.

(After we purchased our property on Woodland Heights, we kept the horses with us. However, we appreciated the time they were allowed to reside on our friends' property on the River.)

But our horse adventures didn't end with just three horses. More than thirty years and several horses later -- long after the original three horses were gone -- we returned from a trip, and there was a new horse in the corral.

Brent had one horse when we left for our trip, and when Dewey went for his walk on our first morning home, he discovered a new resident. Dewey stopped by Brent's house, and said, "Brent, there's a new white horse in the corral. Do you know anything about it?"

Brent said, "No, I don't. You don't suppose that Holly had a colt, do you?" Dewey replied, "No, I don't. This is no colt. This is an adult horse. Now, what's the deal? Did you buy another horse?"

A BAREFOOT BOY FROM OKLAHOMA

The banter went on for several minutes before Dewey walked back to the corral. When he became acquainted with the new resident, he was hooked. He learned that the new horse was Babe, and he fell in love with her, just as Brent had. Dewey enjoyed her for the rest of the time he was allowed here on earth.

In an amusing aside, Jerry and Shawn Sutton lived down the hill from our home. Shawn had a horse she wanted to have bred, and she kept a stud with her. One morning Shawn called Dewey, and asked how to determine if the mare were in season. Dewey said, "Well, is she 'winking'?" ("Winking" is a term for checking a mare's readiness for breeding.) Shawn said, "I don't know." The next time she saw Dewey she asked, "What did you mean, is she 'winking'?" She demonstrated by winking her eye, and Dewey almost collapsed in fits of laughter from her interpretation.

CHAPTER **56**

"Sullivan's Mountain"

For years Dewey dreamed of owning a small acreage, so he spent several summers searching for a rural property within our price range. One evening he came in with the news, "I've found the place I've been looking for." He had found a lot on Woodland Heights in Amity, which was in foreclosure. He bid on it, but had to wait several weeks to learn if his bid had been accepted. When I got the call that his bid was successful, I called him and said, "You're now a landowner. Your offer was accepted." He shouted, " Oh, Boy!"

He spent the next six weeks in preparation, and when summer came, he got things underway for building a house. He was excited as he scrambled to get started. He designed our home, and he worked on blueprints. He lined up people to help, and did the plumbing and much of the work. Brent also helped, and Candy spent a lot of time staining and finishing the trim. He spent the entire summer working on our house, and we moved into it in October of 1976. We named our homestead "Sullivan's Mountain and enjoyed being landowners. (That home was on Woodland Heights in Amity. I consider it ironic that Dewey's physical address here on earth was Amity, Oregon – in light of the rivalry described earlier between Dayton and Amity!)

I had worked with Dewey on two previous homes, so I said, "I'm not going anywhere near that house until it's finished, or we'll probably get a divorce." I did not work well with him as he was the boss, and I thought I should be. Of course, I had to periodically check on the construction, and I helped with what I could. Anyway, he got the house built, and we remained married.

After we built our home on Woodland Heights, we decided to look for a place for Dewey's parents. They lived in Oklahoma, and we and their other children, were far away from them. So during the spring of 1980, we looked at several properties.

That spring, Dewey and I flew to Los Angeles for a conference. While we were in L.A., Dewey ran around with a Latino gent whose wife also attended the conference. He and Dewey zipped around the city in that fellow's Datsun 240Z. The other fellow's wife could not understand their friendship, because her husband detested "gringos," but for some reason, he and Dewey were practically inseparable. They were almost like brothers.

The night before we returned to Oregon, we had a call from Candy. She said, "There's a letter here from Grandpa. Do you want me to open it?" Dewey said, "Yes, open it so we can see what he has to say." She did, and said, "There's a check here for one hundred and fifty dollars." Dewey's father never sent money unless he was serious. We had tried for several years to get them to move, but had been unsuccessful. When we learned that Mr. Sullivan was serious about making the move, we were happy.

The next day we re-routed Dewey's itinerary to Oklahoma City, and I returned to Oregon alone. When he arrived in Muskogee, he found Windle and Norman already there, so he helped them finish packing. When the truck was loaded and ready to leave for Oregon, Dewey's father decided he wanted to delay the departure. Dewey informed him that he was low on medication for high blood pressure (his father appreciated the need for medication), and that was enough to get the move underway.

The night before they left, Oklahoma thunderheads rolled in and they experienced the "mother of all thunderstorms." Dewey said, "The noise was incredible, and the thunder and lightning were amazing. The lightning zigged across the horizon in a dramatic

"SULLIVAN'S MOUNTAIN"

display of power, and the sky lit up like a summer afternoon. The thunder boomed in deafening claps. We went to the storm cellar, for fear there would be a tornado. The cellar smelled musty, but it gave us shelter. It was a relief when the storm was over."

They awoke to a cloudless sky, and were ready for their cross-country trek. It was hard to believe that such an incredible storm had visited the previous night. Dewey drove his parents' 1977 Honda Accord with his mother at his side. Norman drove the moving van with his father "supervising" him. Mr. Sullivan directed the way to Jonell's house. When they arrived in Denver, Norman said, "How in the heck did he find this place?" (Dewey's father had an uncanny sense of direction.) They spent the night with Jonell and got an early start the next morning.

After two days on the road, the entourage arrived at our home on Dewey's mother's birthday, June 21, 1980. That was as nice a birthday present as she ever received. (Her brother, John Evans, had moved to the Brookings-Harbor area of Oregon thirty-five or so years previous, and had written that it was the "Garden of Eden," with all the wild blackberries, etc. She dreamed of living here.)

She later wrote, "Willis had always wanted to move back to Oklahoma, so we sold our home in Fowler, and moved to Muskogee after he retired. We didn't like Muskogee very much. It was dry and hot in the summer, and cold and windy in the winter. We sat up many nights listening to tornado warnings, and wondering if we would be killed in a tornado. Deward and his family had moved to Oregon, and had lived there for several years, and we often visited them there. Willis finally had all of Oklahoma that he wanted, so we moved to Oregon."

She loved the abundance of fruits and vegetables, and as she and Dewey's dad were gardeners, they soon had a productive garden growing. Before they moved to Oregon, she told me I was not keeping up with the blackberry harvest. When they got settled, I told her it was her responsibility to keep all the berries picked. She did a good job of it for six years, and they lived in "Paradise" during that time.

◄ A BAREFOOT BOY FROM OKLAHOMA

Before they moved, we put earnest money on one property, but couldn't get water, so our money was returned. After the move, it took several weeks of looking and negotiating before we found the ideal property and "sealed the deal." A month after our earnest money was returned, an acreage adjoining our property came on the market. We made an offer on it, and were successful. That property is located on Walnut Hill in Amity.

Dewey's parents settled on a mobile home, and had a well drilled and a septic system installed. They moved into their own home in September of 1980, and were delighted. They did not bring much with them, so they furnished their home with new furniture.

Rice Furniture in McMinnville had a plan with no payments and no interest for one year. I encouraged Mr. Sullivan to purchase a mattress and box springs there, and to put it on that plan so he could collect the small amount of interest. One evening something was said, and I asked, "Did you pay that off?" He replied, " Yes, I did." He could not abide the feeling of owing someone. (When he received his property tax statement he went immediately to McMinnville and paid it. I always waited until the deadline to pay ours.)

Norman accepted a position teaching social studies and coaching basketball at St. Paul in 1981, so he moved to Oregon and lived with us for several months. A barking dog annoyed him one night, so he got up about one o'clock, and called a woman. Irately he said, "Can't you hear that dog barking?" Her reply was, "No, I don't hear a dog barking." Again he said (a little more heatedly), "Can't you hear that dog? How can you not hear that dog?" She said, "No, I can't hear a dog." (She was not the owner of the dog – she did not have a dog. Norman later learned that he had a wrong number. I'm thankful that caller ID was not readily available in the early '80s.)

When Dewey's parents moved to Oregon, we made it a family tradition to visit the Coast the day after Christmas. (Dewey's mom loved the Coast.) The second time we made the trip, Dewey and I were in the front of the caravan. His parents were in the car with us, and I was seated in the front seat next to Dewey. I urged him to stay at the speed limit, so he would not get a ticket. I nagged him until a patrol car with red and blue flashing lights approached from the rear. (I had not thought of the cars behind us.)

The "arresting" officer came to our car, and Dewey greeted him with, "Good morning, Officer. What can I do for you?" The officer said, "Do you realize you have a line of traffic behind you?" Dewey replied, "Well, my wife has been nagging me to not exceed the speed limit, so I have been very cautious. I didn't realize we had people following us." *(WE GOT A TICKET!!)*

Our kids were at the back of the procession, and they made the comment, "Someone's going to get a ticket for going too slow." When they got to the front of the line of traffic, and discovered it was their father who got the ticket they cracked up. They teased him unmercifully. They often said, "Dad, how about your ticket?" They didn't let him forget.

For several summers Dewey persuaded me to sleep with him on a mattress on the ground in our backyard. It was wonderful to look up at the summer sky, and to see the falling stars on an August evening. To see those stars "up-close-and-personal," was fantastic. But when I realized we often had visitors of the black kitty variety (with white stripes down their backs), I became reluctant to sleep outdoors.

Dewey's parents had six wonderful years in Oregon, but his father was diagnosed with cancer in 1986, and he died in 1987. When his father died, Dewey grieved more for his mother who lost the love of her life. He knew how difficult life would be for her without her soul mate. She suffered a hip fracture in March of 1991, and she struggled with that and other health problems until she died in September of 1992.

CHAPTER 57

Time Out!!

Dewey ruptured both his Achilles tendons (fortunately not at the same time) – the first in Meeker, Colorado in 1963. He played town team basketball, and pulled up lame. He first thought someone had stepped on his heel, but soon realized what had happened. He went to our local doctor the next day. That doctor had never treated a ruptured Achilles tendon, so he wrapped it in an Ace bandage. (We should have gone to Denver to a specialist.)

For five months Dewey hobbled around school and his coaching activities on crutches. He often slipped in the snow as he walked to school (we lived about half a block away). The tendon got better, and calcified -- it was nearly three times the normal size, but with diligent work and exercise on his part, Dewey was able to reduce its size.

He ruptured his other tendon after we moved to Dayton. He was once again playing town team basketball. One of the other players took him home where he crawled up the stairs to our bedroom. The next day we consulted our doctor in McMinnville, and then drove to Portland for surgery.

Dewey looked at his impending surgery as another adventure in life's journey. He said, "This will be something to look back on." Before the operation he asked to be allowed to watch. (He asked as he was being put under anesthesia, and the doctor said he could watch.) The next thing that Dewey remembered was awakening in the recovery room.

He told the operating surgeon that he had ruptured the other tendon eight years previous, but had not had it repaired. The doctor scoffed, and told him he would not be walking around if he had. I managed to change the conversation. I did not want Dewey to challenge the doctor on that premise. Later the doctor stated, "It's possible you did rupture your other tendon, and a few strands were not broken. It might have been possible for it to grow back." (Dewey assumed the doctor examined the tendon while he was sedated.)

The surgeon used his own technique, a wire in the tendon, which facilitated the healing process. Even though Dewey had been instructed not to use that leg while recuperating, he exercised it as much as possible to prevent it from atrophying. When the cast was removed, the doctor instructed him to kick out gently. He did, and almost knocked the doctor over. The surgeon was delighted, and said that his technique really did work – that Dewey had not lost much of his muscle mass. (Dewey did not tell the doctor he cheated – that he had worked his leg while it was in the cast.)

CHAPTER **58**

The Worst Day of My Life

"I have fought a good fight, I have finished the course, I have kept the faith . . . "

-- II Timothy 4:7

The sun has set . . . the day is done!

At the beginning of the football season in 1995, Dewey experienced some health problems. He and several Dayton teachers (Jim Connelly, Wayne Herring and Hal Tanaka) started to McMinnville for lunch, and he was overcome by a strange sensation and leaned to the right. He asked one of the others to drive him to his doctor's office, where the doctor put a monitor on him to keep tabs on his blood pressure (the doctor thought that might be the problem). He told his companions, "Don't tell Vera."

The others thought that was hilarious, as it would have been impossible for me not to see the contraption to which he was attached. After being under observation for several days, he was taken off the monitor, but his blood pressure was closely watched.

Several weeks later he was again overcome by a strange sensation, so he went to the hospital in McMinnville. He missed the game between Dayton and Amity that year. Tom McKay (whose son, Andy, was on that team and whose other son, Paul, had played for Dewey), called Dewey at the hospital, and kept him apprised of what was happening.

Dewey tried to keep Tom on the phone, so he could have a play-by-play account. Dayton won the game, and Mark Hawley took the game tape and a video recorder to the hospital room afterward. Twenty or more people clustered around to watch the game on tape. It's a wonder the hospital did not kick us out.

As Dayton prepared for the game between Dayton and Santiam-Christian the next week, Emory Blackwell came across the field. He told me that Dewey was again experiencing difficulty, so we agreed he should go to the hospital if it did not go away.

The problem persisted, so we took him to the hospital. He stayed overnight at the Corvallis Hospital (Mary Budke, a former student and statistician for the Pirates, was one of the emergency room doctors). Dewey had an angiogram done, but everything looked okay.

During all that turmoil, we stayed in contact with our family physician for months. Dewey was referred to Oregon Health and Science University (OHSU) for further evaluation. He underwent tests there, but nothing definitive was found. His cardiovascular system was the point of focus. He continued to experience difficulties during the ensuing years, but no suggestion was made that the problem might be with his head or his brain.

Eleven years later, Dewey began experiencing difficulty again. After we returned from lunch after church on the last Sunday in April of 2006, Dewey decided to take his walk (he walked about two miles up and down the hill near our home on a daily basis). Forty-five minutes later he came down the hill, and skidded into our yard out of control. He had no sense of balance, and was terrified. (Our happily-ever-after was about to be turned upside down.)

He called John Patterson, a friend who previously had a problem with his ear and his balance, and Windle who had also experienced similar health problems. He discussed his symptoms with them. On Monday he went to a doctor who examined him, but had no

THE WORST DAY OF MY LIFE

diagnosis for his problem. In August we went to our family physician, and it was suggested he might have a brain tumor. He was referred to a neurologist in Tualatin, and an MRI was scheduled.

We stopped by our doctor's office about a week after the MRI, and the doctor told Dewey that he indeed had a brain tumor. My heart plummeted. A brain tumor! How frightening! I think you could have knocked either of us over with a feather. Even though our doctor had said that was a possibility, we had not considered it seriously.

After that disclosure, my life would never be the same. While we had been going merrily along with life, something insidious had been growing in Dewey's head. We had been unaware of it until that day. I was devastated! (He was being destroyed by a beast from within!) The seriousness of the situation began to sink in, and I waited for the world to right itself. That time is forever etched in my memory.

An alien object would end his life here on earth. He was referred to a specialist at Oregon Health and Science University in Portland, and we visited that doctor on September 8. Dewey was admitted to the hospital on September 11.

When we met with the surgeon before Dewey's surgery, our first question was whether the tumor might have been the cause of his concern in 1995. The operating surgeon assured us he did not believe that to be the case, but we were not convinced.

Once again, Dewey looked at surgery as another adventure – another bridge to be crossed. When he was diagnosed with a brain tumor, he accepted his fate – not with anticipation – but with curiosity. He knew it was to be a challenge, but he worked diligently until the last. He lifted weights the morning he was admitted to the hospital, and wanted to be in the best possible physical condition.

After Dewey's diagnosis, I was angry that an MRI had not been ordered sooner. My thought was that he could have had three months more in which to recuperate. But I later realized that the outcome would most likely have been the same. The last five months of his life might have been more compromised than they were.

A BAREFOOT BOY FROM OKLAHOMA

Dewey would have missed Zack's graduation. He would have missed working with the Pirates at the Linfield football camp. He would have missed the first three weeks of football practice. He would have missed the first two games of the 2006 football season. He would have missed Zack playing in the Shrine game.

Then, I went further back, and regretted that we did not discover the tumor eight or nine years previous to his diagnosis. When I did that, I came to the realization that had Dewey had surgery then, he might have been comatose, paralyzed, or otherwise compromised for that period of time.

In Psalm 139:16 it is written, "You saw me before I began to breathe. Every day was recorded in your Book." That is my consolation.

After Dewey's admission to OHSU, it was more than twenty-four hours before the MRI was performed. MRI procedures are performed first on emergency patients and children. When they tapped into Dewey's skull to alleviate the pressure, fluid gushed. He asked Candy to take a photo of him (to be used for scientific purposes later). He wanted to see what had been done to him, and he asked that no one else be in the picture.

After the surgery, the operating physician informed us that the tumor was older and larger than originally determined. And there were complications. Dewey was taken to the recovery room, where he struggled with his condition. He exercised his hands and his arms, but was unable to communicate verbally. He said a few words, but it was a struggle. He had a tracheotomy, and that imposed hardship on him.

There were mistakes made in his care, but for the most part, he was well cared for. When insurance mandated a move from ICU into regular hospital care, we knew we were in trouble. Dewey could not speak or press a button to summon assistance. If he needed anything, it would not be readily forthcoming. He did not have the round-the-clock observation he had in ICU, so Brent opted to stay in the room with him at night.

When he was later transferred to a care facility in McMinnville,

THE WORST DAY OF MY LIFE

Brent or another family member stayed with him. Someone stayed there with him 24/7. One of the last things Dewey said was, "I need guanabenz." (Guanabenz was one of his prescription medicines for hypertension.) I said, "You're on guanabenz." But, when he repeated that statement, I went to the nursing station where the nurse said, "No, he is not on guanabenz."

I went home and brought the medication back to the hospital where it was administered. (I do not know when guanabenz was removed from his regimen, but it was crucial to him in his daily living. He had tried several times to wean himself from it, but was never successful. He was agitated without it.) The nurses told me his sinus rhythm was normal soon after the guanabenz was administered.

Every night when I left the hospital I hurried home in dread of a phone call telling me the worst. And when the phone rang, I cringed. I lived in fear of the outcome. I wanted to go back to the way things had been for fifty years, but that was not possible. In this world where little can be counted on, Dewey had filled my days with sunshine and light.

Dewey aspirated twice during his recuperation, and contracted pneumonia. The pneumonia was not successfully overcome. I turned him over to God, and I thank God for giving him the time he had here on earth, and for what he accomplished. He was hospitalized from September 11 until November 8 and that period was excruciating for all of us. His loss left me devastated.

His beautiful blue eyes are now seeing for another. We donated them to the Lions Eye Bank, and it is refreshing to know that he enabled someone else to see. His other organs were so ravaged by his interminable hospitalization that they could not be harvested, but I am thankful that he gave someone else the gift of sight.

CHAPTER **59**

Dear Coach —
Tributes to Dewey While He Was Hospitalized

There were many tributes paid to Dewey on YouTube and carepages during his hospitalization. Here are a few:

Logan Malloy wrote: "No words could ever describe the passion for life that this amazing man, Dewey Sullivan, possessed. I transferred to Dayton my freshman year of high school, a skinny boy with hopes of playing for Coach Sullivan. From the day I met him till the last time I spoke with Coach his voice carried so much inspiration, not only for football, but for his church, the community and life. Coach taught me how to want to succeed in all that I did. He taught me football etiquette, weight lifting skills, and was always a light to lead the kids in the dark if we were to ever lose track of our path. Coach was a friend, brother and a grandfather to all who were blessed with his presence. He had so much passion for life in all he did, and when the *"McMinnville News-Register* quoted, 'Just let me go,' I knew that he wasn't giving up. You see Coach was a strong-hearted man that never gave up. He just knew it was his time to 'win again.' Heaven is Dewey Sullivan's last championship and the sweetest victory to have ever been accomplished. He will always be in my heart and memories . . ."

Shane Blanchard wrote: "Dear Coach, as the years of my life

have passed, I've found myself relearning many of the lessons you once taught me. Some were studied and deliberate, some accidental, none of them lost. 'Blanchard, trap right and put your heart into it' . . . today those words still ring true when I need to put my heart into it and don't know if I have the strength. You used to tell us that winning was important, but integrity and sportsmanship were vastly more so. You were right, of course. In your quiet (and not so quiet voice), you taught my team, teams before and teams after that the mark of a man was his character. You taught me to lead, to protect and to sacrifice . . . these I still struggle with to this day. In a few short years, you became an endearing mentor for a rancorous kid and an example for a man."

"He's been the face of small-level football in Oregon for four decades and you can't look at what we do today anywhere in the state, in the playoffs, without thinking about what he's done in the past," said Blanchet coach Jeff Flood, who coached Dayton's rival, Amity, to four straight state titles.

Former Scio coach, Mike Jones, "Guys like 'Coach Sullivan,' you think he's going to live forever. I'll miss the old guy. He was always gracious. For a man with a lot of success, he always made everybody feel good."

Bill Poehler of the *Salem Statesman-Journal* – November 9, 2008 – "Dewey Sullivan had a knack for leaving people wanting more." "Walking away after practice one day last fall, Sullivan said to a reporter, after sharing one of wife Vera's 'healthful' cookies, that a paper had written that that week's game would come down to Santiam Christian quarterback Joel Mason against Sullivan. 'You know' said the then 70-year-old in his slow, Oklahoma drawl, 'I don't believe I could cover him.' Dewey never stopped learning."

When his Pirates weren't playing or practicing, Dewey could be found watching college, high school, junior high or "pee-wee" football games. He was a frequent visitor to coaches' clinics, as a student. He could be found at any number of events, from wrestling tournaments to track meets to pancake breakfasts. He was always quick with his dry humor and compliments.

DEAR COACH - TRIBUTES TO DEWEY WHILE HE WAS HOSPITALIZED

"I'm going to miss him," said Marshfield coach Kent Wigle, who is second on the wins list. "I'll miss him when the clinics start because that's when I would normally see Dewey."

Santiam Christian coach, Steve Woods said, "One of the things that when we beat them at Dayton three years ago, we won that league championship for the first time in twenty years. Dewey came up after the game and said some positive things."

Matt Yaskovic wrote: "In the spring of 1975 my father, John Yaskovic, accepted a position as a business teacher at Dayton High School. I can remember attending Pirate football games with my dad when I was in grade school and thinking how much larger than life Coach Sullivan seemed. When I was about eight years old I attended some function for the teachers at the high school with my dad, during which he introduced me to Coach Sullivan. I remember Coach saying to my father 'He looks like a footballer to me, Yaskovic. You make sure he comes to see me when he gets up here.' as he winked at me. I felt 10 feet tall that day and couldn't wait to be one of Dewey's Pirates."

James Yount wrote: "Coach, I was talking to an old friend today and you know the greatest thing about you wasn't that you won a lot of football games. It was the fact you brought people together and taught us all life lessons, sometimes by putting it right in our faces and sometimes without us ever knowing it. Your legacy lives on in the thousands of lives you touched. I'm so proud to say I played football for you. Thank you for all you did and gave to our small town. All our lives are better for having you in them."

David Flores wrote: "It's so amazing the amount of people whose hearts Coach Sullivan had touched through God. We all had the honor of having him as a coach, teacher and most importantly as a friend. Probably the best memories I have of Coach is the way he was able to simply look at you and you knew what he wanted done, Years later, after playing for Coach and being thousands of miles away from the great Dayton community, he still has an influence on me to keep going forward no matter what!"

A BAREFOOT BOY FROM OKLAHOMA

Jesse Everett wrote "I remember being a scared freshman intimidated by the towering legendary man whose voice boomed throughout practice. I did my best to avoid his gaze, unless, of course, I was doing something right . . . standing in the small office to call my mom for a ride home, I could not hide. So when he interrupted my phone call by asking ' Is that your mother?' I immediately answered 'Yes, Coach.' 'Tell your mother you love her.' 'Yes, Coach. Mom, I love you.' That was the first great lesson he taught me, always, always tell others how you feel, because time may be shorter than you think.

"Years later as I was preparing to enter my senior year, Coach knew something had to change if I was going to be an effective leader. While I was visiting him one day, he played films from two past games in which character and determination led both teams to come back from near impossible odds. 'Do you know why they could come back like that?' he asked. 'No, Coach.' He paused, then looked me square in the eye and said, 'Because, they didn't get angry when things went wrong. They stayed calm, and the captain reminded them that everything would be fine. That is your job. You can't yell at everyone when things go bad, you have to show them that it's all right.'

"I have never forgotten that central lesson. I have taken it into my Sunday School class, management positions, school and, God willing, one day my high school classroom and before my own football team." . . . "It is not possible to summarize the massive effect that Coach Sullivan has had on my life, and the lives of all who knew him. Words are simply too feeble and inadequate to fully express the influence and love that helped countless boys grow into men. Even so, the following expressions of love, loyalty, respect, admiration and appreciation are our best effort to express our love for such a kind, beautiful, and wise man."

CHAPTER **60**

The Final Goodbye — A Legacy of Love

In Dewey's last days, we insisted that his hospital room be opened to any who wanted to say goodbye. There was a constant stream of visitors, and more than fifty people waited to see him the morning he died. They came en masse.

When it became evident that Dewey was not going to recover, we had a talk with the doctor who explained what the outcome would be. He would not have been able to eat again, and he would have had to be fed from a feeding tube for the rest of his days. Had he recovered, he would have had restrictions on his life.

We decided to withdraw the support system that had kept him through that long, difficult struggle, and we tried to make his last days as comfortable as possible. We told him of our decision, and he had a brilliant beaming smile and relaxed. (He had often asked me not to try to sustain him in the event he were in that situation.)

I hate to think of the turmoil we put my beautiful husband through, just to prolong his life here on earth — the agonies he had to endure so we could keep him with us a few more weeks. I kissed him goodbye on his final morning here on earth with the knowledge that I will see him again. As I go about my rituals of living, I carry him with me in my heart. His memory is with me, and I enjoy the remembering.

A hospital is a hard place to be when someone you love is

dying. I met Dewey decades before when we were in grade school. We didn't date until we were teens, but I was with him as he lay on his deathbed. All those years, all that football, all those players, all those games, it was all a blur, a painful blur. When I met him he was full of spark, and he lived a life that gave off fireworks . . . that handsome, devil-may-care smile, that vigorous body . . . were all wasting away in front of me.

It could have been any hospital in the country. They all look the same. The smell of antiseptic air, the plastic curtains, and the crunch of hospital linens are always prevalent. The whir and click of machines was muted amidst the rush of oxygen that ran into the vent tube, a twin to the plastic tubing channeling the pain-killer that ran down to the needle in his arm.

His arm. His arm had been so big, so strong, but had withered in the last two months. Those two months were awful. His arm was once so muscular. Dewey lifted weights, and I remember what he looked like when we moved to Dayton, even as the man he was in his fifties, a strong muscular man with a regal bearing, his crew-cut held high in the era of lengthening hair styles . . . a beacon of the continuing values of less confusing days. He was part Native American Indian. He was proud, and there was a bit of the proud Indian chief in him.

I sat by holding his hand. A hospital cart clattered down the hall. A nearby toilet flushed. His breathing wheezed. I looked at his arm which was much smaller now, and I thought back to when we'd first come to Dayton those many years before, and the amazing things that had happened. I thought about the struggles and the victories. I was with him when he came to Dayton, and I was with him at the end.

When my father died, I told my mother, "I know how you feel." She said, "No, you don't." She was right. I didn't know how she felt. I understood grief, but when I experienced the loss of Dewey, it was overwhelming. A part of me died when he did. I could not believe the loneliness – the devastation. It was the worst day of my life.

My world turned upside down, and the perfect "Happily-Ever-

THE FINAL GOODBYE - A LEGACY OF LOVE

After" that I had lived up until his death came to a screeching halt. There was a hole in my heart the size of Alaska. Hearts really do break!

Life here on earth is just a test — a test for eternity. With God's help, Dewey passed the test and is enjoying the rewards for his efforts. I'm still working on my test, but I'm certain of the rewards that are waiting.

Dewey was the one who held me when my father died; he was the one who comforted me when my mother died; he was the one who dried my tears when my brother died; and now he was gone. He could no longer comfort or hold me. Even though I knew I was not saying "goodbye" for the final time, it was still devastating to say, "Until we meet again."

Dewey coached the first two games of the 2006 football season, and his team defeated Regis 21-20 in one of his most challenging victories. Dayton also defeated Scio in his final game. After the Scio game, he told his team that he would miss a couple of games, but that he would be back. He came to the car after the game, and said, "I cried. It felt as though I was delivering my retirement speech." (He was, but he did not realize it at the time).

Dewey said he would have to retire from coaching before he reached one hundred losses at Dayton, and God made that a possibility for him. Dewey planned to coach for another two or three years. But when he was diagnosed with a brain tumor it was not possible. The surgery was portrayed that he would miss a couple of games at the beginning of the season, and he decided he would be able to coach when Dayton went to Rainier for the fifth game of that season (he felt that Rainier was near Portland so he could get there if he ran into difficulty.

When the time came for Dewey to go "Home," God made the final decision. Dewey didn't make the decision to leave the "Game of Football." God made it for him. He walked out that door, and went "Home to Heaven."

And fifty-three years and three months after we were married, after four kids and five grandchildren, after two great grandsons, our journey through life together ended. Dewey left me here on earth to forge ahead on my own. The pall of my grief hung over me like a dark cloud. My life stretched before me without Dewey, and things looked bleak. The gray skies reflected my sadness.

My sadness reverberated through my being. I could not believe it. Morning had just arrived but it seemed as black as night. I faced the fact that the nightmare I was living was real.

For over fifty years Dewey led the way, but now that he was gone, I learned that he taught me well. With Dewey every day was a honeymoon. It's not where you are, but who you're with that matters. So many games – so many years – so much emotion – and now it was finished.

By the grace of God, I am making it. I am still learning, but I have gotten this far on my trip, and I know I will make it "Home." Life is not made by the dreams we dream, but by the choices we make. Dewey's choices served us both well, and his death helped me value life more. The bridge between the living and the dead – between memory and eternity is fleeting.

CHAPTER **61**

The Stuff of Legends – The Last Football Game

I rolled over in bed, and suddenly *DEWEY WAS THERE!* I couldn't believe it. I reached to touch him, but I couldn't feel him. It had been so long since I had seen him. I said, "I haven't seen you for so long, and I have missed you so much. What have you been doing?"

He replied, "Oh, I have had the most wonderful time. I have been in the most marvelous place. The sun is always shining, and everyone is so friendly. I have been encouraged to sing, and am in a choir. Do you remember my singing?" I said, "Yes, and I enjoyed it, but I know that some people didn't appreciate it." He said, "Well, I've been singing and it is so much fun. There is so much light here. I've been waiting for you to join me."

I rolled over again, and then I sat upright. I reached out to touch him, but he was gone. I realized that I had been dreaming. In that strange netherworld between awareness and sleep, I didn't want to waken, but couldn't go back to my dream state. I basked in the wonder of my encounter for several more minutes. I couldn't get him back no matter how hard I tried. But the sun streamed into my room. I floated on clouds the rest of the day as I remembered my brief encounter.

I have consolation in that Dewey told me he had accomplished everything he ever wanted. He said, "Don't mourn when I die. I have done everything I ever wanted to do. I married the girl of my dreams, and my football teams have won numerous league championships. They have won five state championships, and set the state record for winning football games. I went to Africa five times (Africa was a life-long dream), Hawaii three times, Mexico four times, St. Maarten once, Alaska once, and I own my own classic '53 Ford. I can't think of anything else that I would like to do."

Dewey was the winningest football coach (at all levels, including college), west of the Mississippi River. His official (or maybe unofficial record) for football games won, was 361-102-2 as reported by *USA Today* (August 30, 2006 edition). He won two games at the beginning of the 2006 season, which made his record 363-102-2.

Dewey's record for wins at Dayton was 352-84-2 (in forty-one years and three weeks). At the last he was setting small goals, one of which was to coach a grandson of one of his former players, and he did that at the beginning of the 2006 football season, by coaching Jacob Gonzales and Joey Flores, two grandsons of a former player.

There were many final tributes to Dewey when he died. Before the first round of the playoffs in 2006, Shawn Stanley, the head football coach at West Salem High School, had his players observe a moment of silence in Dewey's honor. Brent and I attended that game, and it was moving to see the tribute.

When Dewey got up in the morning, he said, "What do I get to do today? Let's get moving. We have places to go and things to see." He looked forward to each day, and he achieved the goals he set for himself.

Each day, Dewey eagerly unwrapped the "present" that God gave him. He knew what was important, and he held tightly to that. He knew that life is over in the "blink of an eye," and he savored each moment.

If you saw the 2008 movie, *The Bucket List*, it is evident that Dewey Sullivan accomplished everything on his "bucket list." I cannot think of anything on his "to-do" list, that he did not do. He lived each day to the fullest, as though it were his last.

THE STUFF OF LEGENDS - THE LAST FOOTBALL GAME

The only thing that Dewey had a yen for, and did not get was a rubber tractor. When he was a boy, he was intrigued (those tractors are now made of metal or plastic), but he did not acquire one. He said, "I remember the smell of those tractors, and I wanted one so badly." (But I will have to say, if that was the only thing he wanted, and did not get, he was more fortunate than most of us. His family could not afford "toys," and later when Dewey grew up, things had changed – as had Dewey.)

Dewey knew that acclaim here on earth is fleeting, and his focus was on helping others rather than building his own reputation. He said, "I love my job. I love coaching. I love football, but mostly I love God and my life here on earth. I can walk away from this if it is God's will. I have better waiting for me on the other side.

"I realize that within a year of my death, most people will not know who Dewey Sullivan was. I want to be remembered as a man of God, rather than a man who won many football games. I hope my legacy will be measured in those I have helped, and not in championships." (Even man's biggest successes here on earth are only for a moment. Life is a vapor that appears for a short time and quickly vanishes.)

I recently read a quote from *Lost Horizon* by James Hilton, "The first quarter century of your life is lived under the cloud of being too young for things while the last quarter century is shadowed by the cloud of being too old for them. Between those two clouds what small and narrow sunlight illumines a human lifetime – a slender, breathless and far too frantic interlude." How true!

From the tribute to Dewey Sullivan from the Dayton School District at the end of his life, one of the quotes was, "When hired in 1965, Dewey answered the application question, "If chosen how long would you plan to remain in Dayton?" Dewey's response was, "As long as conditions are favorable." Dewey was twenty-nine at the time and we are thankful as a school and a community that for forty-two years the 'conditions were favorable.'"

Dewey wanted Dayton to be the team against which all others

would be measured, and he attained that goal. Dayton became the measuring stick for the West Valley League, and it was deemed, "If you can beat Dayton you can beat anyone." The bar was set, and the other league schools had something to strive for.

There are many in the community who deserve our undying gratitude. We appreciated the support of those who were there for us for forty-two years. Several years ago, I mentioned to one of the Dayton supporters (she would probably not want her name mentioned as she is quite modest) that the football pants being worn by the team were the same ones her grandson had worn about eight years previous.

That lady's husband called Dewey several days later. He asked if they could help. (Could they help??) They had a car that they donated to the Booster Club to be auctioned or raffled off with the proceeds going to the football program. Two weeks after the phone call, Dewey was asked if it were okay if they sold the car themselves and gave the money to the program. That was better, as there did not have to be a raffle or some other activity, and the money was accessible immediately.

Dewey welcomed their assistance and support. Others have also come forward during pinches. Dewey appreciated all that such elected to do for the football program. I cannot name everything that was done over the years that Dewey spent coaching at Dayton, nor can I name all the people who made it all possible, but thanks are due to many in the Dayton community for their love and support.

In the third revision of, *X's and O's, The Tradition of Dayton Football*, Jim Connelly wrote, "It is known that all rivers gain their might and origin from the streams that trickle down from the lofty heights of the mighty Cascades, the Sierra Nevada, and the Rockies. Streams that begin as fresh, clear springs knowing not whence nor when they shall join up with other flowing bodies. To drink from a spring and not rise and follow its slow, ever-increasing flow, simply quenches the thirst for a moment but to follow and discover its size gives one the chance to tap into the river's full strength.

"Ideas and action are analogous to the river. Ideas find their

THE STUFF OF LEGENDS - THE LAST FOOTBALL GAME

beginning as small springs, fresh and clear. They become wider and deeper as action issues and because of action, may eventually overflow their banks. Eventually the idea will return to the confines of the river channel and continue the journey in a more refined manner and will, in due course, reach the sea . . . and this, the third revision of the *X's and 'O's"* makes for great reading pleasure. It stirs the memories of yesterday and that is the book's lifeblood."

This is where my musings have taken me. This work was difficult to put down once I started. It is the result of the meanderings my mind has taken down the trails of memory. My faith has been sorely tested as I have asked God, "Why me? What do you want of me?"

In writing this, I have stood outside my life with Dewey and watched it unfold before my eyes. It has been surreal. We shared so many thrilling moments. This has been therapeutic and I have enjoyed the memories. I cannot have one more day here on earth with Dewey, but I thank God daily for what I had, and for what I still have. We are all travelers in this world from birth until death and life is a bridge between memory and eternity.

I have so many wonderful memories – memories of the fun times as well as the struggles – memories of tiny babies – memories of warm fuzzy kittens – memories of love – memories of sorrow – memories of football games (won and lost) – memories of trips – memories of celebrations – the joy we experienced in the loving and in the living. What a wonderful joyful, tear-filled life – what a life of rejoicing – of expectations. Our marriage – our love – our lives – all were a growing process. We grew up together – we loved together – we cried together. And now that our time together here on earth is over, I still have those memories. (All the wasted moments in our lives are more precious because they cannot be repeated.)

Dewey once shared a snippet with me about a woman who complained unceasingly to her husband about having to pick up after him. Her husband died, and that woman wrote, "Oh, how I wish I could pick up after him at least one more time." Dewey and I cried over that simple statement, and now I cry alone.

Dewey was loved by many, and admired by even more. He was

an icon in Oregon football history, but that is not what he wanted to be remembered for. He wanted to be remembered for what he contributed to people – he loved people and he loved life. He transitioned, and left a rich heritage of love.

I ask myself, "What if? What if we had not married at such a young age? What if we had not decided Dewey should go to college? What if we had chosen a different path for our lives together? What if??? The "what ifs" in life – IF is such a tiny word, but we all ask ourselves (some of us on a daily basis) "What if I had done this? – What if I had gone there? – What if I had done that?" I contemplate those questions, but I feel Dewey listened to God's call, and did what God wanted with his life. When I asked the question "Would you like to go to college?" his decision was made, and he did his best with what he was given.

The six short years between the time I met Dewey, and the time we embarked on our lives together are a fantastic memory. When you're five it takes an eternity for a birthday or Christmas to arrive – at sixty-five those celebrations seemingly occur every other day or week.

Sometimes the greatest come from the least – the richest come from the poorest. Dewey Sullivan was one of the richest men I have ever known. He was rich in self-satisfaction -- in happiness here on earth – in his desire to assist others. He came from humble beginnings, but far exceeded any expectations he or anyone else had for him.

Dewey didn't seek fame or fortune – he wanted to be a coach. He became a coach, not only of football, but a coach of life. His legacy lives on in those he touched. He didn't need the new thing if what he had worked. He was not pretentious. He was not rich by earthly standards, but was rich beyond measure in what really matters. To him, a Toyota Camry was a luxury car. He was a success.

The passage from the Bible that best exemplifies Dewey's life is Proverbs 18:7, "A pretentious showy life is an empty life; a plain and simple life is a full life."

After a few years at Dayton, Dewey fell in love with the kids and the community. He was often told, "Dewey, I want you to coach my kids (and later their grandkids)." He said, "I don't know if I can ever retire. I'll feel as though I'm letting someone down." He could have left the small town atmosphere for larger and better circumstances, but he hung on, and stayed true to what he believed.

I once told him, "I don't care what happens to Dayton football after you leave." His response was, "I do. I worked hard to build this program, and I hope it goes on long after I am gone." That gave me the incentive to carry on Dewey's legacy. He wanted Dayton football to continue, so that is what I am trying to perpetuate.

The Dewey Sullivan Little Guy Football Camp was started several years ago, and is quite popular with the young set. Shawn Sutton organized the first *Dewey Sullivan Golf Scramble* in 2006, and is now the *Dewey Sullivan Classic*. That tourney now funds the *Dewey Sullivan Memorial Scholarship Fund*. The first two players to be awarded $1,000 scholarships were Nick Olheiser and Jordan May. We hope to be able to have the golf tourney, and the scholarship fund ongoing from year to year.

We are also trying to get funding for a Dayton Sports Museum through the *Dayton Historical Society*, or some other such venue. I have forty-two years of Dayton history: plaques, trophies, footballs, scrapbooks, etc., I would like to share.

When Dewey came to Dayton in 1965, Dayton was definitely a basketball town. There were basketball hoops all around the parking lot, and kids were shooting hoops before and after school, as well as during lunch break. The town mothers discouraged their sons from playing football because they feared they might get injured, and not be able to play basketball.

It took twenty years to equal, but not overcome the basketball influence in Dayton. As we drove by the high school on our way to church after winning the state championship in 1985, some kids were playing football in the snow. I told Dewey, "I think you have finally succeeded in bringing football into its own at Dayton."

Dayton is still a basketball community, but for forty-two years, the footprints left on the football field were huge. For four decades Dewey's face was the face of Oregon small-town football.

In this world where many schools change football coaches as routinely as most of us change our undergarments, it is unusual for a football coach to stay in one small school for forty-two years. If his teams lose, he is fired. If his teams win, he is courted by larger schools.

When you consider the lure of coaching elsewhere -- the lure of larger turnouts -- the lure of better equipment -- the lure of more support -- the lure of more money -- the lure of more publicity -- most successful coaches move on. In Dewey's case, money would have been nice, but he did not do it for money, and he was not into publicity. He settled into Dayton and didn't look back.

He was once referred to as "A man with many victories, but few words." But he did not start his career in 1959 to be a "high profile" coach." He loved kids and football. He was content to stay in the background. He tried to stay out of the limelight, but somehow he became an "icon." It wasn't easy to get where we ended, but the journey was worth the struggle.

Dewey entered life here on earth as *DEWARD SULLIVAN*, a barefoot boy from Oklahoma, and left as *DEWEY SULLIVAN*, the football coach from a small high school in Oregon whose shoes are too big to fill.